Invisible Revolutionaries

Invisible Revolutionaries sheds light on the critical role women play in a contemporary revolution. The book argues that women's engagement in contentious politics is often far less visible than men's participation, when measured by the physical presence of women in protest space. Using the case of the 2013–2014 Revolution of Dignity in Ukraine, the book outlines the different modes of women's participation in a revolution and illustrates how women can be at the forefront of civil resistance, fighting for national independence and democratic development. Drawing on data from large-N surveys and oral history projects, the book uncovers the diverse motivations and forms of women's involvement in mass mobilization and traces the multifaceted outcomes of their activism in the post-revolutionary period. The book proposes an original typology of women's engagement in a revolution and explores a pivotal moment in Ukraine's history that precedes the Russia–Ukraine War.

Olena Nikolayenko is a professor of political science at Fordham University and an associate at the Davis Center for Russian and Eurasian Studies at Harvard University. She is also a board member of the American Association for Ukrainian Studies and the Shevchenko Scientific Society in the United States. Her research has appeared in *Comparative Politics, International Journal of Sociology, International Political Science Review, International Sociology, Slavic Review, Social Movement Studies*, and other journals.

Cambridge Studies in Contentious Politics

General Editor
David S. Meyer *University of California, Irvine*

Editors
Mark Beissinger *Princeton University*
Donatella della Porta *Scuola Normale Superiore*
Jack A. Goldstone *George Mason University*
Michael Hanagan *Vassar College*
Doug McAdam *Stanford University and Center for Advanced Study in the Behavioral Sciences Si*
Holly J. McCammon *Vanderbilt University*
Sarah Soule *Stanford University*
Suzanne Staggenborg *University of Pittsburgh*
Sidney Tarrow *Cornell University*
Charles Tilly (d. 2008) *Columbia University*
Elisabeth J. Wood *Yale University*
Deborah Yashar *Princeton University*

Edmund W. Cheng and Samson Yuen, *The Making of Leaderful Mobilization: Power and Contention in Hong Kong*
Patrick Rafail and John D. McCarthy, *The Rise, Fall, and Influence of the Tea Party Insurgency*
Manfred Elfstrom, *Workers and Change in China: Resistance, Repression, Responsiveness*
Olivier Fillieule and Erik Neveu, editors, *Activists Forever? Long-Term Impacts of Political Activism*
Marcos E. Pérez, *Proletarian Lives: Routines, Identity and Culture in Contentious Politics*
LaGina Gause, *The Advantage of Disadvantage: Costly Protest and Political Representation for Marginalized Groups*
Corinna Jentzsch, *Violent Resistance: Militia Formation and Civil War in Mozambique*
Abel Bojar *Contentious Episodes in the Age of Austerity: Studying the Dynamics of Government-Challenger Interactions*
Ches Thurber, *Between Mao and Gandhi: The Social Roots of Civil Resistance*
Dana M. Moss, *The Arab Spring Abroad: Diaspora Activism Against Authoritarian Regimes*
Sidney Tarrow, *Movements and Parties: Critical Connections in American Political Development*
Shivaji Mukherjee, *Colonial Institutions and Civil War: Indirect Rule and Maoist Insurgency in India*
Teri L. Caraway and Michele Ford, *Labor and Politics in Indonesia*
Yao Li, *Playing by the Informal Rules*
Suzanne Staggenborg, *Grassroots Environmentalism*
Grzegorz Ekiert, Elizabeth J. Perry, and Yan Xiaojun editors, *Ruling by Other Means: State-Mobilized Movements*

Olena Nikolayenko, *Youth Movements and Elections in Eastern Europe*
Eleonora Pasotti, *Resisting Redevelopment: Protest in Aspiring Global Cities*
Federico M. Rossi, *The Poor's Struggle for Political Incorporation: The Piquetero Movement in Argentina*
Marco Giugni and Maria Grasso, *Street Citizens: Protest Politics and Social Movement Activism in the Age of Globalization*
Robert Braun, *Protectors of Pluralism: Religious Minorities and the Rescue of Jews in the Low Countries during the Holocaust*
Chandra Russo, *Solidarity in Practice: Moral Protest and the US Security State*
Barry Eidlin, *Labor and the Class Idea in the United States and Canada*
Nicole Doerr, *Political Translation: How Social Movement Democracies Survive*
Diana Fu, *Mobilizing Without the Masses: Control and Contention in China*
Nancy Bermeo and Deborah J. Yashar, editors, *Parties, Movements, and Democracy in the Developing World*
Neil Ketchley, *Egypt in a Time of Revolution: Contentious Politics and the Arab Spring*
Wayne P. Te Brake, *Religious War and Religious Peace in Early Modern Europe*
Héctor PerlaJr., *Sandinista Nicaragua's Resistance to US Coercion*
Donatella della Porta, *Where Did the Revolution Go? Contentious Politics and the Quality of Democracy*
Erica S. Simmons, *Meaningful Resistance: Market Reforms and the Roots of Social Protest in Latin America*
Ralph A. ThaxtonJr., *Force and Contention in Contemporary China: Memory and Resistance in the Long Shadow of the Catastrophic Past*
Sheena Chestnut Greitens, *Dictators and their Secret Police: Coercive Institutions and State Violence*
Phillip M. Ayoub, *When States Come Out: Europe's Sexual Minorities and the Politics of Visibility*
Amrita Basu, *Violent Conjunctures in Democratic India*
Mario Diani, *The Cement of Civil Society: Studying Networks in Localities*
Jennifer Hadden, *Networks in Contention: The Divisive Politics of Climate Change*
Michael T. Heaney and Fabio Rojas, *Party in the Street: The Antiwar Movement and the Democratic Party after 9/11*
Christian Davenport, *How Social Movements Die: Repression and Demobilization of the Republic of New Africa*
Ronald Aminzade, *Race, Nation, and Citizenship in Post-Colonial Africa: The Case of Tanzania*
Marisa von Bülow, *Building Transnational Networks: Civil Society and the Politics of Trade in the Americas*
Lesley J. Wood, *Direct Action, Deliberation, and Diffusion: Collective Action after the WTO Protests in Seattle*
Sherrill Stroschein, *Ethnic Struggle, Coexistence, and Democratization in Eastern Europe*
Holly J. McCammon, *The U.S. Women's Jury Movements and Strategic Adaptation: A More Just Verdict*
Sidney Tarrow, *The Language of Contention: Revolutions in Words, 1688–2012*
Lars-Erik Cederman, Kristian Skrede Gleditsch, and Halvard Buhaug, *Inequality, Grievances, and Civil War*
W. Lance Bennett and Alexandra Segerberg, *The Logic of Connective Action: Digital Media and the Personalization of Contentious Politics*

Todd A. Eisenstadt, *Politics, Identity, and Mexico's Indigenous Rights Movements*
Donatella della Porta, *Clandestine Political Violence*
Rina Agarwala, *Informal Labor, Formal Politics, and Dignified Discontent in India*
Daniel Q. Gillion, *The Political Power of Protest: Minority Activism and Shifts in Public Policy*
Doug McAdam and Hilary Boudet, *Putting Social Movements in Their Place: Explaining Opposition to Energy Projects in the United States, 2000–2005*
Clifford Bob, *The Global Right Wing and the Clash of World Politics*
Valerie Bunce and Sharon Wolchik, *Defeating Authoritarian Leaders in Postcommunist Countries*
Andrew Yeo, *Activists, Alliances, and Anti-U.S. Base Protests*
Yang Su, *Collective Killings in Rural China during the Cultural Revolution*
Tamara Kay, *NAFTA and the Politics of Labor Transnationalism*
Christian Davenport, *Media Bias, Perspective, and State Repression*
Joseph Luders, *The Civil Rights Movement and the Logic of Social Change*
Eduardo Silva, *Challenging Neoliberalism in Latin America*
Sarah Soule, *Contention and Corporate Social Responsibility*
Charles Tilly, *Contentious Performances*
Ralph A. Thaxton Jr., *Catastrophe and Contention in Rural China: Mao's Great Leap Forward Famine and the Origins of Righteous Resistance in Da Fo Village*
Sharon Erickson Nepstad, *Religion and War Resistance in the Plowshares Movement*
Silvia Pedraza, *Political Disaffection in Cuba's Revolution and Exodus*
Stuart A. Wright, *Patriots, Politics, and the Oklahoma City Bombing*
Javier Auyero, *Routine Politics and Violence in Argentina: The Gray Zone of State Power*
Kevin J. O'Brien and Lianjiang Li, *Rightful Resistance in Rural China*
Sidney Tarrow, *The New Transnational Activism*
Clifford Bob, *The Marketing of Rebellion: Insurgents, Media, and International Activism*
Gerald F. Davis, Doug McAdam, W. Richard Scott, and Mayer N. Zald, *Social Movements and Organization Theory*
Charles Brockett, *Political Movements and Violence in Central America*
Deborah Yashar, *Contesting Citizenship in Latin America: The Rise of Indigenous Movements and the Postliberal Challenge*
Charles Tilly, *Contention and Democracy in Europe, 1650–2000*
Charles Tilly, *The Politics of Collective Violence*
Jack A. Goldstone, editor, *States, Parties, and Social Movements*
Ronald Aminzade et al., *Silence and Voice in the Study of Contentious Politics*
Doug McAdam, Sidney Tarrow, and Charles Tilly, *Dynamics of Contention*

Invisible Revolutionaries

Women's Participation in Ukraine's Euromaidan

OLENA NIKOLAYENKO
Fordham University

CAMBRIDGE
UNIVERSITY PRESS

Shaftesbury Road, Cambridge CB2 8EA, United Kingdom

One Liberty Plaza, 20th Floor, New York, NY 10006, USA

477 Williamstown Road, Port Melbourne, VIC 3207, Australia

314–321, 3rd Floor, Plot 3, Splendor Forum, Jasola District Centre, New Delhi – 110025, India

103 Penang Road, #05-06/07, Visioncrest Commercial, Singapore 238467

Cambridge University Press is part of Cambridge University Press & Assessment, a department of the University of Cambridge.

We share the University's mission to contribute to society through the pursuit of education, learning and research at the highest international levels of excellence.

www.cambridge.org
Information on this title: www.cambridge.org/9781009607476

DOI: 10.1017/9781009607445

© Olena Nikolayenko 2025

This publication is in copyright. Subject to statutory exception and to the provisions of relevant collective licensing agreements, no reproduction of any part may take place without the written permission of Cambridge University Press & Assessment.

When citing this work, please include a reference to the DOI 10.1017/9781009607445

First published 2025

A catalogue record for this publication is available from the British Library

A Cataloging-in-Publication data record for this book is available from the Library of Congress

ISBN 978-1-009-60747-6 Hardback
ISBN 978-1-009-60743-8 Paperback

Cambridge University Press & Assessment has no responsibility for the persistence or accuracy of URLs for external or third-party internet websites referred to in this publication and does not guarantee that any content on such websites is, or will remain, accurate or appropriate.

To all the Ukrainian women who have fought for Ukraine's national independence, democratic development, and cultural heritage

Contents

List of Figures	*page* xi
List of Tables	xiii
Acknowledgments	xv
Note on Transliteration	xix
1 Introduction	1
2 Women's Activism in a Historical Perspective	39
3 Drivers of Women's Participation in the Revolution of Dignity	72
4 Women's Roles During a Revolution	102
5 Gender Outcomes of the Revolution and the Russia–Ukraine War	129
6 Conclusion	166
Appendix	191
Index	197

Figures

1.1 Women's and men's participation in the Revolution of Dignity	page 24
3.1 Motivations for protesting by age and education	76
5.1 Women's representation in the national parliament	135
5.2 Women's representation in local legislative bodies	137
5.3 Gross domestic product (GDP) per capita growth	150
5.4 Unemployment rate among working-age women and men	152
5.5 Gender wage gap, 2002–2021	153
5.6 Servicewomen in the Armed Forces of Ukraine	154
5.7 Disagreement with the statement, "Women Should Not Hold Leadership Positions"	156

Tables

1.1	Typology of women's participation in a revolution	page 6
1.2	Sociodemographic characteristics of Kyiv-based protesters	26
1.3	Participants in anti-government protests in and outside Kyiv	28
1.4	Gender and protest participation: multivariate analysis	29
2.1	Women in the Ukrainian Central Rada, March 1917	46
2.2	Female delegates from Halychyna at the founding congress of Rukh, 1989	56
2.3	Participants in the 2004 postelection protests	65
3.1	Motivations for participation in Kyiv-based protests: findings from on-site surveys	74
3.2	Determinants of motivations for protesting	77
3.3	Women's motivations for participation in a revolution: insights from oral history projects	79
4.1	Main domains of women's participation in a revolution	103
5.1	Women in the Cabinet of Ministers of Ukraine	140
5.2	Female presidential candidates	145

Acknowledgments

The idea for this book was conceived during Ukraine's Revolution of Dignity, and the importance of telling women's stories and preserving national history has become even more acute since the onset of Russia's brutal war against Ukraine in 2014. Over the past century, Ukrainian women exhibited a great deal of resilience and resourcefulness in fighting for Ukraine's national independence, democratic development, and cultural heritage. This book is dedicated to unsung heroines of the Ukrainian liberation struggle from the early twentieth century to the present day.

I am profoundly thankful to Ukrainian historians who gathered rich qualitative data on citizens' participation in Euromaidan and made it available to the academic community. In particular, I am grateful to Tetiana Kovtunovych, Tetiana Pryvalko, and Volodymyr Viatrovych at the Ukrainian Institute of National Remembrance (*Ukrainskyi instytut natsionalnoi pamiati*) and Leonid Finberg and Anna Prokhorova at the National University of Kyiv-Mohyla Academy for meticulously documenting individuals' engagement in civil resistance. Ukrainian sociologists at the Institute of Sociology of the National Academy of Sciences of Ukraine, the Kyiv International Institute of Sociology, and the Ilko Kucheriv Democratic Initiatives Foundation also collected detailed data on Euromaidan protesters. I thank Iryna Bekeshkina (posthumously) and Viktor Stepanenko for generously granting access to the survey data. Additional thanks go to Nataliya Dovhopol for an excellent transcription of interviews. Furthermore, I am deeply indebted to all the participants in the oral history projects for taking the time to share their experiences and their recollections of this critical juncture in Ukrainian history.

The book has greatly benefited from thoughtful comments by many historians, political scientists, and sociologists. I thank Özlem Altan-Olcay, Mark Beissinger, Cynthia Buckley, Susanne Yuk Ping Choi, Sonja Grimm, Janet Elise Johnson, John Krinsky, Tamara Martsenyuk, Lisbeth Matzer, Olga Onuch,

Kiran Klaus Patel, Kevin M. F. Platt, Daniel Ritter, Jillian Schwedler, Ostap Sereda, Thomas Süsler-Rohringer, Anh Tran, Aili Mari Tripp, and Sophia Wilson for their helpful feedback. I am especially grateful to Henry Hale for organizing a manuscript development workshop at the Institute for European, Russian, and Eurasian Studies at the George Washington University and to workshop participants – Daina Stukuls Eglitis, Eugene M. Fishel, Erik Herron, Miriam Lanskoy, and Kateryna Ruban – for their close reading and constructive criticism of the manuscript. Some of the findings from the book project were presented at the Gender and Transformation: Women in Europe Workshop at New York University; the Politics and Protest Workshop at the Graduate Center of the City University of New York; the Harriman Institute at Columbia University; the research colloquium (Oberseminar) at Project House Europe at the Ludwig Maximilian University of Munich; the Monday Seminar (Oberseminar Osteuropäische Geschichte) at Imre Kertész Kolleg Jena; the international workshop "Why to Fight against Dictatorship at High Personal Costs? Studying Political Activism and Its Leadership in Autocracies" at the Peace Research Institute Frankfurt; the Gender Research Centre at the Chinese University of Hong Kong; the workshop "A Woman's Work Is Never Done: Female Life and Labor across the Imperial, Soviet and Post-Soviet Eras" at the University of Illinois at Urbana-Champaign; the interdisciplinary conference "Contested Bodies: Identities and Spaces in Post-Soviet Territories" at the University of Pennsylvania; Taras Shevchenko Ukrainian Studies Conference at Indiana University; the Center for Russian, East European and Eurasian Studies at the University of Kansas; the Conference of the Ukrainian Studies Association of Australia and New Zealand; the Shevchenko Scientific Society in the United States; and the annual meetings of the American Political Science Association, the Association for Slavic, East European, and Eurasian Studies, and the Association for the Study of Nationalities.

This research was supported by the American Political Science Association (APSA Small Research Grant), the Petrach Program on Ukraine at the George Washington University (Petrach Ukrainian Studies Fellowship), Project House Europe at the Ludwig Maximilian University of Munich (Simone Veil Fellowship), Summer Research Laboratory Program on Russia, Eastern Europe, and Eurasia at the University of Illinois at Urbana-Champaign (Title VIII Research Award), and Fordham University (Faculty Research Grant).

At Cambridge University Press, I thank Rachel Blaifeder and David S. Meyer for their enthusiasm about the book project and their incisive feedback throughout various stages of the review process. My infinite thanks go to anonymous reviewers for their thought-provoking and insightful comments on the manuscript. Laura Blake skillfully guided the book through the production process. I am also deeply appreciative of all the invaluable advice Mark Beissinger has given me.

My family provided unwavering support for my research endeavors. I thank my spouse for his boundless love and immense support. I am also fortunate to

Acknowledgments

have been raised by parents who placed a high value on education and freedom. Being born in 1946, my father grew up with the belief that his generation would never live through a war on their soil. Yet, he now witnesses how the Russian military is destroying Ukrainian towns and villages by dropping aerial bombs in residential areas and launching missile and drone strikes against the critical infrastructure with the intent to occupy the land. My hope is that peace and democracy will prevail on the continent.

Copyright Acknowledgments

> I thank the publishers for granting me the copyright permission to reuse some material previously published in peer-reviewed journals.
>
> Olena Nikolayenko. 2020. "Invisible Revolutionaries: Women's Participation in the Revolution of Dignity." *Comparative Politics* 52 (3): 451–72. https://doi.org/10.5129/001041520X15699553017268.
>
> Olena Nikolayenko. 2024. "Gender Differences in Protest Participation: Findings from the 2004 Orange Revolution and the 2013–2014 Revolution of Dignity in Ukraine." *Journal of Women, Politics and Policy* 45 (3): 350–63. https://doi.org/10.1080/1554477X.2024.2301145.

Note on Transliteration

This book uses a simplified version of the *ALA-LC Romanization Tables: Transliteration Schemes for Non-Roman Scripts* approved by the Library of Congress and the American Library Association (www.loc.gov/catdir/cpso/romanization/ukrainia.pdf). Soft signs and apostrophes have been omitted.

1

Introduction

Over the past two decades, there has been a resurgence of authoritarianism around the globe.[1] A third wave of autocratization – the declining quality of institutions for clean elections, freedom of expression, and freedom of assembly – stalled the global spread of democratic ideas and principles.[2] In 2023, the US nonprofit organization Freedom House registered the seventeenth consecutive year of the decline in state provision of political rights and civil liberties.[3] In particular, the quality of democracy came under assault in postcommunist Europe.[4] According to some estimates, more than two-thirds of the world's

---

[1] Anne Applebaum. 2020. *Twilight of Democracy: The Seductive Lure of Authoritarianism*. New York: Knopf Doubleday Publishing Group; Larry Diamond, Marc F. Plattner, and Christopher Walker, eds. 2016. *Authoritarianism Goes Global: The Challenge to Democracy*. Baltimore: John Hopkins University Press; Erica Frantz. 2018. *Authoritarianism: What Everyone Needs to Know*. New York: Oxford University Press; Steven Levitsky and Lucan A. Way. 2010. *Competitive Authoritarianism: Hybrid Regimes After the Cold War*. New York: Cambridge University Press.

[2] Lührmann and Lindberg define an autocratization wave as "the time period during which the number of countries undergoing democratization declines while at the same time autocratization affects more and more countries." Their empirical analysis is based on data from the Varieties of Democracy (V-Dem) project for 182 countries from 1900 to 2017. For details, see Anna Lührmann and Staffan I. Lindberg. 2019. "A Third Wave of Autocratization Is Here: What Is New About It?" *Democratization* 26 (7): 1095–1113, 1102.

[3] Yana Gorokhovskaia, Adrian Shahbaz, and Amy Slipowitz, eds. 2023. *Freedom in the World 2023: Marking 50 Years in the Struggle for Democracy*. New York: Freedom House. https://freedomhouse.org/report/freedom-world/2023/marking-50-years.

[4] Attila Antal. 2019. *The Rise of Hungarian Populism: State Autocracy and the Orbán Regime*. Bingley: Emerald Publishing; Florian Bieber. 2020. *The Rise of Authoritarianism in the Western Balkans*. Cham, Switzerland: Palgrave Macmillan; Vladimir Gel'man. 2015. *Authoritarian Russia: Analyzing Post-Soviet Regime Changes*. Pittsburgh: University of Pittsburgh Press; Henry E. Hale. 2015. *Patronal Politics: Eurasian Regime Dynamics in Comparative Perspective*. New York: Cambridge University Press; Paul Lendvai. 2017. *Orbán: Hungary's Strongman*. New York: Oxford University Press; Adam Przeworski. 2019. *Crises of Democracy*.

population currently live in autocracies.[5] The persistence of "democratic regression" has far-reaching implications for the pursuit of political change and social justice by ordinary citizens.[6]

A related global trend is an unprecedented frequency, scope, and size of antigovernment protests.[7] Between 2009 and 2019, the incidence of mass protests annually increased, on average, by 11.5 percent worldwide.[8] Based on data from the Nonviolent and Violent Campaigns and Outcomes (NAVCO) project, Chenoweth concludes that the past decade saw the largest number of nonviolent campaigns since 1900.[9] Furthermore, there was a proliferation of urban revolutions, involving a high concentration of protesters in urban spaces and popular demands for political freedoms.[10] Using an original dataset of 345 revolutionary episodes from 1900 to 2014, Beissinger demonstrates that citizens extensively leveraged urban space to bring down autocrats.[11] Thousands of people in the Middle East and North Africa (MENA) poured into the streets to oust long-serving incumbents and demand political change in

---

New York: Cambridge University Press; Regina Smyth. 2020. *Elections, Protest, and Authoritarian Regime Stability: Russia 2008–2020*. New York: Cambridge University Press.

[5] A team of researchers at the V-Dem Institute estimated that 72 percent of the world's population, or 5.7 billion people, lived in autocracies in 2022. For details, see Evie Papada and Staffan I. Lindberg, eds. 2023. *Democracy Report 2023: Defiance in the Face of Autocratization*. Gothenburg, Sweden: Varieties of Democracy Institute, University of Gothenburg.

[6] Larry Diamond. 2021. "Democratic Regression in Comparative Perspective: Scope, Methods, and Causes." *Democratization* 28 (1): 22–42.

[7] Dawn Brancati. 2016. *Democracy Protests: Origins, Features, and Significance*. New York: Cambridge University Press; Valerie J. Bunce and Sharon L. Wolchik. 2011. *Defeating Authoritarian Leaders in Postcommunist Countries*. New York: Cambridge University Press; Thomas Carothers and Richard Youngs. 2015. *The Complexities of Global Protests*. Washington, DC: Carnegie Endowment for International Peace; Hank Johnston, ed. 2019. *Social Movements, Nonviolent Resistance, and the State*. London: Routledge; Sharon Erickson Nepstad. 2015. *Nonviolent Struggle: Theories, Strategies, and Dynamics*. New York: Oxford University Press; Adam Roberts and Timothy Garton Ash, eds. 2009. *Civil Resistance and Power Politics: The Experience of Non-Violent Action from Gandhi to the Present*. New York: Oxford University Press; Kenneth Roth. 2019. "World's Autocrats Face Rising Resistance." In *World Report 2019*. New York: Human Rights Watch. www.hrw.org/world-report/2019/country-chapters/global; Kurt Schock. 2015. *Civil Resistance Today*. Cambridge: Polity Press.

[8] Sam Brannen, Christian Stirling Haig, and Katherine Schmidt. 2021. *The Age of Mass Protests: Understanding an Escalating Global Trend*. Washington, DC: Center for Strategic and International Studies.

[9] Erica Chenoweth. 2020. "The Future of Civil Resistance." *Journal of Democracy* 31 (3): 69–84.

[10] Marco Allegra, Irene Bono, Jonathan Rokem, Anna Casaglia, Roberta Marzorati, and Haim Yacobi. 2013. "Rethinking Cities in Contentious Times: The Mobilisation of Urban Dissent in the 'Arab Spring'." *Urban Studies* 50: 1675–88; Mark Beissinger. 2013. "The Semblance of Democratic Revolution: Coalitions in Ukraine's Orange Revolution." *American Political Science Review* 107 (3): 574–92; Mehmet Barış Kuymulu. 2013. "Reclaiming the Right to the City: Reflections on the Urban Uprisings in Turkey." *City* 17 (3): 274–78.

[11] Mark Beissinger. 2022. *The Revolutionary City: Urbanization and the Global Transformation of Rebellion*. Princeton: Princeton University Press.

Introduction

2010–2011.[12] Large-scale anti-government protests also erupted in Belarus, Chile, Hong Kong, Iran, Sudan, Turkey, and Ukraine, to name a few.[13]

Women play a vital role in civil resistance to the entrenchment of authoritarianism,[14] which is closely intertwined with the persistence of patriarchal norms.[15] Across the Middle East, women rose against multiple forms of oppression during the Arab Spring.[16] Likewise, women in Iran joined the Green Movement during the 2009 presidential election and led the 2022 protests against the curtailment of freedoms, abject poverty, and colossal corruption in the country.[17] In Turkey, women protested against the government's

---

[12] Asaf Bayat. 2017. *Revolution without Revolutionaries: Making Sense of the Arab Spring*. Stanford: Stanford University Press; Jason Brownlee, Tarek E. Masoud, and Andrew Reynolds. 2015. *The Arab Spring: Pathways of Repression and Reform*. New York: Oxford University Press; Jeroen Gunning and Ilan Zvi Baron. 2014. *Why Occupy a Square?: People, Protests and Movements in the Egyptian Revolution*. New York: Oxford University Press; Neil Ketchley. 2017. *Egypt in a Time of Revolution: Contentious Politics and the Arab Spring*. New York: Cambridge University Press; Sarah Anne Rennick. 2018. *Politics and Revolution in Egypt: Rise and Fall of the Youth Activists*. London: Routledge.

[13] Yu Loong Au. 2020. *Hong Kong in Revolt: The Protest Movement and the Future of China*. London: Pluto Press; Willow Berridge, Justin Lynch, Raga Makawi, and Alex de Waal. 2022. *Sudan's Unfinished Democracy: The Promise and Betrayal of a People's Revolution*. London: Hurst Publishers; Terri Gordon-Zolov and Eric Zolov. 2022. *The Walls of Santiago: Social Revolution and Political Aesthetics in Contemporary Chile*. New York: Berghahn Books; Paul Hansbury. 2023. *Belarus in Crisis: From Domestic Unrest to the Russia-Ukraine War*. London: Hurst Publishers; Ngok Ma and Edmund W. Cheng, eds. 2019. *The Umbrella Movement*. Amsterdam: Amsterdam University Press; Esra Ozyurek, Gaye Ozpinar, and Emrah Altindis. 2019. *Authoritarianism and Resistance in Turkey: Conversations on Democratic and Social Challenges*. Cham: Springer; Navid Pourmokhtari. 2021. *Iran's Green Movement: Everyday Resistance, Political Contestation and Social Mobilization*. New York: Routledge.

[14] For an overview, see Marie A. Principe. 2017. "Women in Nonviolent Movements." Special Report No. 399. United States Institute of Peace, Washington, DC.

[15] On the linkage between authoritarianism and patriarchy, see, for example, Cristina Awadalla. 2023. "Authoritarian Populism and Patriarchal Logics: Nicaragua's Engendered Politics." *Social Politics: International Studies in Gender, State and Society* 3 (2): 701–23; Gökten Huriye Dogangün. 2020. *Gender Politics in Turkey and Russia: From State Feminism to Authoritarian Rule*. London: Bloomsbury; Grewal Inderpal. 2020. "Authoritarian Patriarchy and Its Populism." *English Studies in Africa* 63 (1): 179–98; Valerie Sperling. 2015. *Sex, Politics, and Putin: Political Legitimacy in Russia*. New York: Oxford University Press.

[16] Nermin Allam. 2018. *Women and the Egyptian Revolution: Engagement and Activism during the 2011 Arab Uprisings*. New York: Cambridge University Press; Mounira M. Charrad and Rita Stephan, eds. 2020. *Women Rising: In and Beyond the Arab Spring*. New York: New York University Press; Sherine Hafez. 2019. *Women of the Midan: The Untold Stories of Egypt's Revolutionaries*. Bloomington: Indiana University Press; Andrea Khalil, ed. 2016. *Gender, Women, and the Arab Spring*. New York: Routledge; Mona Prince. 2014. *Revolution Is My Name: An Egyptian Woman's Diary from Eighteen Days in Tahrir*, trans. Samia Mehrez. Cairo: American University in Cairo Press; Marwa Shalaby and Valentine Moghadam, eds. 2016. *Empowering Women After the Arab Spring*. New York: Palgrave Macmillan.

[17] Janet Afary and Kevin B. Anderson. 2023. "Woman, Life, Freedom: The Origins of the Uprising in Iran." *Dissent* 70 (1): 82–98; Raheleh Dayerizadeh. 2017. "Iranian Women and Their Strategic Role During the Green Movement." In *The New Global Politics: Global Social*

infringement on women's rights.[18] Moreover, women in Ukraine played a significant role during the 2013–2014 Revolution of Dignity, also known as Euromaidan.[19] Women were also at the forefront of the 2019 revolution that brought down Omar al-Bashir's thirty-year rule in Sudan.[20] In Belarus, women's marches were a hallmark of mass mobilization against gross violations of democratic procedures during the 2020 presidential election and police brutality against participants in peaceful postelection protests.[21] Taken as a whole, women were actively involved in contemporary revolutions and pro-democracy movements that emerged in the aftermath of rigged elections or outside an electoral cycle.

Yet, women's engagement in contentious politics often appears to be invisible in the public discourse. The marginalization of women activists derives, in part, from the media's gendered portrayal of civil resistance, which tends to reinforce a gender-based division of labor within a protest movement. Moreover, the media spotlight often focuses on a handful of movement leaders, which further diminishes the visibility of many rank-and-file female activists. Prior research shows that many African American women who performed various roles comparable to those of African American men were "invisible,

---

Movements in the Twenty-First Century, eds. Harry Vanden, Peter Funke, and Gary Prevost. London: Routledge, pp. 111–27; Victoria Tahmasebi-Birgani. 2010. "Green Women of Iran: The Role of the Women's Movement During and After Iran's Presidential Election of 2009." *Constellations* 17: 78–86.

[18] For an overview, see Zehra F. Kabasakal Arat. 2021. "Gender Politics and the Struggle for Equality in Turkey." In *The Oxford Handbook of Turkish Politics*, ed. Güneş Murat Tezcür. New York: Oxford University Press, pp. 627–48.

[19] In this book, the terms Euromaidan and the Revolution of Dignity are used interchangeably, without a reference to a specific moment in mass mobilization. The term Euromaidan is a combination of the words Europe and Maidan. The Ukrainian-language word *maidan* denotes open space or a town square. Furthermore, given a long record of anti-government protests in the center of Kyiv's Independence Square in the post-Soviet period, the word *maidan* has become synonymous with mass mobilization against the ruling elite. For an overview of sociological research on women's participation in Euromaidan, see Tamara Martsenyuk. 2014. *Henderna sotsiolohiia Maidanu: Rol zhinok u protestah*. Kyiv: Electronic Archive of the National University of Kyiv-Mohyla Academy. http://ekmair.ukma.edu.ua/handle/123456789/3511.

[20] Samia Al-Nagar and Liv Tønnessen. 2021. "Sudanese Women's Demands for Freedom, Peace, and Justice in the 2019 Revolution." In *Women and Peacebuilding in Africa*, eds. Ladan Affi, Liv Tønnessen, and Aili Mari Tripp. Suffolk: Boydell and Brewer, pp. 103–28; Balghis Badri. 2020. "Sudanese Women Leading Revolution: Impact on Transformation." *Femina Politica – Zeitschrift für feministische Politikwissenschaft* 1 (May): 146–50.

[21] Elena Gapova. 2023. "Activating and Negotiating Women's Citizenship in the 2020 Belarusian Uprising." In *Belarus in the Twenty-First Century: Between Dictatorship and Democracy*, eds. Elena Korosteleva, Irina Petrova, and Anastasiia Kudlenko. London: Routledge, pp. 161–78; Natallia Paulovich. 2021. "How Feminist Is the Belarusian Revolution? Female Agency and Participation in the 2020 Post-Election Protests." *Slavic Review* 80 (1): 38–44.

unsung heroes and leaders" of the US civil rights movement.[22] Despite significant advances in our knowledge about women's movements in the US,[23] much less effort has been expended to uncover women's involvement in broad-based pro-democracy movements and contemporary revolutions around the globe.[24] The book seeks to address this empirical gap in contentious politics literature. The empirical focus on women's engagement in a revolution is informed by feminist standpoint theory, positing that our understanding of state–society relations is incomplete without a critical reflection on the experiences of marginalized groups, including women.[25] The book places women at the center of empirical analysis not just as participants in a revolution but also as storytellers.

Theoretically, the book contributes to contentious politics literature by proposing a typology of women's participation in a revolution. This typology is summarized in Table 1.1. Based on women's motivations for engagement, modes of women's participation during a period of mass mobilization, and gender outcomes of revolution, the book distinguishes three models of participation: (1) patriarchal, (2) emancipatory, and (3) hybrid. Reinforcing pre-existing patriarchal norms in society, the patriarchal model of women's participation in a revolution assumes that motherhood is a key driver of women's activism, women primarily perform "support tasks" during a revolution, and female revolutionaries retreat into the private sphere in the wake of mass mobilization. The emancipatory model, on the contrary, views feminism as a catalyst for women's activism, assumes women's access to formal positions of leadership within the movement, and anticipates considerable progress in gender equality in the postrevolutionary period. Located between these two

---

[22] Bernice McNair Barnett. 1993. "Invisible Southern Black Women Leaders in the Civil Rights Movement: The Triple Constraints of Gender, Race, and Class." *Gender and Society* 7 (2): 162–82, 162.

[23] See, for example, Lee Ann Banaszak, ed. 2006. *The U.S. Women's Movement in Global Perspective*. Lanham: Rowman and Littlefield; Karen Beckwith, Dieter Rucht, and Lee Ann Banaszak, eds. 2003. *Women's Movements Facing the Reconfigured State*. New York: Cambridge University Press; Jo Reger, ed. 2019. *Nevertheless, They Persisted: Feminisms and Continued Resistance in the U.S. Women's Movement*. New York: Routledge.

[24] Lisa Baldez. 2010. "The Gender Lacuna in Comparative Politics." *Perspectives on Politics* 8: 199–205; Karen Beckwith. 2000. "Beyond Compare? Women's Movements in Comparative Perspective." *European Journal of Political Research* 37 (4): 431–68; Myra Marx Ferree and Aili Mari Tripp, eds. 2006. *Global Feminism: Transnational Women's Activism, Organizing, and Human Rights*. New York: New York University Press; Margaret Randall. 1995. *Sandino's Daughters: Testimonies of Nicaraguan Women in Struggle*. New Brunswick: Rutgers University Press; Aili Mari Tripp, Isabel Casimiro, Joy Kwesiga, and Alice Mungwa. 2011. *African Women's Movements: Transforming Political Landscapes*. New York: Cambridge University Press; Georgina Waylen. 2003. "Gender and Transitions: What Do We Know?" *Democratization* 10: 157–78.

[25] For an overview of feminist standpoint theory, see Catherine E. Hundleby. 2020. "Thinking Outside-In: Feminist Standpoint Theory as Epistemology, Methodology, and Philosophy of Science." In *The Routledge Handbook of Feminist Philosophy of Science*, eds. Sharon Crasnow and Kristen Intemann. New York: Routledge, pp. 89–103.

TABLE 1.1 *Typology of women's participation in a revolution*

	Women's participation in a revolution		
	Patriarchal	Emancipatory	Hybrid
Main motivations	Motherhood	Feminism	Various motivations, including motherhood, feminism, professional service, and civic duty
Women's roles	"Support tasks"	Leadership roles	Stereotypically feminine, stereotypically masculine, or gender-neutral roles
Outcomes	Retreat into the private sphere	Significant progress in gender equality	Mixed record of gender equality in different domains

extremes, the hybrid model encompasses a variety of motivations for women's engagement in the revolution, underscores the diversity of women's roles over the course of mass mobilization, and acknowledges various degrees of success in gender equality in different spheres. This study suggests that a hybrid model might better capture the diversity of women's experiences during a twenty-first-century revolution.

An in-depth analysis of the Revolution of Dignity in Ukraine provides a superb opportunity to examine various motivations for women's involvement in a revolution, diverse domains of women's engagement, and multifaceted outcomes of mass mobilization in a polity with fragile democratic institutions. Since the collapse of communism, the former Soviet republic located between the European Union, on the one hand, and the Russian Federation, on the other, experienced ebbs and flows in the provision of political rights and civil liberties.[26] In particular, rampant corruption hampered democratization processes and economic development.[27] Nevertheless, Ukrainians repeatedly took to the streets to subvert the entrenchment of authoritarian practices and reaffirm the country's national independence.[28]

---

[26] For a succinct survey of Ukrainian modern history, see Serhii Plokhy. 2015. *The Gates of Europe: A History of Ukraine*. New York: Basic Books, pp. 305–46; Serhy Yekelchyk. 2020. *Ukraine: What Everyone Needs to Know*, 2nd ed. New York: Oxford University Press.

[27] Anders Aslund. 2015. *Ukraine: What Went Wrong and How to Fix It*. Washington, DC: Peterson Institute for International Economics; Erik Herron. 2020. *Normalizing Corruption: Failures of Accountability in Ukraine*. Ann Arbor: University of Michigan Press; Taras Kuzio. 2015. *Ukraine: Democratization, Corruption, and the New Russian Imperialism*. Santa Barbara: Praeger.

[28] Emily Channell-Justice. 2022. *Without the State: Self-Organization and Political Activism in Ukraine*. Toronto: University of Toronto Press; Christine Emeran. 2017. *New Generation*

An advantage of focusing on the Ukrainian revolution is that there is a trove of under-explored data on mass mobilization. Ukrainian historians meticulously documented citizens' recollections of civil resistance through oral history projects. Furthermore, Ukrainian sociologists conducted on-site surveys of participants in Kyiv-based protests and fielded a nationally representative survey shortly after the conclusion of protest events. Local journalists also played an important role in chronicling civil resistance to the regime. Drawing on data from large-N surveys, oral history projects, and newspaper articles, the book traces multiple ways in which women participated in the revolution.

The remainder of this chapter elaborates on the study of women and revolutions, provides background information about the Revolution of Dignity and its participants, identifies the main trends in gender inequality in Ukrainian society, and describes data sources.

WOMEN AND REVOLUTIONS

In recent decades, there has been a growing body of interdisciplinary scholarship on women's involvement in different types of revolutions.[29] To some extent, the mere presence of women in revolutionary movements is seen as an act of

---

Political Activism in Ukraine 2000–2014. New York: Routledge; Paweł Kowal, Iwona Reichardt, Georges Mink, and Adam Reichardt, eds. 2019. *Three Revolutions: Mobilization and Change in Contemporary Ukraine II; An Oral History of the Revolution on Granite, Orange Revolution, and Revolution of Dignity*. Stuttgart: Ibidem Press; David R. Marples and Frederick V. Mills, eds. 2015. *Ukraine's Euromaidan: Analyses of a Civil Revolution*. Stuttgart: Ibidem Press; Olena Nikolayenko. 2015. "Youth Mobilization Before and During the Orange Revolution: Learning from Losses." In *Civil Resistance: Comparative Perspectives on Nonviolent Struggle*, ed. Kurt Schock. Minneapolis: University of Minnesota Press, pp. 93–120; Olga Onuch. 2014. *Mapping Mass Mobilization: Understanding Revolutionary Moments in Argentina and Ukraine*. Basingstoke: Palgrave Macmillan; Sophia Wilson. 2022. "The Ukrainian Revolution: Repression, Interpretation, and Dissent." *Research in Social Movements, Conflicts and Change* 45: 157–88.

[29] Michelle Chase. 2015. *Revolution within the Revolution: Women and Gender Politics in Cuba, 1952–1962*. Chapel Hill: University of North Carolina Press; Sheila Fitzpatrick and Yuri Slezkine, eds. 2000. *In the Shadow of Revolution: Life Stories of Russian Women from 1917 to the Second World War*. Princeton: Princeton University Press; Gail Hershatter. 2019. *Women and China's Revolutions*. Lanham: Rowman and Littlefield; Tabea Alexa Linhard. 2005. *Fearless Women in the Mexican Revolution and the Spanish Civil War*. Columbia: University of Missouri Press; Barbara Oberg, ed. 2019. *Women in the American Revolution: Gender, Politics, and the Domestic World*. Charlottesville: University of Virginia Press; Jocelyn Olcott. 2005. *Revolutionary Women in Postrevolutionary Mexico*. Durham: Duke University Press; Rochelle Goldberg Ruthchild. 2010. *Equality and Revolution: Women's Rights in the Russian Empire, 1905–1917*. Pittsburg: University of Pittsburgh Press; Stephanie Smith. 2009. *Gender and the Mexican Revolution: Yucatán Women and the Realities of Patriarchy*. Chapel Hill: University of North Carolina Press; Marilyn Yalom. 2015. *Compelled to Witness: Women's Memoirs of the French Revolution*. New York: Astor and Lenox LLC.

"gender-bending" (the contestation of dominant gender roles),[30] since the revolutionary struggle is traditionally seen as a man's domain.[31] Nonetheless, growing literature suggests that many women sought to challenge the prevailing gender boundaries by assuming a wide range of roles in the revolutionary struggle. Research on eighteenth-century women's history, for example, shows that women assumed multiple roles during the American Revolution, serving as nurses, soldiers, saboteurs, and spies.[32] Focusing on a more recent case of a social revolution, de Volo excavates data from primary documents, memoirs of rebel women, and US declassified material to demonstrate "women's multiple forms of participation" in the Cuban Revolution (p. 6).[33] Another line of inquiry investigates the causes and consequences of women's involvement in armed rebellions and guerrilla movements.[34] Henshaw, for example, analyzes patterns of women's participation in over seventy rebel groups in the post-Cold War period.[35] Specifically, Loken identifies four dimensions of women's involvement in noncombat labor in rebel organizations: logistics, outreach, governance, and community management.[36] Compared to armed insurgencies, nonviolent revolutions

---

[30] On the concept of gender-bending, see Judith Lorber. 1994. "'Night to His Day': The Social Construction of Gender." In *Paradoxes of Gender*, ed. Judith Lorber. New Haven: Yale University Press, pp. 13–36.

[31] On women's participation in revolutionary movements, see Jane S. Jaquette. 1973. "Women in Revolutionary Movements in Latin America." *Journal of Marriage and Family* 35 (2): 344–54; Linda M. Lobao. 1990. "Women in Revolutionary Movements: Changing Patterns of Latin American Guerrilla Struggle." *Dialectical Anthropology* 15 (2/3): 211–32; Linda L. Reif. 1986. "Women in Latin American Guerrilla Movements: A Comparative Perspective." *Comparative Politics* 18 (2): 147–69; Julie D. Shayne. 2004. *The Revolution Question: Feminisms in El Salvador, Chile, and Cuba*. New Brunswick: Rutgers University Press.

[32] Jeanne Munn Bracken, ed. 2009. *Women in the American Revolution*. Boston: History Compass; Susan Casey. 2015. *Women Heroes of the American Revolution: Twenty Stories of Espionage, Sabotage, Defiance, and Rescue*. Chicago: Chicago Review Press.

[33] Lorraine Bayard de Volo. 2018. *Women and the Cuban Insurrection: How Gender Shaped Castro's Victory*. New York: Cambridge University Press.

[34] Karen Kampwirth. 2002. *Women in Guerrilla Movements: Nicaragua, El Salvador, Chiapas, Cuba*. University Park: Pennsylvania State University Press; Sarah Parkinson. 2013. "Organizing Rebellion: Rethinking High-Risk Mobilization and Social Networks in War." *American Political Science Review* 107 (3): 418–32; Susanne Schaftenaar. 2017. "How (Wo)men Rebel: Exploring the Effect of Gender Equality on Nonviolent and Armed Conflict Onset." *Journal of Peace Research* 54 (6): 762–76; Jakana Thomas and Kanisha Bond. 2015. "Women's Participation in Violent Political Organizations." *American Political Science Review* 109: 488–506; Jocelyn S. Viterna. 2006. "Pulled, Pushed, and Persuaded: Explaining Women's Mobilization into the Salvadoran Guerrilla Army." *American Journal of Sociology* 112 (1): 1–45; Reed M. Wood. 2019. *Female Fighters: Why Rebel Groups Recruit Women for War*. New York: Columbia University Press.

[35] Alexis Henshaw. 2016. *Why Women Rebel: Understanding Women's Participation in Armed Rebel Groups*. London: Routledge.

[36] Meredith Loken. 2022. "Noncombat Participation in Rebellion: A Gendered Typology." *International Security* 47 (1): 139–70.

tend to provide a wider range of opportunities for women's recruitment and participation.

The book proposes a typology of women's participation in a revolution based on three dimensions: (1) women's motivations for participation, (2) forms of their participation, and (3) gender outcomes of revolution. The selection of these criteria is informed by three main questions that animate scholarship on mass mobilization: *Why do individuals join a revolution? How do individuals participate in a revolution? What are the outcomes of mass mobilization?* In this section, I briefly discuss how the book speaks to these strands of research.

Women's Mobilization

An influential argument in contentious politics literature is that the movement's strength depends on the effective recruitment of activists and volunteers.[37] Specifically, women's participation can bolster the movement's viability, since women represent nearly half of the population in most societies. It is widely upheld that a sizable movement might raise the costs of repression and decrease the likelihood of the deployment of lethal force against movement participants.[38] Recent scholarship also shows that a cross-cutting coalition of social forces is a salient feature of contemporary revolutions in non-democracies.[39] Against this backdrop, it is crucial to understand why individuals with diverse backgrounds get involved in civil resistance at the risk of their lives.[40] An examination of factors associated with women's participation in a revolution will enable scholars to provide a partial answer to this question.

The book makes an empirical contribution to contentious politics literature by demonstrating a wide range of women's motivations for engagement in a contemporary revolution. In her influential article on women's participation in the struggle against Anastasio Somoza in Nicaragua, Molyneux distinguishes between strategic gender interests aimed at achieving women's emancipation and eliminating gender subordination and practical gender interests directed

---

[37] James DeNardo. 1985. *Power in Numbers: The Political Strategy of Protest and Rebellion.* Princeton: Princeton University Press; Gerald Marwell and Pamela Oliver. 1993. *The Critical Mass in Collective Action.* New York: Cambridge University Press.
[38] On the unintended effects of repression, see Lester Kurtz and Lee Smitney, eds. 2018. *The Paradox of Repression and Nonviolent Movements.* Syracuse: Syracuse University Press.
[39] Asef Bayat. 2015. "Plebeians of the Arab Spring." *Current Anthropology* 56: 33–43; Beissinger, "The Semblance of Democratic Revolution"; Gianni Del Panta. 2020. "Cross-class and Cross-ideological Convergences over Time: Insights from the Tunisian and Egyptian Revolutionary Uprisings." *Government and Opposition* 55 (4): 634–52; Jack Andrew Goldstone. 2011. "Cross-class Coalitions and the Making of the Arab Revolts of 2011." *Swiss Political Science Review* 17 (4): 457–62.
[40] For an overview of the literature on mass mobilization, see Paul Almeida. 2019. *Social Movements: The Structure of Mass Mobilization.* Oakland: University of California Press.

at tackling the immediate perceived needs of women.[41] This distinction is relevant to identify different models of women's participation in a revolution. An egalitarian model of women's participation in a revolution assumes that the development of feminist consciousness and the pursuit of strategic gender interests is a driving force behind women's activism.[42] Meanwhile, in line with a patriarchal model of women's participation in a revolution, maternal identity might serve as a powerful incentive for women's activism.[43] In her analysis of women's community work in low-income neighborhoods in New York City and Philadelphia, Naples develops the concept of activist mothering to encompass caretaking not only for biologically or legally related children but also for the community as a whole.[44] Thus, the politicization of motherhood "turns needs related to children into political demands and thus promotes political action."[45] The hybrid model assumes that a myriad of social identities, including being a mother or a feminist, might provide a catalyst for women's involvement in contentious politics. In line with a hybrid model, the book illustrates that a broad spectrum of motivations, including motherhood, civic duty, professional service, and solidarity with protesters, provides an incentive for women's engagement in a contemporary revolution. These findings are consistent with Marian Rubchak's astute observation that there are "many faces of women," along with diverse conceptions of feminism, in Ukraine (p. 19).[46]

Moreover, the book contributes to the literature about the impact of biographical availability on protest participation by uncovering conditions under which women might get involved in a revolution. In line with the biographical availability argument, parenthood imposes constraints on

---

[41] Maxine Molyneux. 1985. "Mobilization without Emancipation? Women's Interests, the State, and Revolution in Nicaragua." *Feminist Studies* 11 (2): 227–54.
[42] Eric Swank and Breanne Fahs. 2017. "Understanding Feminist Activism among Women: Resources, Consciousness, and Social Networks." *Socius* 3: 1–9.
[43] See, for example, Valeria Fabj. 1993. "Motherhood as Political Voice: The Rhetoric of the Mothers of Plaza de Mayo." *Communication Studies* 44 (1): 1–18; Jenny Irons. 1998. "The Shaping of Activist Recruitment and Participation: A Study of Women in the Mississippi Civil Rights Movement." *Gender and Society* 12 (6): 692–709; Nancy Naples. 1998. *Grassroots Warriors: Activist Mothering, Community Work, and the War on Poverty*. New York: Routledge; Thomas Shriver, Alison Adams, and Rachel Einwohner. 2013. "Motherhood and Opportunities for Activism Before and After the Czech Velvet Revolution." *Mobilization: An International Quarterly* 18: 267–88.
[44] Nancy Naples. 1992. "Activist Mothering: Cross-Generational Continuity in the Community Work of Women from Low-Income Urban Neighborhoods." *Gender and Society* 6 (3): 441–63, 446.
[45] Graciela Di Marco. 2009. "Social Justice and Gender Rights." *International Social Science Journal* 191: 43–55, 53.
[46] Marian J. Rubchak. 2011. "Turning Oppression Into Opportunity: An Introduction." In *Mapping Difference: The Many Faces of Women in Contemporary Ukraine*, ed. Marian J. Rubchak. New York: Berghahn Books, pp. 1–21.

women's engagement in revolutionary activity.⁴⁷ Data from oral history projects, however, reveal that many Ukrainian women with little children tried to carve out some free time for themselves by turning to their parents or friends as a source of tuition-free childcare. The likelihood of women's physical presence on Maidan increased if grandparents temporarily assumed childcare responsibilities. Concurrently, many women tried to combine their childcare duties with their involvement in the protest movement by virtue of social media. These findings demonstrate how women might come up with creative solutions to overcome barriers to protest engagement.

In addition, the book speaks to a debate about the relative importance of various social ties by exploring women's networks of contention.⁴⁸ Drawing on data from oral history projects, empirical analysis uncovers a wide range of social networks conducive to mass mobilization in a society with a rather underdeveloped party system and a low level of formal membership in civic organizations. Women were embedded in a wide range of mixed-gender social networks, including professional associations and community-based organizations. Additionally, data from oral history projects indicate that Facebook served as an important source of information about protest events in the mid-2010s. Specifically, individuals with weak offline social ties were more likely to get galvanized into action via social media. For others, friendship ties or professional networks were more influential.

Modes of Women's Participation in a Revolution

Over the course of mass mobilization, women can perform stereotypically feminine, stereotypically masculine, or gender-neutral roles. In line with a patriarchal model of participation, women's performance of "caretaking" tasks is traditionally seen as an extension of women's roles within a household. Meanwhile, involvement in confrontational protest tactics is traditionally viewed as masculine. In line with an egalitarian model, women might break down dominant gender hierarchies by taking up stereotypically masculine roles. Additionally, some revolutionary activities might be less clearly demarcated as feminine or

---

⁴⁷ Kraig Beyerlein and Kelly Bergstrand. 2022. "Biographical Availability." In *The Wiley-Blackwell Encyclopedia of Social and Political Movements*, 2nd ed., eds. David A. Snow, Donatella della Porta, Bert Klandermans, and Doug McAdam. Hoboken: Wiley-Blackwell, pp. 262–63.

⁴⁸ On the significance of social networks, see Nick Crossley. 2020. *Social Networks and Social Movements: Contentious Connections*. London: Routledge; Mario Diani and Doug McAdam, eds. 2003. *Social Movements and Networks: Relational Approaches to Collective Action*. New York: Oxford University Press; Valentine Moghadam. 2005. *Globalizing Women: Transnational Feminist Networks*. Baltimore: Johns Hopkins University Press; Dana Moss. 2021. *The Arab Spring Abroad: Diaspora Activism against Authoritarian Regimes*. New York: Cambridge University Press; Zeynep Tufekci. 2017. *Twitter and Tear Gas: The Power and Fragility of Networked Protest*. New Haven: Yale University Press.

masculine and fall into the category of relatively gender-neutral roles. According to the hybrid model, women might adopt three different strategies: (1) acquiescence to a traditional gender-based division of labor, (2) appropriation of the masculine forms of resistance, and (3) switching from stereotypically feminine to stereotypically masculine roles or adoption of gender-neutral roles.

An empirical contribution of this book lies in identifying multiple domains of women's activism. Data from oral history projects demonstrate that Ukrainian women coordinated an extensive network of volunteers, executed a wide range of crowdsourcing initiatives, disseminated information, offered pro bono legal aid and urgent medical care, produced art of resistance, and joined self-defense units. Consistent with resource mobilization theory,[49] women's performance of these critical tasks sustained the encampment in the heart of Kyiv for nearly three months. In general, women's engagement in a revolution can bolster the capacity of regime opponents to self-organize through their use of social, cultural, and economic capital.[50]

In addition, a close analysis of women's engagement in a contemporary revolution contributes to the literature on the interplay between gender and nonviolent action. Conventional wisdom holds that women are more prone than men to oppose the deployment of violence against their adversaries.[51] As a principled proponent of nonviolence, Mahatma Gandhi wrote in 1938, "Woman is more fitted than man to make exploration and take bolder action in *ahimsa* [nonviolence]."[52] Research, for example, shows that the suffragist women in the US fought for the right to vote, using such nonviolent methods as hunger strikes, pickets, and marches.[53] Similarly, women played a prominent role in peace movements and employed such nonviolent tactics as vigils and peace camps.[54] Women's presence at protest events is often seen as a deterrent

---

[49] J. Craig Jenkins. 1983. "Resource Mobilization Theory and the Study of Social Movements." *Annual Review of Sociology* 9 (1): 527–53; John D. McCarthy and Mayer N. Zald. 2001. "The Enduring Vitality of the Resource Mobilization Theory of Social Movements." In *Handbook of Sociological Theory*, ed. Jonathan Turner. Boston: Springer, pp. 533–65.

[50] On the conceptualization of different forms of capital, see Pierre Bourdieu. 1986. "The Forms of Capital." In *Handbook of Theory and Research for the Sociology of Education*, ed. John Richardson. New York: Greenwood, pp. 241–58.

[51] Anne N. Costain. 2000. "Women's Movements and Nonviolence." *PS: Political Science and Politics* 33 (2): 175–80.

[52] Anima Bose. 1975. "Women in Gandhi's India." *India International Centre Quarterly* 2 (4): 280–91, 283.

[53] Selina Gallo-Cruz. 2018. "American Mothers of Nonviolence: Action and the Politics of Erasure in Women's Nonviolent Activism." In *100 Years of the Nineteenth Amendment: An Appraisal of US Women's Activism*, eds. Holly J. McCammon and Lee Ann Banaszak. New York: Oxford University Press, pp. 273–94.

[54] Harriet Hyman Alonso. 1993. *Peace as a Women's Issue: A History of the US Movement for World Peace and Women's Rights*. Syracuse: Syracuse University Press; Cynthia Cockburn. 2007. *From Where We Stand: War, Women's Activism and Feminist Analysis*. London: Zed Books; Maja Korac. 2006. "Gender, Conflict and Peace-Building: Lessons from the Conflict in

to violent clashes with the police. In line with this perspective, the book marshals empirical evidence for the argument that women's participation in a political revolution fosters the use of nonviolent methods of resistance. Meanwhile, the book adds a caveat to this argument. The analysis of state–society relations during the last phase of the Revolution of Dignity reveals that female and male activists were inclined to accept the use of violent tactics when both sides assumed that they reached a point of no return.

Gender Outcomes

One of the main questions in the literature on women and revolutions is, *How do women fare in the aftermath of revolutionary struggle?*[55] Assuming the centrality of gender to state-building, economic development, and the construction of national identity, Moghadam singles out two types of revolution: the woman-in-the-family model "excludes or marginalizes women from definitions and constructions of independence, liberation, and liberty," while the women's emancipation model envisions women as "part of the productive forces and citizenry, to be mobilized for economic and political purposes" in the postrevolutionary period.[56] This book, however, proposes a tripartite typology of women's participation in a revolution. Consistent with a patriarchal model of women's participation in a revolution, women are expected to retreat into the private sphere in the aftermath of a revolution. In contrast, an egalitarian model assumes that women's participation in a revolution will lead to the increasing visibility of women in domestic politics and the advancement of gender equality in the postrevolutionary period. Between these two extremes lies a hybrid model, signifying various degrees of women's empowerment in different domains.

A detailed analysis of women's status in the postrevolutionary period will extend our understanding of outcomes of mass mobilization in new democracies and non-democracies. Prolific research has gauged the impact of social movements on public policies and cultural norms in mature democracies.[57]

---

the Former Yugoslavia." *Women's Studies International Forum* 29 (5): 510–20; Lepa Mladjenovic. 2003. "Women in Black Against War (Belgrade)." In *Feminists Under Fire: Exchanges Across War Zones*, eds. Wenona Giles, Malathi de Alwis, Edith Klein, and Neluka Silva. Toronto: Between the Lines, pp. 41–44; Amy Swerdlow. 1993. *Women Strike for Peace: Traditional Motherhood and Radical Politics in the 1960s*. Chicago: University of Chicago Press.

[55] On this point, see Julie Shayne. 2006. "Women and Revolution." In *Revolutionary Movements in World History: From 1750 to the Present*, ed. James DeFronzo. Santa Barbara: ABC-CLIO, pp. 936–40.

[56] Valentine Moghadam. 1997. "Gender and Revolutions." In *Theorizing Revolutions*, ed. John Foran. New York: Routledge, pp. 137–67.

[57] Lorenzo Bosi, Marco Giugni, and Katrin Uba. 2019. "The Consequences of Social Movements: Taking Stock and Looking Forward." In *The Consequences of Social Movements*, eds. Lorenzo Bosi, Marco Giugni, and Katrin Uba. New York: Cambridge University Press, pp. 3–38; Mario G. Giugni. 1998. "Was It Worth the Effort? Outcomes and Consequences of Social

A related strand of research has investigated the dynamics of democratic reforms and economic development in the aftermath of electoral revolutions in the post-Soviet region.[58] There is also growing literature on reforms and social change in Ukraine since Euromaidan.[59] This study focuses on the advancement of gender equality as an outcome of anti-regime mobilization. Specifically, the book traces patterns of women's representation in government, participation in the labor market, and civic engagement, as well as changes in public policies and public opinion. Data from oral history projects further reveal the biographical consequences of women's participation in a revolution. However, the analysis of gender outcomes is confounded by the temporal proximity of the revolution and the ensuing war. Russia's military intervention began immediately after the conclusion of protest events in Kyiv and the ouster of the incumbent.[60] Still, based on insights from women's narratives, it is clear that participation in the Revolution of Dignity served as a catalyst for women's subsequent activism in multiple ways.[61]

Movements." *Annual Review of Sociology* 98: 371–93; Holly J. McCammon and Lee Ann Banaszak, eds. 2018. *100 Years of the Nineteenth Amendment: An Appraisal of Women's Activism*. New York: Oxford University Press; David S. Meyer, Valerie Jenness, and Helen Ingram, eds. 2005. *Routing the Opposition: Social Movements, Public Policy, and Democracy*. Minneapolis: University of Minnesota Press; Kristina Schulz, ed. 2017. *The Woman's Liberation Movement: Impacts and Outcomes*. New York: Berghahn.

[58] Joerg Forbrig and Robin Shepherd, eds. 2005. *Ukraine After the Orange Revolution: Strengthening European and Transatlantic Commitments*. Washington, DC: The German Marshall Fund of the United States; Stephen Jones, ed. 2010. *War and Revolution in the Caucasus: Georgia Ablaze*. London: Routledge; Lincoln Mitchell. 2009. *Uncertain Democracy: U.S. Foreign Policy and Georgia's Rose Revolution*. Philadelphia: University of Pennsylvania Press.

[59] Henry Hale and Robert Orttung, eds. 2016. *Beyond the Euromaidan: Comparative Perspectives on Advancing Reform in Ukraine*. Stanford: Stanford University Press; George Soroka and Tomasz Stępniewski, eds. 2019. *Ukraine After Maidan: Revisiting Domestic and Regional Security*; Stuttgart: Ibidem Verlag; Viktor Stepanenko and Yaroslav Pylynksyj, eds. 2015. *Ukraine After the Euromaidan: Challenges and Hopes*. New York:Peter Lang; Andreas Umland and Valentyna Romanova, eds. 2018. *Ukraine's Decentralization: Challenges and Implications of the Local Governance Reform After the Euromaidan Revolution*. Stuttgart: Ibidem Verlag.

[60] For an overview, see Serhy Yekelchyk. 2015. *The Conflict in Ukraine: What Everyone Needs to Know*. New York: Oxford University Press.

[61] On different forms of women's wartime activism, see Svitlana Biedarieva and Hanna Deikun, eds. 2020. *At the Front Line: Ukrainian Art, 2013–2019. La línea del frente. El arte ucraniano 2013–2019*. Mexico City: Editorial Diecisiete; Olga Boichak. 2022. "Camouflage Aesthetics: Militarisation, Craftivism, and the In/visibility of Resistance at Scale." *Contemporary Voices: St. Andrew's Journal of International Relations* 3 (1): 1–13; Ganna Grytsenko, Anna Kvit and Tamara Martsenyuk. 2016. *Invisible Battalion: Women's Participation in ATO Military Operations in Ukraine*. Kyiv: Ukrainian Women's Fund; Yuliya Ilchuk. 2017. "Hearing the Voice of Donbas: Art and Literature as Forms of Cultural Protest during War." *Nationalities Papers* 45 (2): 256–73; Christina Olha Jarymowycz. 2020. "Guardians and Protectors: The Volunteer Women of the Donbas Conflict." *Feminist Review* 126 (1): 106–22; Evgeniya Podobna, ed. 2020. *Girls Cutting Their Locks: A Book of Memories, the Russo-Ukrainian*

Contentious Politics in Eastern Europe

A detailed analysis of women's participation in the Revolution of Dignity seeks to expand the scope of empirical research on contentious politics in Eastern Europe.[62] Despite a rich literature on social and political revolutions that swept across the region in the twentieth century, a great deal of historical research has yet to be done to unravel women's engagement in those tumultuous events.[63] On the centennial of the 1917 Russian Revolution, for example, Ruthchild pointed out that "the voices of women arguing for citizenship, equality, respect, and civil rights are the often silenced or ignored sopranos and altos of Russia; without them Russian history is all bass and baritone" (p. 694).[64] Likewise, women's activism has received relatively sparse attention in the literature on velvet revolutions and civil resistance under communism.[65] In her book *Solidarity's Secret: Women Who Defeated Communism in Poland*, Penn challenges a male-centered narrative of resistance and shows how Polish women worked "tirelessly behind the scenes" and "carved out distinctive, influential roles" within the movement in the wake of the 1981 martial law.[66] Similarly, further research should be done to trace women's engagement in twenty-first-century revolutions in Eastern Europe.

The book builds on existing literature on Euromaidan but departs from it by focusing on women's participation in the revolution.[67] A growing body of research investigates the role of social media in facilitating civil resistance and

---

War, trans. Mariia Kovalenko. Kyiv: Ukrainian Institute of National Remembrance and Liuta Sprava; Jessica Zychowicz. 2023. "Women's Activism in Ukraine: Anti-discrimination, Anti-disinformation, and Human Rights in Early Civic Documentations of the Ukraine-Russia War." In *Post-Soviet Women: New Challenges and Ways to Empowerment*, eds. Ann-Mari Sätre, Yulia Gradskova, and Vladislava Vladimirova. Cham, Switzerland: Palgrave Macmillan, pp. 271–93.

[62] For an overview, see Grzegorz Ekiert and Jan Kubik. 2017. "The Study of Protest Politics in Eastern Europe in the Search of Theory." In *The Routledge Handbook of East European Politics*, eds. Adam Fagan and Petr Kopecky. London: Routledge, pp. 197–209.

[63] See, for example, Ruthchild. *Equality and Revolution*; Elizabeth Wood. 1997. *The Baba and the Comrade: Gender and Politics in Revolutionary Russia*. Bloomington: Indiana University Press.

[64] Rochelle Goldberg Ruthchild. 2017. "Women and Gender in 1917." *Slavic Review* 76: 694–702.

[65] Western scholarship on the topic has primarily focused on the case of the Solidarity Movement in Poland. See, for example, Belinda Brown. 2003. *The Private Revolution: Women in the Polish Underground Movement*. London: Hera Trust; Padraic Kenney. 1999. "The Gender of Resistance in Communist Poland." *American Historical Review* 104 (2): 399–425; Kristi Long. 1996. *We All Fought for Freedom: Women in Poland's Solidarity Movement*. Boulder: Westview Press.

[66] Shana Penn. 2006. *Solidarity's Secret: The Women Who Defeated Communism in Poland*. Ann Arbor: University of Michigan Press.

[67] On Euromaidan, see, for example, Hale and Orttung. *Beyond the Euromaidan*; Marci Shore. 2017. *The Ukrainian Night: An Intimate History of Revolution*. New Haven: Yale University Press; Mychailo Wynnyckyj. 2019. *Ukraine's Maidan, Russia's War: A Chronicle and Analysis of the Revolution of Dignity*. Stuttgart, Germany: Ibidem Press.

affording new opportunities for activism.[68] Another line of inquiry has concentrated on the cultivation of offline social networks and citizens' capacity to self-organize.[69] Channell-Justice, for example, meticulously traced how male and female left-wing activists demonstrated the capacity to self-organize despite attacks from far-right groups and the state.[70] Scholars also analyzed sociodemographic characteristics of participants in the Revolution of Dignity.[71] Several studies within this rich literature have examined women's activism during Euromaidan.[72] Phillips, for example, scrutinizes the creation of women's squads as a feminists' response to their exclusion from the barricades.[73] Drawing on visual art, interviews, and other materials, Zychowicz documents a generation of artists and activists who debated the construction of feminism and considered art as a form of resistance in postcommunist Ukraine.[74] Unlike most prior publications, the book explores women's activism in multiple domains critical to the resilience of the protest movement, including the coordination of an extensive volunteer network, the execution of crowdsourcing initiatives, the provision of food, legal aid, and medical services, the formation of self-defense units, the production of art, and the organization of educational activities and library services inside the encampment.

[68] Tetyana Bohdanova. 2014. "Unexpected Revolution: The Role of Social Media in Ukraine's Euromaidan Uprising." *European View* 13: 133–42; Jennifer Dickinson. 2014. "Prosymo maksymanl'nyi perepost! Tactical and Discursive Uses of Social Media in Ukraine's EuroMaidan." *Ab Imperio* 3: 75–93; Tetyana Lokot. 2021. *Beyond the Protest Square: Digital Media and Augmented Dissent*. Lanham: Rowman and Littlefield.

[69] Nadia Diuk. 2014. "EuroMaidan: Ukraine's Self-Organizing Revolution." *World Affairs* 176 (6): 9–16; Olga Onuch. 2015. "EuroMaidan Protests in Ukraine: Social Media Versus Social Networks." *Problems of Post-Communism* 62 (4): 217–35.

[70] Channell-Justice. *Without the State*.

[71] Olga Onuch. 2014. "The Maidan and Beyond: Who Were the Protesters?" *Journal of Democracy* 25 (3): 44–51; Daniel Ritter. 2017. "A Spirit of Maidan? Contentious Escalation in Ukraine." In *Global Diffusion of Protest: Riding the Protest Wave in the Neoliberal Crisis*, ed. Donatella della Porta. Amsterdam: Amsterdam University Press, pp. 191–213.

[72] Emily Channell-Justice. 2017. "'We're Not Just Sandwiches': Europe, Nation, and Feminist (Im)Possibilities on Ukraine's Maidan." *Signs: Journal of Women in Culture and Society* 42 (3): 717–41; Olesya Khromeychuk. 2016. "Negotiating Protest Spaces on the Maidan: A Gender Perspective." *Journal of Soviet and Post-Soviet Politics and Society* 2 (1): 9–47; Olena Nikolayenko and Maria DeCasper. 2018. "Why Women Protest: Insights from Ukraine's EuroMaidan." *Slavic Review* 77 (23): 726–51; Olga Onuch and Tamara Martsenyuk. 2014. "Mothers and Daughters of the Maidan: Gender, Repertoires of Violence, and the Division of Labour in Ukrainian Protests." *Social, Health, and Communication Studies Journal* 1 (1): 105–26; Sabine Rossmann. 2016. "'To Serve Like a Man' – Ukraine's Euromaidan and the Questions of Gender, Nationalism and Generational Change." In *Eastern European Youth Cultures in a Global Context*, eds. Matthias Schwartz and Heike Winkel. London: Palgrave Macmillan UK, pp. 202–17.

[73] Sarah Phillips. 2014. "The Women's Squad in Ukraine's Protests: Feminism, Nationalism, and Militarism on the Maidan." *American Ethnologist* 41 (3): 414–26.

[74] Jessica Zychowicz. 2020. *Superfluous Women: Art, Feminism, and Revolution in Twenty-First-Century Ukraine*. Toronto: University of Toronto Press.

Furthermore, the book makes an empirical contribution to political science literature by enhancing public understanding of sources of Ukraine's fierce resistance to Russia's invasion. Following the fall of Viktor Yanukovych's government, Russia annexed Crimea, a peninsula in the Black Sea, and provided military backing for rebel groups in eastern Ukraine.[75] As a result of Russia's military intervention, over 14,000 people, including approximately 3,000 civilians, were killed in the conflict-affected areas between April 2014 and January 2022.[76] The scale and the severity of human casualties have dramatically risen with the onset of Russia's full-scale invasion of Ukraine on February 24, 2022.[77] Numerous human rights reports and eyewitness accounts documented a high incidence of war crimes, including a systematic rape of women, rampant torture and extrajudicial executions of people in occupied territories, and the shelling of civilian infrastructure.[78] Yet, Ukrainian men and women are stoically fighting against the Russian armed forces, sharing the goal of living in a free, democratic society.

UKRAINE'S REVOLUTION OF DIGNITY

The definition of a revolution is vigorously debated in the literature, especially with the rise of nonviolent revolutions in urban settings.[79] Broadly construed,

---

[75] For an overview, see Paul D'Anieri. 2019. *Ukraine and Russia: From Civilized Divorce to Uncivil War*. New York: Cambridge University Press.

[76] Office of the UN High Commissioner for Human Rights. 2022. *Report on the Human Rights Situation in Ukraine, 1 August 2021–31 January 2022*. www.ohchr.org/en/documents/country-reports/report-human-rights-situation-ukraine-1-august-2021-31-january-2022.

[77] See, for example, Office of the UN High Commissioner for Human Rights. 2023. *Ukraine: Civilian Casualty Update March 13, 2023*. www.ohchr.org/en/news/2023/03/ukraine-civilian-casualty-update-13-march-2023.

[78] On war crimes committed by the Russian military in Ukraine, see, for example, Amnesty International. 2022. *Ukraine: Russian Forces Extrajudicially Executing Civilians in Apparent War Crimes – New Testimony*. April 7. www.amnesty.org/en/latest/news/2022/04/ukraine-russian-forces-extrajudicially-executing-civilians-in-apparent-war-crimes-new-testimony; Human Rights Watch. 2022. *Ukraine: Apparent War Crimes in Russia-Controlled Areas: Summary Executions, Other Grave Abuses by Russian Forces*. April 3. www.hrw.org/news/2022/04/03/ukraine-apparent-war-crimes-russia-controlled-areas; Human Rights Watch. 2022. *Ukraine: Executions, Torture During Russian Occupation: Apparent War Crimes in Kyiv, Chernihiv Regions*. May 18. www.hrw.org/news/2022/05/18/ukraine-executions-torture-during-russian-occupation; United Nations. 2022. "Reports of Sexual Violence in Ukraine Rising Fast, Security Council Hears." *UN News*, June 6. https://news.un.org/en/story/2022/06/1119832.

[79] On different approaches to the study of revolutions, see Mark R. Beissinger. 2023. "The Evolving Study of Revolution." *World Politics* 75 (5): 1–12. https://doi.org/10.1353/wp.0.a920225; Donatella della Porta. 2016. *Where Did the Revolution Go? Contentious Politics and the Quality of Democracy*. New York: Cambridge University Press; Jack A. Goldstone. 2014. *Revolutions: A Very Short Introduction*. New York: Oxford University Press; Nepstad, *Nonviolent Struggle*; Kurt Schock, ed. 2015. *Civil Resistance: Comparative Perspectives on Nonviolent Struggle*. Minneapolis: University of Minnesota Press; Stephen Zunes. 1994.

the concept of revolution denotes "a collective mobilization that attempts to quickly and forcibly overthrow an existing regime in order to transform political, economic, and symbolic relations."[80] Here, the usage of the concept is not meant to suggest that a profound transformation in political institutions and economic structures actually occurred in the aftermath of mass mobilization. It should also be emphasized that contemporary revolutions differ from social ("great") revolutions in several ways.[81] Twenty-first-century revolutions tend to be less violent, encompass a cross-class coalition, take place in urban areas, and have the regime, rather than the state, as a primary target.[82]

The book considers the 2013–2014 mass mobilization in Ukraine as a case of a contemporary revolution. Consistent with a broad-based conceptualization of a twenty-first-century revolution, participants in the revolution represented a cross-cutting coalition of social forces united by their utmost dissatisfaction with the current regime.[83] According to various estimates, more than four million people, comprising approximately 10 percent of Ukraine's adult population, joined anti-government protests across the country.[84] In addition, thousands of people provided in-kind support, donated money for protesters, and disseminated information through civic initiatives on social media.[85] Given a large concentration of protesters in the urban space and popular demands for political freedoms, the Revolution of Dignity falls into the category of what Beissinger defines as an "urban civic revolution."[86]

The main square in the center of Kyiv – Independence Square (*Maidan Nezalezhnosti*, or simply *Maidan*) – was the epicenter of a three-month-long confrontation between the ruling elite and ordinary citizens. It was a site of large protest rallies and an encampment during the Revolution of Dignity. The choice of Independence Square as a meeting place for regime opponents was not accidental. Over the past century, the square located within a short distance

---

"Unarmed Insurrections Against Authoritarian Governments in the Third World: A New Kind of Revolution." *Third World Quarterly* 15: 403–26.

[80] George Lawson. 2019. *Anatomies of Revolution*. New York: Cambridge University Press, p. 5.

[81] On this point, see Daniel P. Ritter. 2019. "The (R)evolution Is Dead, Long Live the (R)evolution!" *Contention* 7 (2): 100–107.

[82] Colin J. Beck, Mlada Bukovansky, Erica Chenoweth, George Lawson, Sharon Erickson Nepstad, and Daniel P. Ritter. 2022. *On Revolutions: Unruly Politics in the Contemporary World*. New York: Oxford University Press.

[83] Onuch. "The Maidan and Beyond"; Vladimir Paniotto. 2013. "Ukraina: Evromaidan." *Vestnik obshchestvennogo mnenia* 116 (3–4): 17–23; Ritter. "A Spirit of Maidan?".

[84] Oleksandr Reznik. 2016. "From the Orange Revolution to the Revolution of Dignity: Dynamics of the Protest Actions in Ukraine." *East European Politics and Societies* 30 (4): 750–65. See also The Ilko Kucheriv Democratic Initiatives Foundation (DIF). 2014. "Dva misiatsia protestiv v Ukraini – shcho dali? – zahalnonatsionalne opytuvannia." www.dif.org.ua/ua/polls/2014_polls.

[85] Bohdanova. " Unexpected Revolution"; Dickinson. "Prosymo maksymanl'nyi perepost!"; Lokot. *Beyond the Protest Square*.

[86] Beissinger, *The Revolutionary City*.

from major government buildings has been a major venue for mass gatherings and protests.[87] In particular, this urban space served as the main site of the 1990 student hunger strike, the 2000–2001 Ukraine without Kuchma movement, and the 2004 Orange Revolution. Moreover, given the political significance of this urban space, the ruling elite frequently renamed it to reaffirm the reconfiguration of power in a changing political landscape. Originally known as Khreshchatyk Square (*Khreshchatytska Ploshcha*), it was named Dumska (1878–1919) after the Russian Tsar Nicholas I abolished Kyiv's Magdeburg Rights and Alexander II established a new system of local self-government, including the City Duma. Under the Soviet rule, the square was named Soviet (*Radianska Ploshcha*) and later Kalinin (*Ploshcha Kalinina*) after the Russian Bolshevik Mikhail Kalinin. In 1977, the square was renamed again to mark the sixtieth anniversary of the 1917 October Revolution. For several years, the October Revolution Square (*Ploshcha Zhovtnevoi revoluitsii*) served as a site for military parades and demonstrations in support of the communist regime. Since the demise of the Soviet Union, the square became the most popular venue for mass protests against the ruling elite.

Another salient feature of the Ukrainian Revolution is that it exemplifies mass mobilization demanding the government's recognition of human dignity.[88] Nowadays, the concept of dignity is widely seen as a critical element of international human rights law and an essential attribute of the democratic political system.[89] The idea of human dignity as an inherent, inviolable quality of every human being is enshrined in the Universal Declaration of Human Rights adopted by the United Nations, and the Charter of Fundamental Rights of the European Union.[90] Drawing upon the human rights discourse, participants in the Indignados movement in Spain, the Occupy Wall Street in the US, and the 2011 Egyptian Revolution articulated their demands for the government's

---

[87] On the political significance of the square, see Roman Cybriwsky. 2014. "Kyiv's Maidan: From Duma Square to Sacred Space." *Eurasian Geography and Economics* 55 (3): 270–85; Dmytro Vortman. 2021. "Maidan Nezalezhnosti." In *Entsyklopediia istorii Ukrainy*, ed. Valerii Smolii. Kyiv: Institute of History, the National Academy of Sciences and Naukova Dumka, pp. 351–52; Serhy Yekelchyk. 2020. "The Ideological Park: How the Tsar's Garden in Kyiv Became a Modern Political Space." In *Postsocialist Landscapes: Real and Imaginary Spaces from Stalinstadt to Pyongyang*, eds. Thomas Lahusen and Schamma Schahadat. Bielefeld: Transcript Verlag, pp. 25–46.

[88] On this point, see Olena Nikolayenko. 2020. "The Significance of Human Dignity for Social Movements: Mass Mobilization in Ukraine." *East European Politics* 36 (3): 445–62.

[89] Paolo Carozza. 2013. "Human Dignity." In *The Oxford Handbook of International Human Rights Law*, ed. Dinah Shelton. New York: Oxford University Press, pp. 345–59; Josiah Ober. 2012. "Democracy's Dignity." *American Political Science Review* 106 (4): 827–46; Michael Rosen. 2012. *Dignity: Its History and Meaning*. Cambridge: Harvard University Press.

[90] Article 1 of the Charter states, "Human dignity is inviolable. It must be respected and protected." The Charter's full text is retrieved from https://eur-lex.europa.eu/legal-content/EN/TXT/HTML/?uri=CELEX%3A12012P/TXT.

respect of dignity.⁹¹ As noted by Fukuyama, mass mobilization in the name of dignity represents "a large part of the political struggles of the contemporary world, from democratic revolutions to new social movements."⁹² A close examination of the Ukrainian Revolution sheds light on this global phenomenon and in particular unravels women's claim-making within a heterogeneous pro-democracy movement.

The incumbent's abrupt decision to abandon the idea of political association and economic integration with the EU sent shockwaves in Ukrainian society. At the Vilnius Summit in November 2013, President Yanukovych was expected to sign an Association Agreement with the EU, which would liberalize EU–Ukraine trade, introduce a visa-free travel regime for citizens of Ukraine, and spearhead a series of reforms in education, energy, environment, transportation, and other sectors of the economy.⁹³ In particular, Yanukovych punctured the hopes of many young people to witness Ukraine's movement toward European integration.

The Ukrainian government reportedly declined to sign a treaty with the EU and changed its foreign policy orientation under the Kremlin's pressure.⁹⁴ Since the demise of the Soviet Union, Russia has been trying to reassert its control over the former Soviet republics and install a revamped model of the Soviet Union, with the solo power center in Moscow.⁹⁵ Putin's fixation on Ukraine was, in no small degree, driven by his fear of democratic tendencies in the neighboring country, which undermined his grip on power in the authoritarian regime.⁹⁶ As a part of Putin's grand plan, Ukraine was supposed to join the Eurasian Economic Union, consisting of such corruption-ridden autocracies as

---

⁹¹ Marlies Glasius and Geoffrey Pleyers. 2013. "The Global Moment of 2011: Democracy, Social Justice and Dignity." *Development and Change* 44 (3): 547–67; Susana Narotzky. 2016. "Between Inequality and Injustice: Dignity as a Motive for Mobilization During the Crisis." *History and Anthropology* 27 (1): 74–92; Diane Singerman. 2013. "Youth, Gender, and Dignity in the Egyptian Uprising." *Journal of Middle East Women's Studies* 9 (3): 1–27.

⁹² Francis Fukuyama. 2018. *Identity: The Demand for Dignity and the Politics of Resentment*. New York: Macmillan Press.

⁹³ The full text of the agreement is available at: https://trade.ec.europa.eu/doclib/docs/2016/november/tradoc_155103.pdf.

⁹⁴ Christoph Hasselbach. 2013. "A Frosty Meeting in Vilnius After EU Snub." *Deutsche Welle*, November 29. https://p.dw.com/p/1AQKO.

⁹⁵ Svante E. Cornell and S. Frederick Starr, eds. 2009. *The Guns of August 2008. Russia's War in Georgia*. London: M.E. Sharpe; D'Anieri. *Ukraine and Russia*; Timur Dadabaev. 2022. *Decolonizing Central Asian International Relations: Beyond Empires*. New York: Routledge; Mark Galeotti. 2023. *Putin's Wars: From Chechnya to Ukraine*. Camden: Bloomsbury Publishing; Marcel van Herpen. 2015. *Putin's Wars: The Rise of Russia's New Imperialism*. Lanham: Rowman and Littlefield; Elizabeth A. Wood, William E. Pomeranz, E. Wayne Merry, and Maxim Trudolyubov. 2016. *Roots of Russia's War in Ukraine*. Washington, DC: Woodrow Wilson Center Press.

⁹⁶ Mark Edele. 2023. *Russia's War Against Ukraine: The Whole Story*. Melbourne: Melbourne University Press; Maria Popova and Oxana Shevel. 2024. *Russia and Ukraine: Entangled Histories, Diverging States*. Cambridge: Polity Press.

Russia, Belarus, and Kazakhstan.[97] Yet, despite the Kremlin's information warfare,[98] the majority of Ukrainians rejected Russia's model of political and socioeconomic development. In March 2013, for example, only 31 percent of the voting-age population and in particular 19 percent of eighteen–twenty nine-year-old Ukrainians favored a customs union with Russia.[99] Against this backdrop, Yanukovych's policy shift upset many Ukrainians.

The revolution began with a Facebook post by Mustafa Nayyem, a thirty-two-year-old Ukrainian journalist of Afghani descent. "Come on guys, let's be serious. If you really want to do something, don't just "like" this post. Write that you are ready, and we can try to start something," he wrote on November 21. Over 600 Facebook users made a comment within an hour of the original post, and Nayyem suggested meeting on Independence Square that night.[100] Hundreds of people filled the square. A group of university students and civic activists subsequently decided to occupy the urban space to demand the government's commitment to European integration.[101] Ukrainian youth waved the national flag, consisting of two equally sized horizontal bands of blue and yellow, and chanted the slogan "Ukraine Is Europe." The incumbent responded with a violent dispersal of youthful protesters at dawn on November 30.[102] Yet, police violence backfired.

A peaceful protest against the government's reversal of Ukrainian foreign policy has rapidly evolved into a broad-based movement, demanding the incumbent's resignation, respect for human dignity, eradication of corruption, and implementation of democratic reforms.[103] On December 1, 2013, between

[97] Alexander Libman and Anastassia V. Obydenkova. 2018. "Regional International Organizations as a Strategy of Autocracy: The Eurasian Economic Union and Russian Foreign Policy." *International Affairs* 94 (5): 1037–58.
[98] Todd Helmus, et al. 2018. *Russian Social Media Influence: Understanding Russian Propaganda in Eastern Europe*. Santa Monica: Rand Corporation; Marcel van Herpen. 2015. *Putin's Propaganda Machine: Soft Power and Russian Foreign Policy*. Lanham: Rowman and Littlefield.
[99] Mariia Zolkina and Olexiy Haran. 2017. "Zminy u zovnishnopolitychnykh orientatsiiakh pislia Evromaidanu: zahalnonatsionalnyi ta rehionalnyi rivni." In *Transformatsii suspilnykh nastroiv v umovakh protydii ahresii Rosii na Donbasi: rehionalnyi vymir*, ed. Olexiy Haran. Kyiv: Stylos, pp. 112–41, 121.
[100] Mustafa Nayyem. 2014. "Uprising in Ukraine: How It All Began." *Voices*, April 4. www.opensocietyfoundations.org/voices/uprising-ukraine-how-it-all-began.
[101] Emily Channell-Justice. 2014. "Flexibility and Fragmentation: Student Activism and Ukraine's (Euro)Maidan Protests." *Berkeley Journal of Sociology* 58: 59–65; Tom Junes. 2016. "Euromaidan and the Revolution of Dignity: A Case Study of Student Protest as a Catalyst for Political Upheaval." *Critique and Humanism* 46 (2): 73–96.
[102] Human Rights Watch. 2013. "Ukraine: Excessive Force against Protesters." December 3. www.hrw.org/news/2013/12/03/ukraine-excessive-force-against-protesters; Kharkiv Human Rights Protection Group. 2015. "Euromaidan Events and Human Rights." May 26. https://khpg.org/en/1432629035.
[103] For an overview, see Olena Nikolayenko. 2022. "EuroMaidan (The Revolution of Dignity)." In *The Wiley-Blackwell Encyclopedia of Social and Political Movements*, 2nd ed., eds. David

100,000 and 350,000 people joined the March of Millions to denounce police violence and demand political freedoms.[104] "People felt that if they [police] had beaten students today, then they [police] would beat everyone tomorrow," remarked Sviatoslav Shevchuk, Major Archbishop of the Ukrainian Greek Catholic Church (UGCC).[105] Many individuals who aspired to "change the world ... change Ukraine" got involved in civil resistance.[106] As a result, the encampment on Maidan swelled in size, and protesters occupied a few adjacent buildings to provide shelter and medical services for revolutionaries.[107]

The riot police made another attempt to clear the square on December 11, 2013. That night, the bells of St. Michael's Golden-Domed Cathedral, originally built in 1108, rang the alarm for the first time in modern history since the city's seizure by the Golden Horde in the thirteenth century.[108] In response, hundreds of Kyivites rushed to the protest site to prevent the police's destruction of the encampment. Over time, protesters built more formidable barricades to protect themselves against a police assault.

Another escalation in state–society relations was triggered by the adoption of draconian anti-protest laws in January 2014. These laws introduced prison terms of up to fifteen years for the violation of public order, as well as criminal responsibility for the defamation of state officials and the distribution of the so-called extremist materials.[109] To decimate the protest movement, the riot police deployed tear gas, stun grenades, water cannons, rubber bullets, and live ammunition, which resulted in the deaths of nearly 100 civilians.[110] As a result of the shootings on February 20, 2014, alone, at least forty-eight protesters

Snow, Donatella della Porta, Doug McAdam, and Bert Klandermans. Hoboken: Wiley-Blackwell, pp. 745–47

[104] BBC. 2013. "Clashes amid Huge Ukraine Protest Against U-Turn on EU." December 1. www.bbc.com/news/world-europe-25176191.
[105] Qtd. from *Winter on Fire: Ukraine's Fight for Freedom*. 2016 [Netflix documentary]. Directed by Evgeny Afineevsky.
[106] On this point, see UINP interview with Oleksandra Navrotska, April 15, 2016.
[107] Protesters occupied the Trade Unions building (Khreshchatyk Street 18/2), the October Palace (Instytutska Street 1), and the Kyiv City Administration Building (Khreshchatyk Street 36).
[108] Den. 2013. "The Bell Ringer of St. Michael's About the Clearing of the Maidan at Night on December 11." December 25. https://day.kyiv.ua/uk/video/dzvonar-mihaylivskogo-pro-rozgin-ievromaydanu-v-nich-na-11-grudnya-video.
[109] Radio Free Europe/Radio Liberty. 2014. "Ukrainian Parliament Pushes Through Antiprotest Measures." January 16. www.rferl.org/a/urkaine-parliament-antiprotest-law/25232537.html; Daisy Sindelar. 2014. "Does 'Black Thursday' Mark End of Ukraine's Democratic Decade?" *Radio Free Europe/Radio Liberty*, January 17. www.rferl.org/a/ukraine-end-democratic-decade/25233555.html.
[110] Oleksandra Matviichuk and Oleksandr Pavlichenko, eds. 2015. *The Price of Freedom: Public Report by Human Rights Organizations on Crimes Against Humanity Committed During Euromaidan (November 2013–February 2014)*. Kyiv: International Renaissance Foundation. https://issuu.com/irf_ua/docs/hr-2015-2engl.

were killed and 200 people sustained injuries.[111] The slain revolutionaries became known as the Heavenly Hundred. Numerous eyewitness accounts testify that snipers deliberately aimed at protesters' eyes or spines to physically maim Euromaidan participants, including journalists with flash cameras and nurses with a red cross on their clothes, and thus break their will to resist the regime.[112] In turn, some revolutionaries threw Molotov cocktails, while others burnt tires to create a smoke screen and hinder the advancement of the riot police.[113] Since the dissolution of the Soviet Union in 1991, it was the bloodiest standoff between the incumbent government and regime opponents in Ukraine.

The Revolution of Dignity culminated in a parliamentary vote on February 22, 2014, declaring Yanukovych's removal from office and scheduling snap elections for May 25, 2014.[114] When leaders of opposition political parties announced that the incumbent had agreed to hold early presidential elections in December 2014, most ordinary citizens rejected the terms of elite-led negotiations and threatened to oust the autocrat by force. On February 21, Volodymyr Parasiuk, a twenty-six-year-old commander of a self-defense unit (*sotnik*), climbed onto Maidan's stage and articulated public disapproval of the politicians' deal with the incumbent. "No Yanukovych is going to be a president for a whole year," Parasiuk said. "Tomorrow, by 10:00 a.m., he must be gone!"[115] Out of concern for his personal safety, Yanukovych fled the capital city and found refuge in Russia, albeit he refused to accept the legitimacy of his removal from power. Meanwhile, the newly elected president Petro Poroshenko signed the Association Agreement with the EU, fulfilling one of the protesters' demands.

A PORTRAIT OF PARTICIPANTS IN THE REVOLUTION

Over the span of three months, thousands of Ukrainians participated in the Revolution of Dignity. Figure 1.1 displays the level of women's and men's participation in different types of activities. According to a nationally representative survey conducted in July 2014, 6 percent of men and nearly 3 percent of

---

[111] Jay Aronson, McKenna Cole, Alex Hauptmann, Dan Miller, and Bradley Samuels. 2018. "Reconstructing Human Rights Violations Using Large Eyewitness Video Collections: The Case of Euromaidan Protester Deaths." *Journal of Human Rights and Practice* 10 (1): 159–78.

[112] Leonid Finberg and Uliana Holovach, eds. 2016. *Maidan. Svidchennia. Kyiv, 2013–2014 roky.* Kyiv: Duh i Litera, pp. 95, 329, 407, 412, 413, 464, 525, 599, 658, and 768.

[113] See, for example, Shore. *The Ukrainian Night*, pp. 42 and 89.

[114] BBC. 2014. "Ukrainian MPs Vote to Oust President Yanukovych." February 22. www.bbc.com/news/world-europe-26304842.

[115] Richard Balmforth. 2014. "In Ukraine Turbulence, a Lad from Lviv Becomes the Toast of Kiev." *Reuters*, February 25. www.reuters.com/article/us-ukraine-crisis-hero/in-ukraine-turbulence-a-lad-from-lviv-becomes-the-toast-of-kiev-idUKBREA1O0HP20140225.

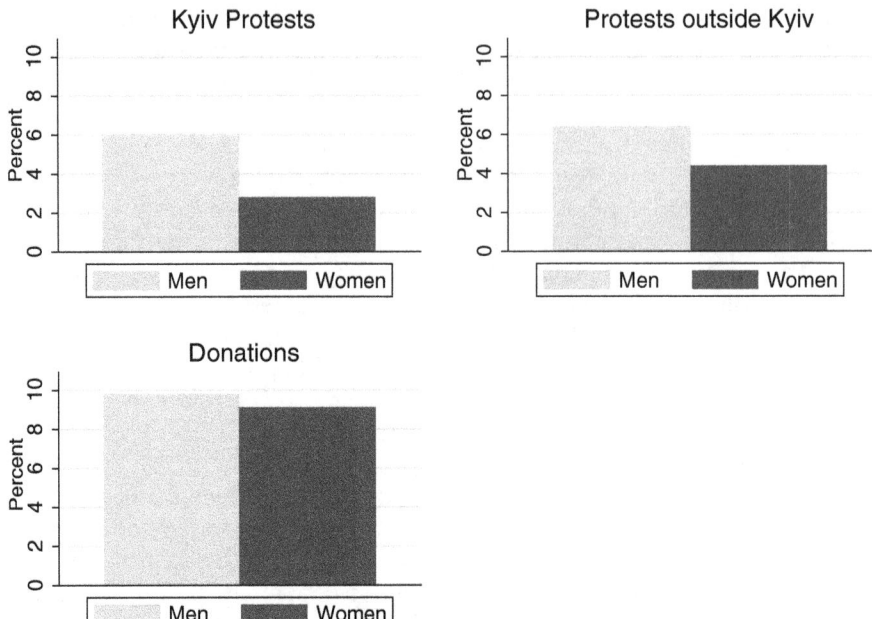

FIGURE 1.1 Women's and men's participation in the Revolution of Dignity.
Note: Percentages are displayed in the figure.

Source: Institute of Sociology, the National Academy of Sciences of Ukraine, *Ukrainian Society–2014: Social Monitoring*.

women joined anti-government protests in the capital city.[116] In addition, 6.4 percent of men, as well as 4.4 percent of women, were involved in protests outside Kyiv. Moreover, 9 percent of women and men provided in-kind support and donated money for the protest movement. Overall, the survey results show a high level of women's and men's engagement in civil resistance to the regime.

What is remarkable about this case of an urban revolution is that on-site surveys conducted by the Ilko Kucheriv Democratic Initiatives Foundation (DIF) and the Kyiv International Institute of Sociology (KIIS) in downtown Kyiv enable scholars to explore cross-time patterns in protest participation.[117]

---

[116] Survey data come from the nationally representative survey *Ukrainian Society-2014: Social Monitoring* conducted by the Institute of Sociology, the National Academy of Sciences of Ukraine in collaboration with the Kyiv-based SOCIS Centre for Social and Marketing Research in July 2014. N = 1,800.

[117] For an overview, see Kyiv International Institute of Sociology. 2014. "Vid Maidanu-taboru do Maidanu-sichi: Shcho zminylosia?" Press Release of February 6. http://kiis.com.ua/?lang=ukr&cat=reports&id=226&page=2.

Ukrainian sociologists distinguished three phases of mass mobilization: *Student Maidan* (November 21–30, 2013), with a high rate of student participation in protest events; *Maidan Tabir* (December 1, 2013–January 15, 2014) marked by the construction of barricades and the growth of the encampment on Maidan; and *Maidan Sich* (January 16, 2014–February 22, 2014), signifying an escalation in state violence and the radicalization of protest tactics. Consistent with this typology, survey respondents represented participants in peaceful protest rallies on December 7–8, 2013 (N = 1,037), inhabitants of the encampment on December 20, 2013 (N = 515), and defenders of barricades on February 3, 2014 (N = 502). Remarkably, 86.3 percent of Maidan participants stated in February 2014 that they were going to stay inside the encampment "as long as it takes" (*skilku bude treba*) to achieve the movement's goals. Meanwhile, the survey results indicate that the share of women inside the encampment drastically dropped from 42.8 percent in early December 2013 to 11.8 percent in February 2014. Some women were turned away from the encampment in response to an escalation in police violence.[118] Yet, despite their physical absence from the Kyiv-based encampment, many women remained actively involved in the revolutionary movement.

As seen in Table 1.2, there were gender differences in the sociodemographic characteristics of participants in Kyiv-based protests. Women, on average, had a higher level of education than men. Furthermore, the share of female protesters with higher education remained quite stable over the course of anti-regime mobilization. In contrast, among men, the percentage of protesters with a university degree decreased more markedly with an increasing level of police violence. Despite the visibility of young people, especially university students, at the start of anti-government protests in November 2013, the survey results show that thirty–fifty four-year-old Ukrainians made up the plurality of participants in the Revolution of Dignity. Among women, the percentage of 18–29 protesters dropped from 42.8 percent in early December 2013 to 25.4 percent in February 2014, signifying the greater physical presence of middle-aged women in the epicenter of civil resistance. Among men, youth made up one-third of protesters throughout the period.

Another statistically significant gender difference is related to the geographical origin of protesters. In early December 2013, one-third of female and two-thirds of male participants in Kyiv-based protests were non-Kyivites. By February 2014, 75.9 percent of female and 89.2 percent of male protesters on Maidan came from outside the capital city. Half of the protesters arrived in Kyiv from western Ukraine, 23 percent came from central Ukraine, and 21 percent were from eastern or southern parts of the country. Reflecting the linguistic situation in

---

[118] The Maidan commandant Andrii Parubii reportedly advised women against participating in direct combat on the barricades.

TABLE I.2 *Sociodemographic characteristics of Kyiv-based protesters*

Variable	Date of the survey					
	December 7–8, 2013		December 20, 2013		February 3, 2014	
	Women	Men	Women	Men	Women	Men
Age						
18–29	42.8	34.2	39.0	33.3	25.4	34.4
30–54	41.5	54.3	46.8	53.0	55.9	55.9
≥55	15.7	11.5	14.3	13.7	18.6	9.7
Education						
Secondary/vocational	11.7	30.0	26.3	41.0	22.4	45.8
University student	17.4	9.4	15.8	9.3	12.1	9.1
Higher education	70.4	59.4	53.9	47.8	65.5	40.3
Language spoken at home						
Ukrainian	46.4	58.6	53.2	52.3	57.6	59.5
Russian	35.4	21.6	18.2	19.9	13.6	16.1
Ukrainian and Russian	17.0	19.5	28.6	27.4	28.8	23.6
Kyiv resident	65.6	37.5	67.5	17.4	24.1	10.8
Membership in organizations						
Political party	2.0	5.5	15.6	14.8	15.3	6.8
Civic organization	2.9	3.9	3.9	9.8	10.2	8.1
Number of respondents	453	584	77	438	59	443

Note: Percentages are reported in the table. The three-wave survey Student Maidan (N = 1,037), Maidan Tabir (N = 515), and Maidan Sich (N = 502) was conducted by the Ilko Kucheriv Democratic Initiatives Foundation and the Kyiv International Institute of Sociology.

Ukrainian society,[119] 59.3 percent of protesters mostly spoke Ukrainian at home, 15.8 mostly spoke Russian, and 28.8 percent used either Ukrainian or Russian in their interactions with family members.

A salient feature of the Revolution of Dignity is the development of horizontal social networks and citizens' distrust in politicians of different stripes.[120]

---

[119] As an outcome of the long-term Russian policy of Russification, imposition of Russian culture and language, Stalin-era purges, wiping out a stratum of Ukrainian intellectuals, and the Ukrainian government's inept policies in the post-Soviet period, Ukraine on the eve of Euromaidan was de facto a bilingual country. Most citizens of Ukraine comprehended Ukrainian and Russian, while they mostly spoke one language at home or switched between languages, depending on the social circumstances. On language policies and practices in Ukraine prior to Euromaidan, see Volodymyr Kulyk. 2011. "Language Identity, Linguistic Diversity and Political Cleavages: Evidence from Ukraine." *Nations and Nationalism* 17 (3): 627–48.

[120] On this point, see Diuk. "Euro Maidan".

A Portrait of Participants in the Revolution

More than two-thirds of out-of-town protesters reported that they had traveled to Kyiv on their own, without any assistance on the part of a political party or a nonprofit organization. At that time, a lot of car owners offered free rides to Kyiv by making posts on social media. Only 2 percent of female and 5.5 percent of male participants in protest rallies on December 7–8, 2013, were members of a political party. By February 2014, the presence of protesters with a party affiliation rose to 15.3 percent among women and 6.8 percent among men. Likewise, 10.2 percent of female protesters and 8.1 percent of male protesters reported affiliation with a nonprofit organization during the revolution's last phase. Apparently, opposition political parties played a minor role in mobilizing the population against the regime.[121]

Additional data from the nationally representative survey *Ukrainian Society – 2014: Social Monitoring* conducted by the Institute of Sociology, the National Academy of Sciences of Ukraine in collaboration with the Kyiv-based SOCIS Centre for Social and Marketing Research in July 2014 provide insights into patterns of protest participation in and outside the capital city (N = 1,800). Consistent with the results of on-site surveys, the analysis finds that the plurality of protesters was aged between thirty and fifty-four. The majority of protesters were Ukrainian-language speakers. Though a sizeable portion of participants in anti-government protests came from western Ukraine, the protest movement embodied people from different parts of the country.[122] In line with prior findings, the analysis finds that a minuscule fraction of protesters was affiliated with a political party or a civic organization. Compared to on-site surveys, however, the results of nationally representative surveys suggest that the proportion of protesters with a university degree was lower. As seen in Table 1.3, only one-third of participants in anti-government protests reportedly received higher education. Apart from educational attainment, opinion polls conducted during and shortly after mass protests sketch a similar portrait of a typical participant in the Revolution of Dignity.

---

[121] From 1994 to 2014, less than 5 percent of voting-age population annually reported that they were members of a political party in Ukraine. For details, see Valerii Vorona and Mykola Shulha, eds. 2016. *Ukrainske suspilstvo: monitorinh sotsialnykh zmin*. Kyiv: Institute of Sociology, National Academy of Sciences of Ukraine, p. 433.

[122] The variable *region* is constructed by grouping Ukraine's administrative units (oblasts) into four macro regions. *West* is comprised of Chernivtsi, Ivano-Frankivsk, Lviv, Rivne, Ternopil, Volyn, and Zakarpattia. *Center* includes Cherkasy, Chernihiv, Khmelnytskyi, Kirovohrad, Kyiv, Poltava, Sumy, Vinnytsia, and Zhytomyr. *South* covers southern and southeastern oblasts: Dnipropetrovsk, Kharkiv, Kherson, Mykolaiv, Odesa, and Zaporizhzhia. *East* includes Donetsk and Luhansk oblasts. Given Russia's annexation of Crimea, the survey was not administered in the autonomous republic and the city of Sevastopol. On regional cleavages in Ukraine, see Oleksandr Vyshniak. 2015. *Shcho ob'iednuie ta shcho roz'iednuie ukraintsiv: Rezultaty opytuvan hromadskoi dumky*. Kyiv: Ilko Kucheriv Democratic Initiatives Foundation.

TABLE 1.3 *Participants in anti-government protests in and outside Kyiv*

Variable	Protests in Kyiv		Protests outside Kyiv	
	Women	Men	Women	Men
Age				
18–29	25.0	39.6	13.6	25.5
30–54	42.9	45.8	61.4	49.0
≥55	32.1	14.6	25.0	25.5
Education				
Secondary/vocational	67.8	72.3	63.7	60.0
Higher education	32.2	23.4	28.9	32.0
Language spoken at home				
Mostly Ukrainian	50.0	64.6	65.9	76.5
Mostly Russian	14.3	14.6	11.4	7.8
Ukrainian and Russian	35.7	20.8	22.7	15.7
Region				
West	41.7	28.6	56.8	54.9
Center	50.0	57.1	13.6	29.4
South	8.3	10.7	20.5	13.7
East	0	3.6	9.1	2.0
Membership in organizations				
Political party	3.6	2.1	4.5	5.9
Civic organization	3.6	0	2.3	3.9
Number of respondents	28	48	44	51

Note: Percentages are reported in the table.
Source: Institute of Sociology, the National Academy of Sciences of Ukraine, *Ukrainian Society-2014: Social Monitoring*.

The results of binary logistic regression analysis, with participation in Kyiv-based protests as the dependent variable, are summarized in Table 1.4.[123] As shown in the table, gender had a significant impact on citizens' engagement in anti-government protests in the capital city, controlling for a variety of variables. Women were less likely than men to participate in anti-government protests in Kyiv. Across the models, age had a significant impact on the odds of protest participation. Young people were twice as likely as persons aged between thirty and fifty-five to join anti-government protests. The results of multivariate analysis also suggest that *Higher education* and *Income* had weak effects on the odds of citizens' involvement in the Revolution of Dignity. In addition, being married did not appear to affect the likelihood of protest

---

[123] Binary logistic regression models estimate the probability of falling into a certain category (protest participation versus nonparticipation) given a set of predictors. Stata's logit command is used to calculate odds ratios.

TABLE 1.4 *Gender and protest participation: multivariate analysis*

Variables	Model		
	1	2	3
Gender (1 = female)	0.512**	0.513**	0.516**
	(0.137)	(0.138)	(0.139)
Under 30	2.430***	2.460***	2.374***
	(0.760)	(0.770)	(0.750)
Over 55	0.760	0.757	0.739
	(0.254)	(0.253)	(0.249)
Higher education	1.314	1.292	1.337
	(0.395)	(0.395)	(0.401)
Income	1.000	1.000	1.000
	(8.35e-05)	(8.36e-05)	(8.59e-05)
Married	1.051	1.063	1.017
	(0.297)	(0.301)	(0.288)
Preschool child	0.265***	0.265***	0.277**
	(0.134)	(0.135)	(0.141)
Ethnic Ukrainian	1.469	1.480	1.508
	(0.826)	(0.836)	(0.864)
Ukrainian language	1.922**	1.897**	1.824**
	(0.526)	(0.526)	(0.512)
Party membership		1.761	
		(1.461)	
Membership in civic organization		1.359	
		(1.594)	
Trust in compatriots			1.404**
			(0.222)
Constant	0.0250***	0.0244***	0.007***
	(0.017)	(0.016)	(0.007)
Observations	1,640	1,640	1,638
Log likelihood	-268.4	-268.1	-265.4
Pseudo R-square	0.062	0.063	0.072

Note: Odds ratios are reported in the table, with robust standard errors in parentheses.
***$p < 0.01$, **$p < 0.05$, *$p < 0.10$.
Source: Institute of Sociology, the National Academy of Sciences of Ukraine, *Ukrainian Society-2014: Social Monitoring*.

engagement.[124] Concurrently, having a preschool child decreased the odds of participation in Kyiv-based protests by 73 percent.[125] The analysis also finds that Ukrainian-language speakers were almost twice as likely to get involved in

---

[124] The variable *Married* is coded 1 if a respondent is legally married or in a common-law relationship, and 0 otherwise.
[125] The binary variable *Preschool child* takes the value of 1 if a respondent has a child under the age of six.

protest activity in the capital city. As seen in Model 2, membership in political parties and civic organizations did not boost the likelihood of protest engagement. In contrast, trust in compatriots is positively associated with protest engagement.

This book focuses on female participants in anti-government protests held in the capital city because Kyiv's Maidan was a prime site of the confrontation between the incumbent government and regime opponents. Methodologically, it is advantageous to focus on mass mobilization in one city to control for within-country variation in political conditions.[126] For example, the costs of participation in local protests were much higher in Donetsk, Yanukovych's home base in eastern Ukraine, than in Lviv, a stronghold of Ukrainian culture, located on the western edge of the country. In part, the book highlights how women from different parts of the country joined forces to sustain anti-government protests in the capital city.

GENDER INEQUALITY IN UKRAINIAN SOCIETY

Women, albeit comprising 53.8 percent of the country's 45-million population, faced a great deal of gender discrimination in Ukrainian society in the early 2010s.[127] Global rankings suggest that the former Soviet republic lagged behind many European countries in terms of women's empowerment. The 2013 Global Gender Gap Index, for example, ranked Ukraine 64th of 136 countries, indicating wider gender disparities in labor market participation and political representation in Ukraine than in Latvia (12th) and Lithuania (28th).[128] Similarly, Ukraine was ranked sixty-first of 149 countries on the 2013 Gender Inequality Index, scoring 0.326 on a scale from 0 to 1, with a higher value indicating a higher level of gender inequality.[129] A brief overview of the status of women in education, economy, and politics further illustrates the magnitude of

---

[126] On mass mobilization outside the capital city, see Olga Zelinska. 2015. "Who Were the Protestors and What Did They Want? Contentious Politics of Local Maidans Across Ukraine, 2013–2014." *Demokratizatsiya: The Journal of Post-Soviet Democratization* 23: 379–400.

[127] A greater share of women in the total population began in the age group of those over thirty-five and became especially pronounced in the oldest age groups. The average life expectancy was seventy-six years for women and sixty-six years for men in 2013. For details, see O. O. Karmazina, ed. 2014. *Dity, zhinky ta sim'ia v Ukraini*. Kyiv: State Statistics Service of Ukraine.

[128] For details, see World Economic Forum. 2015. *The Global Gender Gap Report 2015*. Geneva: World Economic Forum. http://reports.weforum.org/global-gender-gap-report-2015.

[129] The index measures the level of inequality in achievement between women and men in three dimensions: reproductive health, empowerment, and the labor market. Empowerment is measured by the share of parliamentary seats held by women and the share of the population with at least some secondary education. For details, see the United Nations Development Program. 2014. *Human Development Report 2014*. New York: UNDP. http://report.hdr.undp.org/.

Gender Inequality in Ukrainian Society

gender inequality prior to the onset of anti-government protests in November 2013.

Women, on average, have a higher level of educational attainment than men in contemporary Ukraine. At the start of the 2013–2014 academic year, women made up 51.2 percent of all the students enrolled in institutions of higher education.[130] In the class of 2013, women comprised 51.3 percent of graduates with a bachelor's degree, 54.4 percent of those with a specialist (five-year) degree, and 59.6 percent of those with a master's degree.[131] Yet, despite women's access to higher education, there remained a high degree of occupational segregation.[132] In the fall of 2013, for example, 96.7 percent of undergraduate students majoring in elementary education, as well as 90.1 percent of library science majors and 87.7 percent of philology majors, were women.[133] In contrast, women made up 23 percent of computer science, 57.4 percent of international law, and 60.2 percent of marketing majors. Gender differences in educational attainment affected women's participation in the labor market.

In the past two decades, the gender wage gap in Ukraine has reduced, but it remained higher than the EU mean.[134] The average monthly wages were UAH 2,866 ($362) for women and UAH 3,711 ($469) for men in 2013, meaning that female full-time workers made seventy-seven cents for every dollar earned by men.[135] Gender disparities in wages were even larger in higher-paying sectors of the economy and, for example, stood at 66.7 percent in the financial and insurance sectors.[136] Access to a smaller pool of economic resources put women at a significant disadvantage in the political sphere.

---

[130] Based upon the type of academic programming, institutions of higher education used to be divided into four tiers: I – vocational schools, II – colleges, III – institutes, and IV – institutes and universities. Statistics on student enrollment in institutions of higher education with III–IV level of accreditation are reported in the text. Data are retrieved from Karmazina. *Dity, zhinky ta sim'ia v Ukraini*, p. 263.

[131] I. V. Kalachova, ed. 2014. *Osnovni pokaznyky diialnosti vyshchykh navchalnykh zakladiv Ukrainy na pochatok 2013/14 navchalnoho roku*. Kyiv: State Statistics Service of Ukraine, p. 77.

[132] Iryna Kohut. 2014. "Chym vidrizniaiutsia zhinky i choloviky: Pro hendernu (ne)rivnist v vyshchyi osviti." July 10. Cedos, Kyiv. www.cedos.org.ua/uk/discrimination/chym-vidrizniaiutsia-zhinky-i-choloviky-pro-hendernu-ne-rivnist-u-vyshchii-osviti.

[133] Kalachova. *Osnovni pokaznyky diialnosti vyshchykh navchalnykh zakladiv Ukrainy na pochatok 2013/14 navchalnoho roku*, pp. 126–30.

[134] Norberto Pignatti. 2012. "Gender Wage Gap Dynamics in a Changing Ukraine." *IZA Journal of Labor Development* 1 (7): 1–44.

[135] The estimates of the gender pay gap are based upon the author's calculations. Data are retrieved from the online archive of the State Statistics Service of Ukraine. "Average Monthly Wages and Salaries of Women and Men by Type of Economic Activity in 2013." www.ukrstat.gov.ua/operativ/operativ2013/gdn/Szp_ed/Szp_ed_e/Szp_ed_2013_e.html. According to the National Bank of Ukraine, the exchange rate for Ukrainian national currency *hryvnia* (UAH) to US dollar was 7.9 in 2013. https://bank.gov.ua/control/uk/publish/category?cat_id=7693080.

[136] State Statistics Service of Ukraine, "Average Monthly Wages and Salaries."

Women were underrepresented in national and local legislatures.[137] The share of women in Verkhovna Rada, Ukraine's national parliament, ranged from 2.9 percent in 1991 to 9.4 percent in 2012.[138] There is mixed empirical evidence regarding the effects of new electoral rules – the introduction of the proportional electoral system – on women's representation in the national parliament.[139] Women edged out a slightly better representation in local governments.[140] Female candidates, for example, secured 12 percent of seats in provincial councils (*oblasni rady*) as a result of the 2010 local elections.

A myriad of structural and cultural factors impeded women's representation in government.[141] First, the ruling elite tossed away the Soviet-era practice of allotting a certain proportion of parliamentary seats for women to maintain a façade of gender equality. Second, the collapse of communism created a fertile ground not only for the emergence of a multiparty political system but also for the rise of oligarchs with enormous political clout.[142] Oligarchs lobbied their business interests, in part, by financing fledgling political parties and placing their loyalists in positions of power. The costs of election campaigning were also on a steady rise. According to some estimates, it cost up to $5 million to win a race for a parliamentary seat in a single-member district in 2012.[143] Moreover, dominant cultural norms created enormous barriers to women's

---

[137] For an overview, see Tamara Martsenyuk. 2015. "Women's Top-Level Political Participation: Failures and Hopes of Ukrainian Gender Politics." In *New Imaginaries. Youthful Reinvention of Ukraine's Cultural Paradigm*, ed. Marian J. Rubchak. New York: Berghahn Books, pp. 33–52.

[138] Olena Zakharova, Anatolii Oktysyuk, and Svitlana Radchenko. 2017. *Participation of Women in Ukrainian Politics*. Kyiv: International Centre for Policy Studies, p. 6. www.icps.com.ua/en/our-projects/publications/participation-of-women-in-ukrainian-politics/.

[139] Elena Semenova. 2012. "Patterns of Parliamentary Representation and Careers in Ukraine: 1990–2007." *East European Politics and Societies* 26 (3): 538–60; Frank Thames. 2018. "The Electoral System and Women's Legislative Underrepresentation in Post-Communist Ukraine." *Comparative Politics* 50: 251–73.

[140] Ukrainian Women's Fund. 2010. *Henderna arifmetika vlasti*. Kyiv: UWF. www.uwf.kiev.ua/files/arifmetika_ukr2010-1.pdf.

[141] See, for example, Sarah Birch. 2003. "Women and Political Representation in Contemporary Ukraine." In *Women's Access to Political Power in Post-Communist Europe*, eds. Richard Matland and Kathleen Montgomery. New York: Oxford University Press, pp. 130–53; Tetiana Kostiuchenko, Tamara Martsenyuk, and Svitlana Oksamytna. 2015. "Women Politicians and Parliamentary Elections in Ukraine and Georgia in 2012." *East/West: Journal of Ukrainian Studies* 2: 83–110.

[142] In Ukrainian society, the term "oligarch" refers to "a very wealthy and politically well-connected businessman ... who was the main owner of a conglomerate of enterprises and had close ties to the president." For details, see Anders Aslund. 2009. *How Ukraine Became a Market Economy and Democracy*. Washington, DC: The Peterson Institute for International Economics, p. 107.

[143] Andriy Meleshevych. 2016. *Cost of Parliamentary Politics in Ukraine*. London: Westminster Foundation for Democracy, p. 4. www.wfd.org/2016/09/05/cost-of-politics-ukraine/.

empowerment.[144] Opinion polls showed that gender equality was not at the top of public agenda. When asked to identify the top five public policies that should be implemented by the national parliament, only 8 percent of voting-age Ukrainians in 2012 mentioned equal rights and opportunities for women and men.[145] Under these circumstances, Ukrainian women had to overcome a plethora of structural and cultural constraints to realize their political ambitions.

Women played an active role in the nongovernmental sector to tackle a broad spectrum of issues, including domestic violence, human trafficking, and gender equality. According to some estimates, there were over 700 women's organizations in Ukraine in the early 2010s.[146] But few women's organizations captured as much media attention as FEMEN. Since its emergence in 2008, FEMEN stirred up a storm by using topless body as a method of resistance to patriarchal norms in Ukraine and beyond.[147] Bare-breasted activists, for example, protested against prostitution and sex tourism during the Euro-2012 soccer championship cohosted by Poland and Ukraine.[148] Another group of women formed the Feminist Offensive (*Feministychna Ofenzyva*) in 2010 to advance the development of critical gender studies and advocate women's empowerment through public events.[149] The Feminist Offensive, for example, organized marches on March 8 to reclaim the political significance of International Women's Day and raise public awareness of women's rights.[150]

Overall, despite some progress in the education sector and the labor market, Ukrainian women fell far behind in terms of their political empowerment. Women held less than 15 percent of seats in the national parliament and oblast

---

[144] On this global trend, see Ronald Inglehart and Pippa Norris. 2003. *Rising Tide: Gender Equality and Cultural Change Around the World.* New York: Cambridge University Press.

[145] The poll was conducted on August 21–September 6, 2012 (N = 2,000). For details, see International Republican Institute. 2012. "IRI Poll: Majority of Ukrainians Think Country Is Moving in Wrong Direction." October 17. www.iri.org/resources/iri-poll-majority-of-ukrainians-think-country-is-moving-in-wrong-direction.

[146] Liana Iatsenko. 2008. "Zhinochyi rukh Ukrainy: Etapy stanovlennia." *Naukovy zapysky z ukrainiskoi istorii* 21: 386–90. Pereiaslav-Khmelnytskyi State Pedagogical University named after Hryhorii Skovoroda, Department of History and Culture of Ukraine.

[147] Emily Channell. 2014. "Is Sextremism the New Feminism? Perspectives from Pussy Riot and Femen." *Nationalities Papers* 42: 611–14; Theresa O'Keefe. 2014. "My Body Is My Manifesto! SlutWalk, FEMEN and Feminist Protest." *Feminist Review* 107 (1): 1–19; Marian J. Rubchak. 2012. "Seeing Pink: Searching for Gender Justice Through Opposition in Ukraine." *European Journal of Women's Studies* 19 (1): 55–72; Jessica Zychowicz. 2011. "Two Bad Words: FEMEN and Feminism in Independent Ukraine." *Anthropology of East Europe Review* 29 (2): 215–27.

[148] Cerelia Athanassiou and Jonah Bury. 2014. "On Caretakers, Rebels and Enforcers: The Gender Politics of Euro 2012." *European Journal of Women's Studies* 21 (2): 148–64.

[149] Feminist Offensive, https://ofenzyva.wordpress.com/about/#_eng.

[150] Mark Rachkevych. 2012. "New Feminist Offensive Aims to Lift Women." *Kyiv Post,* March 22. www.kyivpost.com/article/guide/about-kyiv/new-feminist-offensive-aims-to-lift-women-124777.html.

legislatures. Furthermore, women were typically denied high-level positions in government. Nonetheless, women en masse joined the 2013–2014 protests to reassert the country's right to choose its own path of political development. Some of them seized an opportunity to raise a feminist voice at a critical juncture in Ukrainian modern history.

DATA SOURCES

Using the case study approach, the book analyzes quantitative and qualitative data from multiple sources. The abovementioned on-site surveys conducted in December 2013 and February 2014 provide an empirical basis for sketching a portrait of participants in anti-government protests in the capital city. Furthermore, nationally representative surveys administered by the Institute of Sociology of the National Academy of Sciences of Ukraine in July 2014 allow for a comparison of protesters and non-protesters across different strata of the country's population. To assess gender outcomes of the revolution, statistical data are retrieved from publications and online archives of the State Statistics Service of Ukraine, the Central Election Commission of Ukraine, Verkhovna Rada, other government agencies, and nongovernmental organizations. Qualitative data primarily come from oral history projects carried out by Ukrainian historians immediately upon the conclusion of protest events.

Oral history as a research method is best suited to uncover "hidden realities" and elucidate women's perspectives on their engagement in a revolution.[151] Oral history helps us better understand women's activism because it documents not only what women did but also how they felt about it.[152] In particular, data from in-depth interviews with female protesters offer valuable insights into diverse ways in which women engage in civil resistance.

The book leverages rich qualitative data from two oral history projects on the Revolution of Dignity. The oral history project "Maidan: Oral History" (*Maidan: Usna istoriia*) was administered by the Ukrainian Institute of National Remembrance (*Ukrainskyi instytut natsionalnoi pamiati*, UINP).[153] Between 2014 and 2017, a nationwide team of Ukrainian historians, coordinated by Tetiana Kovtunovych and Tetiana Pryvalko, interviewed over 1,000 Euromaidan participants across the country. Focusing on Kyiv as a key venue for revolutionary events, I retrieved raw data for a randomly selected subset of

---

[151] Joan Sangster. 1994. "Telling Our Stories: Feminist Debates and the Use of Oral History." *Women's History Review* 3 (1): 5–28.

[152] Kathryn Anderson, Susan Armitage, Dana Jack, and Judith Wittner. 1987. "Beginning Where We Are: Feminist Methodology in Oral History." *Oral History Review* 15 (1): 103–27.

[153] The Ukrainian Institute of National Remembrance is a government agency that was established in 2006 with the mission to restore and preserve national memory of Ukrainian people.

Data Sources 35

women who participated in civil resistance in the capital city.[154] The sample consisted of eighty five interviewees, ranging in age from eighteen to sixty-four in 2014, with a mean of 34.5. The youngest one was a freshman at the National University of Kyiv-Mohyla Academy, one of the most prestigious Ukrainian universities. Born in 1950, the poets Mariia Makhovets (Volynska) and Olha Strashenko were the oldest respondents. Most interviewees received a university degree or were enrolled in an institution of higher education. Approximately one-third of the interviewees presented themselves as Kyiv-born residents (*korinna kyianka*). More than half of the interviewees lived in Kyiv at the start of anti-government protests. Others came to the capital city during the Revolution of Dignity with the intent to sustain civil resistance. The interviewed women performed a wide range of roles, including crowdsourcing, food provision, hospital guard, legal aid, public relations, shield painting, street actions, and urgent medical care. Approximately half of the interviews (N = 46) were conducted in 2014, and twenty-nine interviews were completed in 2015. Eight women were interviewed in 2016, and only one interview in the sample dates back to 2017.[155] A list of eighty-five female interviewees, including their place of birth and their age in 2014, is provided in Appendix 1.[156]

Most interviews were transcribed by a professional Ukraine-born transcriber. A compilation of transcripts with thirty-two female interviewees was published in two UINP books. The first book, *Maidan vid pershoi osoby: 45 istorii Revoliutsii hidnosti* [Maidan from the first person: forty-five stories of the Revolution of Dignity], showcased the occupational diversity of participants in the revolution, ranging from university students and journalists to clergy and entrepreneurs. Of forty-five interviewees featured in the book, ten were women.[157] The second book, *Maidan vid pershoi osoby: Mystetsvo na barykadakh* [Maidan from the first person: Art on the barricades] featured thirty-six artists, poets, and musicians, including twelve women.[158]

Another oral history project, titled "Maidan. Testimonies" (*Maidan. Svidchennia*), was implemented by the Center for the Studies of History and Culture of East European Jewry at the National University of Kyiv-Mohyla Academy (NaUKMA). The project was coordinated by Leonid Finberg, distinguished professor of Jewish Studies and the Center's director, and Anna Prokhorova, senior lecturer in sociology and the Center's deputy director. Between late February and July 2014, a team of researchers conducted in-depth

---

[154] The UINP video-recorded interviews and made audio files available for academic research upon request. Most interviews were transcribed by a professional Ukraine-born transcriber.
[155] Information about the date of the interview was missing in one case.
[156] The age of respondents in 2014 is calculated by subtracting the year of birth from 2014.
[157] Tetiana Kovtunovych and Tetiana Pryvalko, eds. 2015. *Maidan vid pershoi osoby: 45 istorii Revoliutsii hidnosti*. Kyiv: Ukrainian Institute of National Remembrance.
[158] Tetiana Kovtunovych and Tetiana Pryvalko, eds. 2016. *Maidan vid pershoi osoby: Mystetsvo na barykadakh*. Kyiv: Ukrainian Institute of National Remembrance.

interviews with 300 participants in the revolution.[159] The quota sampling was employed to reflect the sociodemographic diversity of protesters. Interviews were conducted in Russian or Ukrainian (depending upon the interviewee's language preference) and transcribed in the original language. One of the main outputs from this oral history project was the 784-page long book, *Maidan. Svidchennia. Kyiv, 2013–2014 roky* [Maidan. Testimonies. Kyiv, 2013–2014].[160] This compilation of transcripts with 147 protesters, including sixty women, provides a trove of qualitative data on protest participation.[161] Female interviewees ranged in age from sixteen to seventy, with a mean of 34.6. The youngest respondent was a high-school student during the protest events. Almost half of the respondents self-identified as natives of Kyiv. Others moved to the capital city from all over the country, including Dnipro, Ivano-Frankivsk, Kharkiv, and Lviv. Most interviewees either had higher education or were university students. Many participants in the oral history project were employed in the healthcare sector or the media sector. The interviewed women were responsible for art production, food distribution, legal aid, medical assistance, organization of street actions, public relations, patrol of the encampment, religious services, and transportation of the wounded. A list of female respondents whose interviews were transcribed in the original language (Ukrainian or Russian) and published in the abovementioned book in 2016 is provided in Appendix 2. All the translations of transcribed interviews from Ukrainian or Russian are my own.

AN OVERVIEW OF THE BOOK

The book is divided into six chapters. Following the introductory chapter, the book places women's engagement in the Revolution of Dignity in the context of women's activism over the past century. Chapter 2 examines women's participation in three revolutions that had far-reaching repercussions for Ukraine's political development. The 1917 February Revolution ended the Romanov dynasty's rule over the Russian Empire and opened up an opportunity for the establishment of the Ukrainian National Republic.[162] The 1990 student hunger strike, also known as the Revolution on Granite, exposed the diminishing legitimacy of

---

[159] Anna Prokhorova. 2017. "Metodolohichni osoblyvosti doslidzhennia osobystyh svidchen' uchasnykiv Maidanu 2013–2014 rokiv metodom napivstrukturovannoho interv'ui." *Naukovi zapysky NaUKMA: Sotsiolohichni nauky* 196: 32–37.

[160] Finberg and Holovach. *Maidan. Svidchennia. Kyiv, 2013–2014 roky.*

[161] A subsequent oral history project focused on activists who were primarily responsible for the provision of medical services and the development of transnational networks during the Revolution of Dignity. For details, see Leonid Finberg, Iryna Berliand, and Olena Andreeva, eds. 2018. *Maidan. Svidchennia. Dopomoha postrazhdalym. Mizhnarodna solidarnist* [Maidan. Testimonies. Aid for the Injured. International Solidarity]. Kyiv: Dukh i Litera.

[162] Stephen Velychenko. 2011. *State Building in Revolutionary Ukraine: A Comparative Study of Governments and Bureaucrats, 1917–1922.* Toronto: University of Toronto Press.

the communist regime and presaged Ukraine's exit from the Soviet Union the next year.[163] The 2004 Orange Revolution was triggered by gross violations of democratic procedures during national elections and culminated in an unprecedented rerun of the second round of the presidential election, signifying the victory of pro-democracy forces.[164] Although women were involved in these tumultuous events, women's stories of resistance tend to be marginalized in Western historiography on the topic. The chapter aims to address this oversight and trace continuities or ruptures in Ukrainian women's activism over the past century.

Chapters 3–5 illustrate the applicability of a hybrid model to the case of women's participation in Ukraine's Euromaidan. Chapter 3 uncovers a myriad of women's motivations for participation in the revolution. In addition, data from oral history projects show that a variety of social networks, including family ties, professional associations, and community-based organizations, galvanized women into action. Chapter 4 demonstrates that women performed a broad spectrum of roles to sustain civil resistance under precarious political conditions. Additionally, the chapter chronicles how women's multifaceted participation expanded the resisters' access to a considerable pool of material and nonmaterial resources. Chapter 5 traces the political, socioeconomic, and cultural outcomes of the revolution, with a focus on women. The analysis begins with an assessment of women's representation in government and describes women's bids for the presidency. Next, the chapter analyzes patterns of women's participation in the labor market. Moreover, the chapter examines how women contested gender hierarchies in the armed forces during the early phases of the Russia–Ukraine war (2014–2021). Finally, the chapter analyzes public opinion on women's role in society in the post-2013 period. Overall, the analysis registers some variation in the degree of gender equality in different domains.

The concluding chapter underscores the book's contribution to contentious politics literature and elaborates on the implications of the main findings for the study of contemporary urban revolutions. The chapter brings up the cases of the 2013 Gezi Park uprising in Turkey and the 2020 electoral revolution in Belarus to elucidate various forms of women's engagement in civil resistance. The Turkish government's infringement on women's rights ignited women's involvement in anti-government protests and fueled their demands for gender equality. In particular, young college-educated women with a feminist agenda

---

[163] Ihor Ostrovskii and Serhii Chernenko. 2000. *Velykyi zlam: Khronika 'revoluitsii na hraniti' 2-17 zhovtnia 1990 roku.* Kyiv: Ahentsvo Ukraina.

[164] Anders Aslund and Michael McFaul, eds. 2006. *Revolution in Orange: The Origins of Ukraine's Democratic Breakthrough.* Washington, DC: Carnegie Endowment for International Peace; Paul D'Anieri, ed. 2010. *Orange Revolution and Aftermath: Mobilization, Apathy, and the State in Ukraine.* Baltimore: Johns Hopkins University Press.

actively participated in the 2014 uprising.[165] Additionally, middle-aged women responded to the government's call to bring their rebellious children home by forming human chains around the encampment and protecting youngsters against police violence.[166] Meanwhile, Sviatlana Tsikhanouskaya positioned herself as a loving wife and a caring mother who ran for the presidency in the aftermath of her spouse's imprisonment on the promise to create more favorable conditions for the conduct of free and fair elections and subsequently resign from the post.[167] Nonetheless, despite the invocation of maternalist frames and a high level of state repression, many Belarusian women subverted patriarchal stereotypes and reasserted their agency.[168] A cursory look at women's activism in Turkey and Belarus reveals the diversity of women's voices within a protest movement.

In addition, the concluding chapter suggests that an in-depth analysis of women's activism during Euromaidan enhances our understanding of women's multifaceted engagement in the Russia–Ukraine war. Since 2014, Ukrainian women have been fighting for national independence on the frontlines, the home front, and abroad. At the time of this writing, thousands of Ukrainian women serve in the armed forces to defend the country's territorial integrity and protect the Ukrainian nation against Russia's aggression. Women's struggle for democracy and gender equality is far from over in today's world so the book might inform women's ongoing efforts to have a say in domestic politics in Eastern Europe and beyond.

---

[165] For an overview, see Joyce Marie Mushaben. 2018. "'I'm Here Too, Girlfriend ...': Reclaiming Public Spaces for the Gendering of Civil Society in Turkey." In *Civil Society and Gender Relations in Authoritarian and Hybrid Regimes: New Theoretical Approaches and Empirical Case Studies*, eds. Gabriele Wilde, Annette Zimmer, Katharina Obuch, and Isabelle-Christine Panreck. Leverkusen, Germany: Verlag Barbara Budrich, pp. 185–216.

[166] Öykü Potuoğlu-Cook. 2015. "Hope With Qualms: A Feminist Analysis of the 2013 Gezi Protests." *Feminist Review* 109: 96–123.

[167] See, for example, the full text of the address by the presidential candidate Sviatlana Tsikhanouskaya on the TV channel *Belarus 1* on July 28, 2020 (translated in English). https://babariko.vision/en/news-en/speech-by-presidential-candidate-svetlana-tsikhanouskaya.

[168] On the significance of women's agency during the 2020 protests, see, for example, Gapova. "Activating and Negotiating Women's Citizenship"; Paulovich. "How Feminist Is the Belarusian Revolution?".

2

Women's Activism in a Historical Perspective

Since the start of the twentieth century, at least three episodes of contention preceding Euromaidan had a profound impact on the development of Ukrainian statehood and the dynamics of state–society relations. The 1917–1921 Ukrainian Revolution provided a fertile ground for the birth of the Ukrainian National Republic (*Ukrainska Narodna Respublika*, UNR).[1] However, the victory of the Russian Bolsheviks stalled the development of an independent state and entailed the establishment of the Ukrainian Soviet Socialist Republic as a constituent part of the Soviet Union. Following a gruesome period of purges, famines, and Russification (imposition of Russian culture),[2] the rise of the Popular Movement of Ukraine for Perestroika (*Rukh*) in the 1980s and the 1990 student hunger strike, later dubbed the Revolution on Granite (*Revoluitsiia na hraniti*), propelled Ukraine's exit from the Soviet Union.[3] Yet, transition from

---

[1] Wolfram Dornik, ed. 2015. *The Emergence of Ukraine: Self-Determination, Occupation, and War in Ukraine, 1917–1922*, trans. Gus Fagan. Edmonton: University of Alberta Press; Taras Hunczak, ed. 1977. *The Ukraine, 1917–1921: A Study in Revolution*. Cambridge: Harvard Ukrainian Research Institute; Stephen Velychenko. 2011. *State Building in Revolutionary Ukraine: A Comparative Study of Governments and Bureaucrats, 1917–1922*. Toronto: University of Toronto Press.

[2] Anne Applebaum. 2017. *Red Famine: Stalin's War on Ukraine*. New York: Doubleday; Timothy Snyder. 2010. *Bloodlands: Europe between Hitler and Stalin*. New York: Basic Books; Lynne Viola. 2017. *Stalinist Perpetrators on Trial: Scenes from the Great Terror in Soviet Ukraine*. New York: Oxford University Press.

[3] Olexiy Haran. 1993. *Ubyty drakona: Z istorii Rukhu ta novykh partii Ukrainy*. Kyiv: Lybid; Olga Onuch. 2019. "The Forgotten Revolution on the Granite (1990): A Legacy of Contention in Independent Ukraine." In *Three Revolutions: Mobilization and Change in Contemporary Ukraine I: Theoretical Aspects and Analyses on Religion, Memory, and Identity*, eds. Paweł Kowal, Georges Mink, and Iwona Reichardt. Stuttgart: Ibidem Press, pp. 175–94; Ihor Ostrovskii and Serhii Chernenko. 2000. *Velykyi zlam: Khronika "revoluitsii na hraniti" 2–17 zhovtnia 1990 roku*. Kyiv: Ahentsvo Ukraina.

communism was replete with setbacks, in part, due to the political clout of oligarchs and systematic violations of the rule of law.[4] Electoral malpractices, along with rampant corruption, socioeconomic inequality, and the government's foreign policy, triggered another wave of mass mobilization in the fall of 2004.[5] The Orange Revolution culminated in the rerun of the second round of the presidential election and brought into power a pro-Western candidate. Despite voluminous research on these critical moments in Ukrainian history, scant attention, especially in Western scholarship, has been devoted to the role of Ukrainian women in bringing about dramatic political change.

These episodes of contention can be broadly construed as revolutions. In each case, there was mass mobilization in favor of regime change. Using urban space as an arena for the contestation of power, participants in protest events demanded the establishment of democratic institutions and advocated the idea of Ukrainian statehood. As noted by Tatiana Zhurzhenko, a common theme across these revolutions is a narrative "about freedom, solidarity, and people's empowerment, [...] about choosing Europe as a political goal and the ability of people to defend their choice."[6] It should also be acknowledged that there are substantial cross-time differences in political conditions. The 1990 student hunger strike occurred in Ukraine under the Soviet rule, and the 2004 Orange Revolution unfolded in the post-Soviet period, which influenced modes of women's engagement in contentious politics. Yet, given ruptures in political structures and geographical boundaries of the Ukrainian state, "Ukraine's history does not lend itself to configuration as linear national history modeled on the Western historical narratives of a nation-state."[7]

Notably, the dominant public discourse in contemporary Ukraine frames the abovementioned tumultuous events as a sequence of revolutions, laying the foundation for the development of Ukrainian statehood. In 2017, the Ukrainian

---

[4] Paul D'Anieri. 2007. *Understanding Ukrainian Politics: Power, Politics, and Institutional Design*. Armonk: M. E. Sharpe; Taras Kuzio. 1997. *Ukraine Under Kuchma: Political Reform, Economic Transformation and Security Policy in Independent Ukraine*. London: Macmillan Press; Lucan Way. 2015. *Pluralism by Default: Weak Autocrats and the Rise of Competitive Politics*. Baltimore: John Hopkins University Press.

[5] Anders Aslund and Michael McFaul, eds. 2006. *Revolution in Orange: The Origins of Ukraine's Democratic Breakthrough*. Washington, DC: Carnegie Endowment for International Peace; Paul D'Anieri and Taras Kuzio, eds. 2007. *Aspects of the Orange Revolution I: Democratization and Elections in Post*. Stuttgart: Ibidem Verlag Press; Andrew Wilson. 2005. *Ukraine's Orange Revolution*. New Haven: Yale University Press.

[6] Tatiana Zhurzhenko. 2017. "The Making and Unmaking of Revolutions: What 1917 Means for Ukraine, in Light of the Maidan." *Eurozone*, November 30. www.eurozine.com/the-making-and-unmaking-of-revolutions/.

[7] Kataryna Wolczuk. 2019. "In Search of a Tradition: Discontinuities of Statehood in Ukraine's History." In *The Moulding of Ukraine: The Constitutional Politics of State Formation*. Budapest: Central European University Press, pp. 29–58.

government marked the centennial of the Ukrainian liberation struggle.[8] In particular, the Ukrainian Institute of National Remembrance emphasized "state-building continuity from the Ukrainian National Republic to independent Ukraine."[9] As a successor to the UNR, post-Soviet Ukraine, for example, adopted UNR symbols of statehood: the blue and yellow banner became the national flag, and the song based on the 1862 poem "Ukraine Has Not Yet Perished" by Pavlo Chubynskyi regained its prominence as the national anthem.[10] Moreover, dominant accounts of the Ukrainian Revolution highlighted the role of such (male) public figures as Mykhailo Hrushevsky and Volodymyr Vynnychenko in propelling state-building processes in the wake of the 1917 February Revolution.

This chapter provides a concise overview of women's activism over the course of the abovementioned revolutions. The concept of women's activism is here used to encompass women's engagement in a wide range of activities, including participation in street actions, public outreach, fundraising, production of art, and provision of first aid and food for an encampment. Furthermore, women's leadership positions in such political institutions and civic organizations as the Ukrainian Central Rada (*Ukrainska Tsentralna Rada*, UCR) and the social movement Rukh are here treated as indicators of women's activism in Ukrainian society. This chapter shows how women in the UNR, the Soviet Union, and postcommunist Ukraine engaged in the liberation struggle and challenged dominant gender norms. The study demonstrates that such educational organizations as Prosvita and student unions served as mobilizing structures for many young women. Overall, the findings suggest that women gradually gained greater visibility in contentious politics.

THE UKRAINIAN REVOLUTION, 1917–1921

The liberation struggle in Ukraine unfolded against the backdrop of broader political processes in the Russian Empire. The popularity of the Russian Tsar Nicholas II dwindled in the aftermath of Russia's defeat in the Russo-Japanese War of 1904–1905, the 1905 Revolution, heavy losses in World War I, and the deteriorating quality of living standards for the majority of the population. Acute food and fuel shortages caused strikes and riots in the winter of 1917.

---

[8] Serhiy Kvit. 2017. "The 100th Anniversary of the Ukrainian Revolution (1917–1921)/ Reflections One Hundred Years of the Ukrainian Liberation Struggle." *Kyiv-Mohyla Humanities Journal* 4: 145–52.

[9] Volodymyr Viatrovych, Yaroslav Faizulin, Victoria Yaremenko, Maxym Mayorov, Vitalii Ohiienko, and Anatoliy Khromov. 2019. *100 Years of Struggle: The Ukrainian Revolution 1917–1921*. Kyiv: Ukrainian Institute of National Remembrance, p. 2.

[10] Originally, the first line of the poem stated, "Ukraine has not yet perished, neither her glory, nor her freedom." However, in accordance with the 2003 Law on the national anthem, the first line of the national anthem now reads as follows, "Ukraine's glory hasn't perished, nor her freedom."

Many Ukraine-born women and men returned from Petrograd to Kyiv and subsequently became involved in state-building processes in Ukraine.

Women on the Streets

Women's demonstrations were a hallmark of the February Revolution in Petrograd.[11] Thousands of women from different social classes, including "many ladies, even more lower-class women" (*mnogo dam, eshche bol'she bab*), took to the street on February 23, according to the Julian calendar, or March 8 on the Gregorian calendar.[12] The prevailing view is that women protested against bread shortages and meager rations for soldiers' families. Feminist scholars, however, challenge the portrayal of women's demonstrations as spontaneous events devoid of any concerns over women's rights.[13] Different political forces entertained the idea that women's suffrage could serve as a focal point for mobilizing a sizeable stratum of women.[14] Another women's demonstration held on March 6 (March 19, new style) focused on the issue of women's suffrage. Approximately 40,000 people joined the march organized by the All-Russian League for Women's Equal Rights (*Vserossiiskaia liga ravnopraviia zhenshchin*).[15] Vera Figner, a leader of the socialist organization People's Will and an accomplice in the assassination of Tsar Alexander II in 1881, rode in a car in the middle of

---

[11] For an overview, see Soma Marik. 2009. "Women in the Russian Revolution." In *The International Encyclopedia of Revolution and Protest*, ed. Immanuel Ness. Malden: Willey-Blackwell, pp. 3550–55.

[12] Since Russia used the Julian calendar until 1918, dates related to the 1917 Russian Revolution are usually reported following the Julian calendar. The Julian calendar (old style) was 13 days behind the Gregorian calendar (new style) in the twentieth century. For an account of protest events, see Aleksandr Pavlovich Balk. 1991 [1929]. "Gibel tsarskogo Petrograda: Fevralskaia revoliutsiia glazami gradonachalnika A.P. Balk: Vospominaniia A.P. Balka iz arkhiva Guverskogo instituta voiny, revoliutsii i mira (Stenford, SShA), 1929 g." *Russkoe proshloe* 1: 7–72, 26.

[13] On this point, see Rochelle Goldberg Ruthchild. 2017. "Women and Gender in 1917." *Slavic Review* 76 (3): 694–702.

[14] Barbara Evans Clements. 1979. *Bolshevik Feminist: The Life of Aleksandra Kollontai*. Bloomington: Indiana University Press; Jane McDermid and Anna Hillyar. 1999. *Midwives of Revolution: Female Bolsheviks and Women Workers in 1917*. London: UCL Press; Rochelle Goldberg Ruthchild. 2010. *Equality and Revolution: Women's Rights in the Russian Empire, 1905–1917*. Pittsburg: University of Pittsburgh Press; Richard Stites. 1978. *The Women's Liberation Movement in Russia: Feminism, Nihilism, and Bolshevism, 1860–1930*. Princeton: Princeton University Press; Elizabeth A. Wood. 1997. *The Baba and the Comrade: Gender and Politics in Revolutionary Russia*. Bloomington: Indiana University Press.

[15] Rochelle Goldberg Ruthchild, trans. 2012. "Kak v revoliutsionnoe vremia vserossiiskaia liga ravnopraviia zhenshchin dobilas izbiratelnykh prav dlia russkikh zhenshchin" ["How in the Revolutionary Time the All-Russian League for Women's Equal Rights Won Suffrage for Russian Women"]. *Aspasia* 6: 117–24.

the procession.¹⁶ Under public pressure, the Petrograd Soviet of workers and soldiers, as well as the State Duma, agreed to extend voting rights to women.¹⁷

Among participants in women's marches were Ukraine-born women who studied or worked in Petrograd.¹⁸ According to some estimates, over 1,000 Ukrainians were students at various institutions of higher education in the capital of the Russian Empire in the early 1910s.¹⁹ The civic organization Ukrainian Community (*Ukrainska hromada*) published the magazine *Ukrainian Student* and organized a variety of cultural events to promote Ukrainian culture. Student activities were a part of the long-term opposition to Russification, the policy of forced cultural assimilation of non-Russians in the Russian Empire. In 1720, Tsar Peter I banned printing Ukrainian-language books, except state-censored church books. The 1876 decree by Emperor Alexander II further banned the import of Ukrainian-language books, the performance of Ukrainian-language plays, and the delivery of Ukrainian-language lectures at universities. The 1906 Fundamental Laws bolstered the use of the Russian language in the education sector and the army. Yet, the Ukrainian community in the Russian Empire sought to preserve and promote their cultural heritage.

The public celebration of Taras Shevchenko's birthday was a hallmark of Ukrainian resistance to Russian imperialism.²⁰ Born a serf in Kyiv governorate, Shevchenko had a talent for drawing and poetry. With the help of local artists, he was bought out of serfdom at the age of twenty-four and provided with an opportunity to study art at the Imperial Academy of Arts. His paintings and writings vividly conveyed Ukrainians' aspirations for freedom. Moreover, Shevchenko became involved in the activities of the Cyril and Methodius Brotherhood, a secret society that called for the abolition of serfdom, the provision of equal opportunities for all Slavic nations, and the creation of a federation

---

¹⁶ Lynne Hartnett. 2014. *The Defiant Life of Vera Figner: Surviving the Russian Revolution*. Bloomington: Indiana University Press.
¹⁷ Andrii Kobaliia. 2017. "Vid 'rivnopravky' do 'radianskoi zhinky'. Khto v Ukraini vpershe nadav zhintsi pravo holosu?" *Povaha*, August 23. https://povaha.org.ua/vid-rivnopravky-do-radyans koji-zhinky-hto-v-ukrajini-vpershe-nadav-zhintsi-pravo-holosu/.
¹⁸ Valeria Motuz. 2020. "The Famous Women of the Period of the Central Council of Ukraine and Their Contribution to the Building of the National State." In *Transformatsiia suspilnykh nauk: sotsialno-ekonomichnyi, lingvistychnyi, politychnyi ta IT vymiry/Materialy mizhnarodnoi naukovoi konferentsii*, ed. N. R. Rabei. Dnipro: Mizhnadrodnyi tsentr naukovykh doslidzhen, pp. 89–93. https://doi.org/10.36074/11.09.2020.08.
¹⁹ Yurii Bezkrovnyi. 2015. "Ukrainskyi studentskyi rukh u Sankt-Peterburzi na pochatku XX st." *Naukovi zapysky Ternopilskoho natsionalnoho pedahohichnoho universytetu imeni Volodymyra Hnatiuka. Seriia Istoriia* 2 (2): 89–95, 90.
²⁰ See, for example, Volodymyr Mylko. 2014. "Zaborona sviatkuvannia 100-litnoho iuvileiu T. G. Shevchenka: Pozytsiia deputativ Derzhavnoi dumy (1914)." In *T. G. Shevchenko kriz stolittia: Liudyna, tvorets, symvol*, ed. Oleksandr Reent. Kyiv: Institute of Ukrainian History, pp. 24–32.

of Slavic states, with Kyiv as the capital city.²¹ In 1847, members of the society were arrested, and Shevchenko was sent in exile to a fort on the eastern shores of the Caspian Sea. Despite the official ban on public events in honor of the preeminent Ukrainian poet, the Ukrainian community sought to mark Shevchenko's birthday with special events. For example, young Ukrainians organized a demonstration in Kyiv:

The celebration was banned, and our youth decided to show their disapproval by holding a low-key public event [*manifestatsiia*]: a group of male and female students walked up the hill along the former Cadet Street, singing *The Testament* [Shevchenko's poem]. It was wonderful spring weather, the sun was shining in the sky, spring streams were roaring, winding down the street, and young voices of male and female students filled the air. But a squad of Don Cossacks galloped at them down Volodymyrska Street, with lashes in their hands. They rushed to the youthful group, stomped on them, circled, and forced to walk to the Old Kyiv police station at the other end of Volodymyrska Street.²²

Given dramatic changes in the political climate, the Ukrainian community in Petrograd organized a belated celebration of Shevchenko's centennial anniversary on March 12 (March 25, new style). According to some estimates, 25,000 people, including students, soldiers, and workers, attended a special memorial service in Kazan Cathedral to mark Shevchenko's 103rd birthday.²³ In preparation for the festivities, young women were charged with the task of sewing the blue-and-yellow flag.²⁴ Ukrainians marched to the Tauride Palace, the seat of the State Duma, carrying banners with the slogan "Long live free Ukraine."

Following the abdication of Nicholas II, Ukrainians seized an opportunity to revive their culture and reassert their right to self-determination. On March 19 (April 1, new style), over 100,000 people in Kyiv participated in a public rally in support of free Ukraine.²⁵ To advance state-building processes, the Society of Ukrainian Progressives (*Tovarystvo ukrainskykh postupovtsiv*, TUP), in collaboration with Ukrainian political parties, the military, clergy, and cultural organizations, set up the UCR.²⁶ The All-Ukrainian National Congress convened

---

[21] For an overview of the society's activities, see George Luckyj. 1991. *Young Ukraine: The Brotherhood of Saints Cyril and Methodius, 1845–1847*. Ottawa: University of Ottawa Press.

[22] Zinoviia Nahachevska and Oksana Jus, eds. 2012. *Sofiia Rusova. Z malovidomoho i nevidomoho. Chastyna 3: "Ia ne poetesa, Ia ne vchena, Ia hromadianka"*. Ivano-Frankivsk: Prykarpatskii natsionalnyi universytet imeni Vasylia Stefanyka, p. 354.

[23] Mykhailo Hrushevsky. 1989 [1918]. "Spomyny: chastyna II" ["Memoirs: Part II"] *Kyiv* 8: 103–54, 141.

[24] Nadiia Surovtsova. 1996. *Spohady*. Kyiv: Olha Teleha Publishing House, p. 62.

[25] Volodymyr Vynnychenko. 1990 [1920]. *Vidrodzhennia natsii: istoriia Ukrainskoi revoluitsii (berezen 1917 – hruden 1919 rr.)*. Part 1. Kyiv: Dzvin, p. 49.

[26] See, for example, A. Hrytsenko. 1999. *Dialnist ukrainskykh orhanizatsii na terenakh Rosii za dobu Ukrainskoi Tsentralnoi Rady*. Kyiv: Institute of History of Ukraine, National Academy of Science of Ukraine; Oleksandr Kopylenko. 1992. *"Sto dniv" Tsentralnoi Rady*. Kyiv: Ukraina.

in April 1917 further institutionalized the development of the UCR as a prototype of a parliament. The First Universal (decree) by the UCR conveyed the idea of Ukraine's autonomy within the democratic Russian Federation.[27] Yet, in response to the 1917 October Revolution and the ensuing conflict with Russian Bolsheviks, the Fourth Universal issued in January 1918 declared the establishment of "a free, sovereign state of the Ukrainian people."[28] Furthermore, the UNR Constitution adopted in April 1918 granted equal rights for men and women.[29]

Women in the UCR

Women made up 9.6 percent (9 of 94 members) in the first UCR convocation (March 7–April 7, 1917), representing several Kyiv-based organizations.[30] Table 2.1 displays a list of female delegates, summarizing their age, educational background, and organizational membership. The average age of women was forty-six. The youngest female delegate was twenty-two-year-old Vira Nechaivska, a member of the Ukrainian Women's Union. While male delegates represented a wide range of political organizations, labor unions, and religious institutions, more than half of female delegates were nominated by local educational organizations and the Ukrainian Pedagogical Society (*Ukrainske pedahohichne tovarystvo*, UPT). Female delegates were all well educated and embodied the Ukrainian intelligentsia of the early twentieth century. Liubov Yanovska, for example, was an author of numerous novels and plays.[31] Being raised by the Ukrainian writer Mykhailo Starytskyi and Sofiia Lysenko, sister of the well-known composer Mykola Lysenko, Liudmyla Starytska-Cherniakhivska recalled the salience of Ukrainian culture in their lives:

Our generation is an exceptional generation: we were the first Ukrainian children. We were not like those children who grew up in a village, in the home environment, as Ukrainians by chance (*stykhiini ukraintsi*). We were urban kids raised by parents from the cradle under hostile conditions as nationally conscious Ukrainians (*svidomi ukraintsi*).[32]

---

[27] Wolodymyr Stojko. 1975. "The Relations between Ukrainian Central Rada and the Russian Provisional Government." *Nationalities Papers* 3 (1): 34–45.

[28] Serhy Yekelchyk. 2019. "The Ukrainian Meanings of 1918 and 1919." *Harvard Ukrainian Studies* 36 (1/2): 73–86.

[29] I. M. Korostashova. 2021. "Henderne zakonodavstvo v Ukraini (1917–1919 rr) – Shliakh do 'verkhovenstva prava': Istoryko-pravovyi analiz." *Storinky istorii* 52: 181–201, 192.

[30] L. V. Petryshchyna. 2006. "Zhinochyi rukh v Ukraini v 1917 rotsi." *Naukovi zapysky Vinnytskoho derzhavnoho pedahohichnoho universytetu imeni M. Kotsiubynskoho. Seriia: Istorychni nauky* 1: 145–50, 146; Vladyslav Verstiuk and Tetiana Ostashko. 1996. *Diiachi Ukrainskoi Tsentralnoi Rady: Biohrafichnyi dovidnyk*. Kyiv: Kyiv Notna Fabryka, pp. 206–208.

[31] Serhiy Horobets. 2021. "Pysmennytsia z Borznianshchyny Liubov Yanovska." *Svoboda.fm*, July 29. http://svoboda.fm/politics/society/279804.html.

[32] Qtd. from Verstiuk and Ostashko. *Diiachi Ukrainskoi Tsentralnoi Rady*, p. 161.

TABLE 2.1 *Women in the Ukrainian Central Rada, March 1917*

Last name, first name	Age in 1917 (year born)	Education	Organization
Hrushevska, Mariia	49 (1868)	Lviv Seminary for Teachers	Educational organization in Kyiv
Mirna, Zinaida	42 (1875)	Paramedics Courses	Educational organization in Kyiv
Nechaivska, Vira	22 (1895)	Uman Commercial College	Ukrainian Women's Union
O'Connor-Vilinska, Valeriia	51 (1866)	Kyiv Women's Gymnasium	Educational organization in Kyiv
Pashchenko, Olimpiada	38 (1879)	Women's Gymnasium in Kamianets-Podolskyi	Ukrainian Pedagogical Society (UPT)
Rusova, Sofiia	61 (1856)	Kyiv Fundukleiv Gymnasium	Educational organization in Kyiv
Skrypnyk, Liudmyla		Higher Course for Women, Kyiv	Ukrainian Technical-Agrarian Society (UTAT)
Starytska-Cherniakhivska, Liudmyla	48 (1869)	Kyiv Women's Gymnasium	Society of Ukrainian Progressives (TUP)
Yanovska, Liubov	56 (1861)	Poltava Institute for Women	TUP

Sources: L. V. Petryshchyna. 2006. "Zhinochyi rukh v Ukraini v 1917 rotsi." *Naukovi zapysky Vinnytskoho derzhavnoho pedahohichnoho universutetu imeni M. Kotsiubynskoho. Seriia: Istorychni nauky* 1: 145–150; Vladyslav Verstiuk and Tetiana Ostashko. 1998. *Diiachi Ukrainskoi Tsentralnoi Rady: Biohrafichnyi dovidnyk*. Kyiv: Kyiv Notna Fabryka.

One of the pathways to women's representation in the UCR was marriage to a politically active person. Mariia Hrushevska was the spouse of Mykhailo Hrushevsky, a renowned Ukrainian historian and the chair of the UCR. Valeriia O'Connor-Vilinska (Irish on the paternal side) was married to Oleksandr Vilinskii, another UCR delegate and member of the Society of Ukrainian Progressives. Vilinskii studied engineering in Germany and promoted the development of vocational education upon his relocation to Kyiv. Likewise, O'Connor-Vilinska was an active member of the Ukrainian community. Having graduated from a Kyiv women's gymnasium, she published Ukrainian-language books and plays.

Membership in the civic organization Prosvita (Enlightenment) was a major vehicle for women's empowerment. Formed in Lviv in 1868, the organization was a driving force behind the revival of Ukrainian culture throughout Ukraine in 1917–1921.[33] The number of Prosvita chapters swelled from 952 in the fall

[33] Oksana Kalishchuk. 2016. "Suchasni doslidzhennia dialnosti Tovarystva Prosvita: Bibliohrafichnyi ohliad." *Naukovyi visnyk Skhidnoevropeiskoho natsionalnoho universytety imeni Lesi Ukrainky*

of 1917 to 4,227 in June 1921.³⁴ Women played an instrumental role in setting up reading rooms in rural areas and cities, facilitating the opening of Ukrainian-language schools, and organizing a wide range of cultural activities for the population. Olimpiada Pashchenko, for example, was an active member of Prosvita in Kamianets-Podilskyi.³⁵ Likewise, Liubov Yanovska promoted the development of Ukrainian theater through her service as the chair of the dramaturgy department in Kyiv's chapter of Prosvita.

Following the Ukrainian National Congress in April 1917, the UCR was transformed into a political body, representing delegates from different parts of contemporary Ukraine, as well as Ukrainian communities in Kuban and Rostov-on-the-Don. Among female delegates in August 1917 were representatives of different political forces and ethnic minorities: Anna Gerber, H. Zaslavska-Krupovetska, Elia Kaganova, Lidiia Rabinovich, Vira Revzina, and Sarah Fuchs.³⁶ Originally from Kharkiv oblast, Revzina, for example, was a member of the Ukrainian Socialist-Revolutionary Party.³⁷ Yet, the overall share of female delegates in the UCR dropped. Women made up only 2.4 percent, or 16 of 656 members, in the sixth convocation of the UCR elected in August 1917.³⁸

Despite their underrepresentation in the nascent government, women spearheaded a wide range of public policies directed at the advancement of Ukrainian culture and science.³⁹ Trained as a doctor, Valentyna Radzymovska

---

3: 186–98; Vasyl Kupriichuk. 2013. "Vplyv tovarystv Prosvita na derzhavotvorchi protsesy humanitarnoho rozvytku doby ukrainskoi natsionalnoi revoluitsii (1917–1920 rr.)." *Zbirnyk naukovykh prats Natsionalnoi akademii derzhavnoho uprvalinnia pry Prezydentovi Ukrainy* 1: 207–17; Olha Maliuta. 2008. '*Prosvity' i Ukrainska derzhavnivst (druha polovyna XiX – persha polovyna XX st)*. Kyiv: Prosvita Center; Volodymyr Zelenyi. 1999. "Stanovlennia ta dialnist Prosvit u Kharkivskii, Katerynoslavskii ta Poltavskii huberniakh u 1905–1917 rokakh." *Zbirnyk naukovykh prats Kharkivskoho derzhavnoho pedahohichnoho universytetu im. H. Skovorody: Istorychni nauky* 2: 66–71.

³⁴ Ukrainian Institute of National Remembrance. 2018. "Rozvytok osvity i nauky pid chas Ukrainskoi revoluitsii 1917–1921 rokiv." November 16. https://uinp.gov.ua/informaciyni-materialy/vchytelyam/metodychni-rekomendaciyi/rozvytok-osvity-i-nauky-pid-chas-ukrayinskoyi-revolyuciyi-1917-1921-rokiv.

³⁵ Evheniia Sokhatska. 1996. "Olimpiada Pashchenko – vyznachna diiachka ukrainskoho hromadskoho i kulturno-osvitnoho rukhu." *Zhinky Ukrainy: Istoriia, suchasnist ta pohliad u maibutne*. Materials of the international scientific conference, Dnipro, November 4–5, pp. 22–26.

³⁶ Petryshchyna. "Zhinochyi rukh v Ukraini v 1917 rotsi," p. 146; Verstiuk and Ostashko. *Diiachi Ukrainskoi Tsentralnoi Rady*, p. 224.

³⁷ Vitalii Skalsky. 2022. "Khto predstavliav rosiisku menshynu v Ukrainskii Tsentralnii Radi?" In *Perelom: Viina Rosii proty Ukrainy u chasovykh plastakh i prostorakh mynuvshyny. Dialohy z istorykamy*, ed. Valerii Smolii. Kyiv: Institute of Ukrainian History, National Academy of Sciences of Ukraine, pp. 629–30.

³⁸ Petryshchyna. "Zhinochyi rukh v Ukraini v 1917 rotsi," p. 146.

³⁹ Valeria Motuz. 2020. "The Key Stages of the Search of a Place in the 'Men's World' by Representatives of the Ukrainian Women's Movement." *Project Approach in the Didactic Process of Universities – International Dimension* 1: 85–93; Oksana Onishchenko. 2016. "Zhinku v

joined the Central Rada's department of health and worked on the publication of a Russian-Ukrainian dictionary of medical terms.[40] Furthermore, several women, including O'Connor-Vilinska, Starytska-Cherniakhivska, and Mariia Starytska, toiled away to set up the theater department and establish the Ukrainian Academy of Arts.

Being Swedish on the paternal side and French on the maternal side, Rusova (née Lindfors) made an enormous contribution to the development of Ukrainian-language education. As the chair of the department of preschool and extracurricular (*pozashkilna*) education, Rusova played a leadership role in expanding a network of Ukrainian-language libraries in rural areas and organizing the first all-Ukrainian Assembly of Prosvita chapters in Kyiv in September 1917.[41] In addition, Rusova coordinated the publication of new textbooks for public schools and cofounded the Ukrainian Teachers' Union to propel the use of Ukrainian in schools. In general, she enthusiastically propagated the idea of Ukrainian-language education across different types of educational institutions, starting with kindergartens and ending with universities. Rusova described fundamental changes in the education system as follows:

And how great and happy the whole of Ukraine appeared to look back then! In the very Katerynoslav [now – Dnipro], where I served a thirteen-month imprisonment for a Ukrainian-language book, I could now freely, on behalf of state authorities, recite a call for having Ukrainian-language schools "from the top to the bottom." What a miraculous turnaround![42]

Another heroine of the Ukrainian Revolution was Nadiia Surovtsova. Raised in Uman, she attended the Bestuzhev Courses in St. Petersburg, the first educational institution of higher education for women in the Russian Empire.[43] In March 1917, Surovtsova returned to Ukraine and threw her support behind the nascent state. Initially, she worked as an agitator, galvanizing mass support for the UCR in rural areas:

We started visiting villages. Maybe, it was April or May. Many villages did not know at all what happened in Petrograd, about the Provisional Government, or the Central Rada. And our task was to go, inform [people], and replace the village governance structures with village councils. Concurrently, Prosvita chapters were set up.[44]

Ukrainskii Tsentralnii Radi." *Literatura ta kultura Polissia: Zbirnyk naukovykh prats. Seriia Istorychni nauky* 6: 81–90.
[40] Alla Dovzhyk. 2016. "Zhyttevyi shliakh vykladacha, vchenoho Valentyny Vasylivny Radzymovskoi." *Eminak* 3 (3): 98–108.
[41] For an overview of Rusova's work, see Taisiia Kivshar. 1993. "Prosvitianska spadshchyna Sofii Rusovoi." *Pratsi Tsentru pam'iatkoznavstva* 2: 173–87.
[42] Nahachevska and Jus. Sofiia Rusova. Z malovidomoho i nevidomoho. Chastyna 3, p. 368.
[43] On her life and work, see Ihor Kryvosheia and Liudmyla Yakymenko. 2016. *Nadiia Surovtsova (1896–1985): U poshukah vtrachennoho chasu.* Uman: M. M. Sochinskii Press.
[44] Surovtsova. Spohady, p. 64.

Fluent in French and German, Surovtsova subsequently worked in the Secretariat of Foreign Affairs. Surovtsova, for example, conducted prep work for UNR's negotiations regarding the Treaty of Brest-Litovsk, which ended Russia's participation in WWI and recognized Ukraine's independence.

Women's Rights

Women's issues were at the core of the Ukrainian Women's Union formed in the spring of 1917. This organization brought together the young generation of Ukrainian women who pressed for revolutionary change and the older generation of Ukrainians who were actively involved in various cultural initiatives in the early 1900s and in particular the Women's Community (*Zhinocha hromada*).[45] The union's membership was open to both women and men who embraced the idea of gender equality. Furthermore, the union set up chapters across Ukraine, including Chernihiv, Kharkiv, Kherson, Kyiv, Poltava, and Volyn. The founding assembly held in April 1917 defined a woman's role in society as follows:

> For the sake of Ukraine, the Ukrainian woman should perform all the civic duties that are congruent with feminine nature, and, in turn, she should exercise human rights on an equal footing with men.[46]

Yet, the Ukrainian Women's Union did not position itself as a feminist organization. The first issue of the Women's Newsletter (*Zhinochyi vistnyk*) featured the following editorial statement:

> Whoever aspires to find some feminist, suffragist tendencies [in the newsletter] should not subscribe to the *Women's Newsletter*. They won't find this kind of stuff here.[47]

Furthermore, women activists wrestled with the challenge of striking a balance between their political activism and their family life.[48] In her

---

[45] Formed in Kyiv in 1901, the Women's Community coordinated the delivery of Ukrainian-language books for rural libraries and provided financial aid for the education of young women from rural areas. For an overview, see Kateryna Kobchenko. 2009. "Zhinocha hromada." In *Encyclopedia of Contemporary Ukraine*. Kyiv: Institute of Encyclopedic Research, National Academy of Science of Ukraine. https://esu.com.ua/search_articles.php?id=18143; Liudmyla Smoliar. 1998. "Uchast zhinotstva v dialnosti Hromad." *Suchastnist* 9: 76–90.

[46] Qtd. from, Oksana Onishchenko. 2002. "Ukrainskyi Zhinochyi Soiuz." In *Problema vyvchennia istorii Ukrainskoi revoluitsii 1917–1921 rokiv: Zbirnyk naukovykh statei*, ed. V. Verstiuk. Kyiv: Institute of History of Ukraine, National Academy of Sciences of Ukraine, pp. 111–16, 112.

[47] Qtd. from Onishchenko. "Ukrainskyi Zhinochyi Soiuz," p. 113.

[48] Iryna Fatkhutdinova. 2015. "Vplyv ideolohichnoho aparatu prymusu na rol ukrainskoi zhinky u sferi simeino-shliubnykh vidnosyn v period sotsialno-politychnykh potriasin." *Future Human Image* 2 (5): 101–24.

memoirs,[49] Rusova reminisced about her feelings of guilt for not spending enough time with her children due to political activism:

Against my volition, there arose the question whether I had the right to be so consumed by political work when it might inevitably ruin my family life. And my life was crippled by the permanent conflict between these two duties: family, children, spouse – everyone whom I loved – and, on the other hand, community, my homeland.[50]

To unite Ukrainian women in different parts of Ukraine, a group of activists, including Zinaida Mirna and Sofiia Rusova, established the Ukrainian National Women's Council (*Ukrainska natsionalna zhinocha rada*).[51] However, once the Russian Bolsheviks seized power, many council members fled the country and concentrated on the development of a network of women activists in exile.

Outcomes of the Revolution

The Bolshevik victory and the establishment of the Soviet Union entailed state repression against regime opponents.[52] Such organizations as Prosvita were banned in the Soviet Union. Furthermore, most women involved in the UCR became targets of political violence. Surovtsova, for example, was arrested during her research visit to Kharkiv in 1927 and spent nearly three decades in Soviet prisons and labor camps.[53] Having served a term in a labor camp, Starytska-Cherniakhivska was sentenced to exile and died in transit to Kazakhstan. Others were crushed by state violence against their relatives. Hrushevska's daughter Kateryna, for example, was arrested in 1938 for alleged support of anti-Soviet activity by a nationalist organization and perished in a labor camp.[54] A few women escaped the horrors of Stalinism by virtue of their emigration in the 1920s. O'Connor-Vilinska, for example, settled down in Vienna, while Mirna assumed a leadership role in the Union of Ukrainian Women in Prague.

More broadly, the installment of the communist regime had mixed effects on gender equality in the country. Some feminist scholars in the West hailed the

---

[49] Sofiia Rusova. 1937. *Moi spomyny*. Lviv: Khortytsia; Sofiia Rusova. 2004. *Memuary. Schodennyk.* Kyiv: Polihrafichna knyha.

[50] Qtd. from Martha Bohachevsky-Chomiak. 1995. *Bilym po bilomu: Zhinky u hromadskomu zhytti Ukrainy 1884–1939*. Kyiv: Lybid, p. 125.

[51] Liudmyla Smoliar. 2000. "Zhinochi doli v konteksti istorii ukrainkskoi derzhavnosti." *Etnichna istoriia narodiv Evropy* 7: 10–15.

[52] On repression and resistance in Soviet Ukraine, see Oksana Kis. 2021. *Survival as Victory: Ukrainian Women in the Gulag.* Cambridge: Harvard University Press; Olena Palko. 2020. *Making Ukraine Soviet: Literature and Cultural Politics Under Lenin and Stalin.* London: Bloomsbury Publishing.

[53] Nadezhda Surovtseva. 1999. "Vladivostok Transit." In *Till My Tale Is Told: Women's Memoirs of the Gulag,* ed. Simeon Vilensky. Bloomington: Indiana University Press, pp. 181–210.

[54] Vasyl Horyn. 2000. "Kateryna Hryshevska: talan chy dolia." *Postup,* June 27. http://postup.brama.com/000627/108_9_1.html.

1917 Russian Revolution as a harbinger of women's emancipation since the Bolsheviks articulated a new vision of women's role in society and introduced some policies that appeared to be more progressive than those in other European societies.[55] In 1920, the Bolshevik government signed an edict legalizing abortion. Propagating drastic changes in family relations and labor market participation, the ruling party construed marriage as a voluntary union of men and women and endorsed women's economic independence from men.[56] These ideas were enshrined in the Family Code of 1926.[57] To improve women's well-being, the women's sections (*zhinviddily*) were set up as a unit within the Bolshevik Party in 1919.[58] However, the abolishment of *zhinviddily* in the 1930s presaged a conservative turn in Soviet politics.[59] The 1936 Family Code introduced the criminalization of abortion and imposed significant constraints on women's rights.[60] The Soviet government further tightened its control over family life and reasserted the supremacy of state interests in the aftermath of the war. Given heavy human losses during World War II, the 1944 Family Code sought to boost the birth rates.[61] In accordance with the Soviet-era gender order, women were expected to have full-time employment,

---

[55] Valentine Moghadam. 1995. "Gender and Revolutionary Transformation. Iran 1979 and East Central Europe 1989." *Gender and Society* 9 (June): 328–58; Michele Rivkin-Fish. 2017. "Legacies of 1917 in Contemporary Russian Public Health: Addiction, HIV, and Abortion." *American Journal of Public Health* 107 (11): 1731–35.

[56] V. Hrusheva, A. Riabchevska, and A. Sedenkova. 2017. "Sotsialnyi status zhinky v Radianskii Ukraini u 20–30-ti roku XX st." *Naukovi pratsi istorychnoho fakultetu Zaporizhskoho natsionalnoho universytetu* 47: 122–26; Inna Strionova. 2013. "Praktyka podruzhnikh vzaemovidnosyn u period formuvannia radianskoho hendernoho ladu u 1920–1930 rokakh (na materialakh Donbasu)." *Novi storinky istorii Donbasu* 22: 161–80.

[57] Wendy Goldman. 1984. "Freedom and Its Consequences: The Debate on the Soviet Family Code of 1926." *Russian History* 11 (4): 362–88; Lauren Kaminsky. 2011. "Utopian Visions of Family Life in the Stalin-Era Soviet Union." *Central European History* 44: 63–91.

[58] *Zhinviddily* (in Ukrainian), or *zhenotdely* (in Russian), were abolished in Soviet Ukraine in 1930. To facilitate the imposition of the Soviet rule in western Ukraine, *zhinviddily* were temporarily set up in the region in the post-WWII period. For an overview, see Olha Lobur. 2014. "Spohady predstavnyts zhinviddiliv iak dzherelo vyvchannia radianskoi polityky 'zhinochoho rozkripachennia' v Ukraini 1920-kh rokakh." *Storinky istorii* 37: 117–26; Halyna Starodubets. 2019. "Women's Experience of Participation in the Process of the Sovietization in the Western Regions of Ukraine in the Conditions of Stalin's Regime." *Skhidnoevropeiskii istorychnyi vistnyk* 10: 171–80.

[59] Mariia Voronina. 2007. "'Nova radianska zhinka': henderna polityka radianskoi vlady u 1930-kh rokakh." In *Ukrainski zhinky v hornyli modernizatsii*, ed. Oksana Kis. Kharkiv: Klub simeinoho dozvillia, pp. 106–30.

[60] Wendy Goldman. 1993. *Women, the State, and Revolution: Soviet Family Policy and Social Life, 1917–1936*. New York: Cambridge University Press.

[61] For an in-depth analysis of family laws in the postwar period, see Mie Nakachi. 2021. *Replacing the Dead: The Politics of Reproduction in the Postwar Soviet Union*. New York: Oxford University Press.

bear children, and perform the bulk of domestic work.[62] On top, Ukrainian women were charged with the task of preserving Ukrainian culture under precarious conditions in Soviet Ukraine.[63]

Despite women's contributions to the development of Ukraine's statehood in 1917–1921, most Western historiography sidelined women's engagement in revolutionary events and focused on such male figures as Mykhailo Hrushevsky, Serhii Yefremov, and Volodymyr Vynnychenko.[64] In addition, given state censorship in Soviet Ukraine, heroines of the Ukrainian Revolution were underexplored in Ukrainian historiography.[65] Yet, a brief survey of events surrounding the UNR suggests that women took an active part in political processes that facilitated the development of Ukrainian statehood. In her memoirs, Mirna underscored the importance of women's labor in the hostile political climate:

When I now recall all the colossal work made by us, Ukrainian women in the Central Rada, I can state with confidence that it is possible to work like this only once in a lifetime. To work despite the lack of preparedness, with little experience, with people who might have had even less relevant experience, coping with an enormous amount of work and having the boundless commitment to the idea, devotion to the point of self-forgetfulness. And though our work did not produce the results we aspired to achieve, did not lead to the consolidation of our statehood, it was necessary for the sake of our Fatherland, as well as the work of the next generations of women would be necessary for the revival of our state.[66]

Taken as a whole, an examination of women's involvement in state-building processes in the UNR indicates that women played an influential role in advancing the development of Ukrainian culture and the expansion of Ukrainian-language education in the nascent state. In particular, women took an active part in cultural initiatives spearheaded by Prosvita. Involvement in education, health, and art initiatives might be nowadays construed as a vestige of gender stereotyping because these public sectors are traditionally associated

---

[62] Sarah Ashwin. 2000. "Gender, State and Society in Soviet and Post-Soviet Russia." In *Gender, State and Society in Soviet and Post-Soviet Russia*, ed. Sarah Ashwin. London: Routledge, pp. 1–29.

[63] Solomea Pavlychko. 1996. "Feminism in Post-Communism Ukrainian Society." In *Women in Russia and Ukraine*, ed. Rosalind Marsh. New York: Cambridge University Press, pp. 305–15.

[64] Serhii Plokhy. 2005. *Unmaking Imperial Russia: Mykhailo Hrushevsky and the Writing of Ukrainian History*. Toronto: University of Toronto Press; Mykola Soroka. 2012. *Faces of Displacement: The Writings of Volodymyr Vynnychenko*. Montreal: McGill-Queen's University Press; Maxim Tarnawsky. 2017. "Serhii Yefremov: Epitome of the Ukrainian Revolution." *Kyiv-Mohyla Humanities Journal* 4: 1–10.

[65] For an overview, see Tetiana Orlova. 2009. "Zhinky v revoluitsiiakh: Ukrainska istoriohrafiia XX – pochatku XXI st." *Storinky istorii* 2: 111–20.

[66] Qtd. from Liudmyla Smoliar. 2001. "Ta, shcho tvoryla istoriiu: Pam'iati Zinaidy Mirnoi (1875–1950)." *Nashe Zhytiia* 53 (10): 9–12, 12.

with women's labor. Yet, it is remarkable that Ukrainian women exercised the right to vote and assumed leadership roles in several policy domains in the early twentieth century.

THE 1990 REVOLUTION ON GRANITE

Despite decades of repressive policies against ethnic Ukrainians in the Soviet Union, Ukrainian dissidents cherished the idea of restoring Ukrainian statehood and reviving Ukrainian culture.[67] Women played an active role in the dissident movement, albeit they were underrepresented in the movement's leadership. Based on an analysis of the sociodemographic characteristics of 210 Ukrainian dissidents active during the 1963–1981 period, Bilocerkowycz finds that 88.1 percent of prominent dissidents were men.[68] Among ten founding members of the Ukrainian Helsinki Group (UHG) were two women: Oksana Meshko and Nina Strokata.[69] Many UHG members were arrested in 1977, and Meshko assumed a leadership role in the human rights organization. In 1980, seventy-five-year-old Meshko was placed in the Kyiv Psychiatric Hospital named after Ivan Pavlov and subsequently sentenced to a five-year exile in the subarctic village of Aian in the Russian Far East.[70] Following a four-year imprisonment in a Mordovian labor camp and a ban to settle in Ukraine, Strokata was stripped of Soviet citizenship and allowed to leave the communist state. Strokata, along with Nadiia Svitlychna, Petro Hryhorenko, Raisa Rudenko, and Mykola Rudenko, actively participated in the work of the External Representation of the Ukrainian Helsinki Group in the US. Ukrainian activists published an English-language version of *Ukrainskii Visnyk* (Ukrainian Herald), a compilation of human rights violations in Soviet Ukraine.[71] Formed by a group of American women of Ukrainian descent, the Women's Association for the Defense of Four Freedoms for Ukraine appealed to the international community not to remain silent "in the face of such tyranny and injustice."[72]

---

[67] For an overview of state repression and the human rights movement under Leonid Brezhnev (1964–1982), see Myroslav Marynovych. 2021. *The Universe behind Barbed Wire: Memoirs of a Ukrainian Soviet Dissident*, trans. Zoya Hayuk. Rochester: University of Rochester Press.
[68] Jaroslaw Bilocerkowycz. 1988. *Soviet Ukrainian Dissent: A Study of Political Alienation*. London: Routledge, chapter 5.
[69] Marynovych. *The Universe behind Barbed Wire*, p. 96.
[70] Oksana Meshko. 1981. *Between Death and Life*, trans. George Moshinsky. New York: Women's Association for the Defense of Four Freedoms for Ukraine.
[71] See, for example, Nadia Svitlychna, ed. 1981. *Herald of Repression in Ukraine*. New York: External Representation of the Ukrainian Helsinki Group.
[72] Women's Association for the Defense of Four Freedoms for Ukraine. 1977. "An Appeal to the Delegates of the IWY Women's Conference in Houston." Retrieved from Marjorie Randal National Women's Conference Collection, University of Houston Libraries Special Collections, 1996-007, Box 1, Folder 25, Item 5. ark:/84475/do1774qk34k.

A myriad of political and socioeconomic changes in the late 1980s opened up an opportunity for regime change in Ukraine. Elected as the General Secretary of the Communist Party of the Soviet Union in 1985, Mikhail Gorbachev launched a series of reforms aimed at strengthening the Soviet system and stimulating economic growth after a streak of economic stagnation under Leonid Brezhnev.[73] Gorbachev's policies, however, had unintended consequences. The introduction of somewhat competitive elections was originally conceived as a mechanism for boosting the Soviet Union's legitimacy. Yet, the relaxation of state control over society revealed the declining appeal of the Communist Party. As a result of the 1990 election in Soviet Ukraine, 111 candidates affiliated with the Democratic Bloc, a coalition of the Popular Movement of Ukraine for Perestroika (known as *Rukh*, the Ukrainian-language word for "movement"), the Ukrainian Language Society, and the Ukrainian Republican Party, along with other pro-democracy forces, were elected to the 450-member Supreme Council (*Verkhovna Rada*).[74] Furthermore, the government's efforts to cover up the adverse environmental and health effects of the 1986 accident on the Chornobyl nuclear power plant eroded citizens' faith in the Soviet system.[75] Another blow to the regime's legitimacy was delivered by labor strikes in the summer of 1989. Thousands of coal miners arrived in Kyiv to demand better working conditions and greater autonomy from the center.[76] The party's long-term boss Volodymyr Shcherbytsky resigned in September 1989, and his successor, Volodymyr Ivashko, stepped down in July 1990.

In this dynamic political climate, Rukh membership, as well as its goals, underwent rapid change. Rukh membership grew from 280,000 people in September 1989 to 630,000 people in October 1990.[77] Furthermore, Rukh quickly transformed itself "from the popular movement for perestroika to the popular movement of Ukraine for independence."[78] At the movement's second

---

[73] For an overview of economic policies under Brezhnev, see Thomas Crump. 2013. *Brezhnev and the Decline of the Soviet Union*. London: Routledge; Peter Rutland. 1993. *The Politics of Economic Stagnation in the Soviet Union: The Role of Local Party Organs in Economic Management*. New York: Cambridge University Press. On the role of Gorbachev in Soviet politics, see Archie Brown. 1997. *The Gorbachev Factor*. New Haven: Yale University Press.

[74] Anatol Kaminsky. 1990. *Na perekhidnomu etapi: "Hlasnist," "perebudova," i "demokratyzatsiia" na Ukraini*. Munich, Germany: Ukrainian Free University, p. 607.

[75] Serhii Plokhy. 2018. *Chernobyl: History of a Tragedy*. New York: Penguin Books; Marilyn Young and Michael Launer. 1991. "Redefining Glasnost in the Soviet Media: The Recontextualization of Chernobyl." *Journal of Communication* 41 (June): 102–24.

[76] David Marples. 1991. *Ukraine under Perestroika: Ecology, Economics and the Workers' Revolt*. New York: Palgrave Macmillan, pp. 175–217; Lewis Siegelbaum and Daniel J. Walkowitz. 1995. *Workers of the Donbass Speak: Survival and Identity in the New Ukraine, 1989–1992*. Albany: State University of New York Press.

[77] Andrew Wilson. 1997. *Ukrainian Nationalism in the 1990s: A Minority Faith*. New York: Cambridge University Press, pp. 66–67.

[78] Qtd. from Taras Kuzio. 2000. *Ukraine: Perestroika to Independence*. London: Macmillan Press, p. 149.

congress held in October 1990, delegates supported the idea of removing the word perestroika (*perebudova*) from the organization's name and declared that the movement's main goal lay in "the renewal of independent statehood for Ukraine."[79] During her visit to the US in October 1990, the Rukh member Larysa Skoryk warned US policymakers that "the imperial intent of the Soviet Union has not changed" with the start of Gorbachev's tenure.[80] Ukrainian women joined the social movement to press for national independence and cultural revival.

Women's Representation in Civic Organizations

A pinnacle of the growing opposition to the communist regime was Rukh's founding congress held in September 1989. Of 1,109 delegates, 28 percent came from the three western oblasts with the highest levels of Rukh membership. Women made up 10 percent of delegates nationwide.[81] Specifically, women represented 8 percent of delegates (25 out of 311) from Halychyna.

Table 2.2 displays a list of female delegates from Ivano-Frankivsk, Lviv, and Ternopil oblasts.[82] The average age of female delegates was forty-one. The youngest delegate was twenty-one-year-old Oleksandra Turanska, an undergraduate student at the Lviv Conservatory, and the oldest one was sixty-year-old Larysa Krushelnytska, a scholar at the Institute of Social Sciences. More than two-thirds of women (84 percent) had higher education. Most of them were employed in the education, health, or media sectors. With the exception of Olena Koida (ethnic Russian), all the female delegates from Halychyna were ethnic Ukrainians. For comparison, ethnic Ukrainians made up 72.7 percent of the population in Soviet Ukraine, according to the 1989 census.[83]

The social movement Rukh might be considered a "cradle" for two main women's organizations that rose to prominence in the late 1980s. The Union of Ukrainian Women (*Souiz ukrainok*) and the Women's Community (*Zhinocha hromada*) were headed by Atena-Sviatomyra Pashko and Mariia

---

[79] Roma Hadzewycz. 1990. "Rukh Declares Independence as Its Goal." *The Ukrainian Weekly*, November 4, p. 1. www.ukrweekly.com/archive/1990/The_Ukrainian_Weekly_1990-44.pdf.

[80] Irene Jarosewich. 1990. "Dramatic Changes in Ukraine Provide New Opportunities for Contacts." *The Ukrainian Weekly*, November 4, p. 3. www.ukrweekly.com/archive/1990/The_Ukrainian_Weekly_1990-44.pdf.

[81] Vladimir Paniotto. 1991. "The Ukrainian Movement for Perestroika 'Rukh': A Sociological Survey." *Soviet Studies* 43 (1): 177–81, 178.

[82] Data are retrieved from Evhen Zherebytskyi, ed. 2009. *Try dni veresnia visimdesiat dev'iatoho. Materialy Ustanovchoho z'izdu Narodnoho rukhu Ukrainy za perebudovu*. Kyiv: Vydavnytsvo Ukrainska entsiklopediia imeni M. P. Bazhana, pp. 437–72.

[83] Valentyna Steshenko. 2000. "Demographic Situation in Ukraine in the Transition Period." In *New Demographic Faces of Europe: The Changing Population Dynamics in Countries of Central and Eastern Europe*, eds. Tomáš Kučera, Olga V. Kučerová, Oksana B. Opara, and Eberhard Schaich. Heidelberg: Springer-Verlag Berlin, pp. 347–69.

TABLE 2.2 *Female delegates from Halychyna at the founding congress of Rukh, 1989*

Last name, first name	Age	Education	Occupation status
Lviv oblast (N = 14)			
Babii, Mariia		Higher	Engineer
Bakhmai, Hanna	26	Secondary special	Medic
Dadatska, Liubov	38	Higher	Engineer
Horbenko, Liubov	43	Higher	Editor
Hrynnyk, Olesia	42	Higher	Engineer
Kalynets, Iryna	49	Higher	Educator
Koida, Olena	38	Higher	Housewife
Komad, Olena	46	Higher	Pharmacist
Kryp'iakevych, Oleksandra	45	Higher	Worker
Krushelnytska, Larysa	60	Higher	Scientist
Pakholok, Iryna	24	Higher	Professor
Pryveda, Oleksandra	34	Higher	Professor
Shabatura, Stefaniia	50	Higher	Artist
Voitiv, Hanna	36	Higher	Scientist
Ternopilska oblast (N = 7)			
Anheliuk, Lidiia	56	Higher	Pensioner
Danylchenko, Olha	56	Secondary special	Medic
Filinska, Lesia	33	Higher	Doctor
Kuzemko, Mariia	41	Incomplete higher	Philologist
Kurysh, Oksana	30	Higher	Educator
Pliushch, Nadiia	46	Higher	Engineer
Tkachuk, Mariia	41	Higher	Engineer
Ivano-Frankivsk oblast (N = 4)			
Bobrova, Liubov	41	Higher	Speech pathologist
Stefurak, Neonila	38	Higher	Journalist
Turanska, Oleksandra	21	Incomplete higher	Student
Volkovetska, Oksana	50	Higher	Teacher

Source: Evhen Zherebytskyi, ed. 2009. *Try dni veresnia visimdesiat dev'iatoho. Materialy Ustanovchoho z'izdu Narodnoho rukhu Ukrainy za perebudovu*. Kyiv: Vydavnytsvo Ukrainska entsiklopediia imeni M. P. Bazhana, pp. 437–72.

Drach, spouses of Rukh leaders Viacheslav Chornovil and Ivan Drach. Originally formed in Lviv in 1917 on the basis of the Women's Community and the Circle of Ukrainian Women (*Hurt ukrkainskikh divchat*), the Union of Ukrainian Women united thousands of women.[84] In the post-Soviet period, these

---

[84] Roksolana Popeliuk. 2021. "Soiuznytsia Ukrainy: istoriia naibilshoi zhinochoi orhanizatsii XX stolittia." *Lokalna istoriia*, March 18. https://localhistory.org.ua/texts/statti/soiuznitsi-ukrayini-istoriia-naibilshoyi-zhinochoyi-organizatsiyi-khkh-stolittia; Liudmyla Smoliar. 1998. *Mynule zarady maibutnioho: Zhinochyi rukh Naddniprianskoi Ukrainy 2-oi pol. XIX – poch. XX st. Storinky istorii*. Odesa: Astroprynt. https://chtyvo.org.ua/authors/Smoliar_Liudmyla/Mynule_

women's organizations advocated women's economic rights and supported women's entrepreneurship. Moreover, women activists campaigned for the restoration of Mother's Day and the commemoration of Olena Teliha's contributions to the Ukrainian liberation struggle.[85] Yet, according to Solomea Pavlychko, a well-known Ukrainian feminist, these influential women's organizations eschewed the idea of feminism in their public discourse.[86]

The Student Hunger Strike

The 1990 student hunger strike embodied another high point in civil resistance to the communist regime.[87] The strike was organized by the Student Brotherhood in Lviv and the Ukrainian Student Union (*Ukrainska studentska spilka*). Formed in May 1989, the Student Brotherhood coordinated the organization of local protests in favor of students' rights at Lviv universities and played an active part in establishing the Ukrainian Student Union in the fall of 1989.[88] In part, Ukrainian students were inspired by student activism in the People's Republic of China in 1989 and the student strike in Bulgaria in the summer of 1990.[89] As Olha Samborska put it, rebels of the late twentieth century set up a tent city near the monument to a leader of the early twentieth-century revolution [Lenin].[90]

Ukrainian students issued five demands: (1) resignation of Vitaly Masol, head of the Council of Ministers, (2) the conduct of multiparty parliamentary elections no later than spring 1991, (3) the adoption of a government's decree (*postanova*) regarding the nationalization of property owned the Communist Party or the Komsomol on the territory of Ukraine, (4) the government's refusal to sign a union treaty aimed at preserving the Soviet Union, and (5) the military service of Ukrainian soldiers only on the territory of Ukraine.[91] As noted by

---

zarady_maibutnoho_Zhinochyi_rukh_Naddniprianskoi_Ukrainy_II_pol_XIX_-_poch_XX_st_Storinky_ist.pdf.

[85] Tetiana Kozyreva. 2021. "Obrazok do zhyttia Ateny Pashko." *Den*, October 21. https://m.day.kyiv.ua/uk/article/cuspilstvo/obrazok-do-zhyttya-ateny-pashko.

[86] Solomea Pavlychko. 1997. "Progress on Hold: The Conservative Faces of Women in Ukraine." In *Post-Soviet Women: From the Baltic to Central Asia*, ed. Mary Buckley. New York: Cambridge University Press, pp. 219–34.

[87] Oleksandr Boiko. 2001. "Fenomen zhovtnevoi revoluitsii 1990 roku abo chomu alternatyva ne stala realnistiu." *Nova polityka i chas* 4: 40–44.

[88] Yuriy Bobrovnik. 2009. "Vynyknennia ta diialnist Lvivskoho Studentskoho Bratstva v Ukraini (1989–1994)." *Ukrainskii Istorychnyi Zbirnyk* 12: 253–61.

[89] On the student strike in Bulgaria, see Associated Press. 1990. "Bulgaria Students Strike over Elections." *Los Angeles Times*, June 12. www.latimes.com/archives/la-xpm-1990-06-12-mn-416-story.html.

[90] Olha Samborska. n.d. "Editorial: Moia revoluitsiia" [blog entry]. https://revnagraniti.wordpress.com.

[91] Ukrainian Institute of National Remembrance. 2019. "Iak pochynalas studentska 'Revoliutsiia na hraniti'." October 2. https://uinp.gov.ua/pres-centr/novyny/yak-pochynalasya-studentska-revolyuciya-na-graniti.

Viacheslav Kyrylenko, there were five well-formulated political demands, but "deep inside our hearts there was one demand – Ukraine's independence."[92]

The size of the hunger strike grew over time. On October 2, 1990, forty university students placed mats on the granite-covered square in the center of Kyiv and declared the start of their hunger strike.[93] The next day, forty-nine tents were set up on Maidan, and over a hundred students joined the hunger strike.[94] By October 16, 298 people were on a hunger strike.[95] Moreover, according to official estimates, 100,000 of 500,000 university students in Soviet Ukraine participated in the nationwide strike.[96] Some students who arrived from Lviv agitated in favor of the strike at Kyiv-based universities.[97] Furthermore, several artists and dissidents publicly endorsed the student strike. As a laureate of the 1989 Chervona Ruta music festival, twenty-year-old Mariia Burmaka showed her solidarity with striking students by performing Ukrainian-language songs inside the encampment.[98] One of Burmaka's songs based on Oleksandr Oles's poem "Snow in the Grove" conveyed the hope that people would awaken from their slumber.[99]

This protest campaign was remarkably well organized. The striking committee was cochaired by three students, representing different parts of Ukraine: Oleh Barkov (Dniprodzerzhynsk), Oles Donii (Kyiv), and Markiyan Ivashchyn (Lviv). Students designated individuals who coordinated the provision of such services as health, public safety, and public relations. Hunger strikers were supposed to wear white bandanas, often with the handwritten sign "I am on a hunger strike" (*Ia holoduiu*). Others inside the encampment wore black bandanas.

Contestation of Gender Norms Inside the Encampment

An abundance of news reports and public statements by striking students reveals that dominant gender norms influenced patterns of participation in

[92] TV 24. 2011. "Studencheskaia revoluitsiia – simvol natsionalnogo vozrozhdenia." August 15. http://24tv.ua/home/showSingleNews.do?studencheskaya_revolyutsiya__simvol_natsional nogo_vozrozhdeniya&objectId=124956&lang=ru.
[93] Ostrovskii and Chernenko. Velykyi zlam, p. 40.
[94] On the chronology of the student hunger strike, see Denys Prystai. 2020. "30-ta richnytsia Revoluitsii na hraniti. Khronika." *Suspilne*, October 2. https://suspilne.media/67513-30-ta-ricnica-revolucii-na-graniti-hronika/.
[95] Ostrovskii and Chernenko. *Velykyi zlam*, p. 67.   [96] *Literaturna Ukraina*, October 18, 1990.
[97] Kateryna Sadlovka. 2020. "'Tse buly nezabutni chasy. My dumaly, shcho mozhemo shchos zminyty': Spohady uchasnykiv Revoliutsii na hraniti." *Suspilne*, October 2. https://suspilne.media/148011-pocuvausa-bils-zahisenim-u-kurortnomu-morsini-provakcinuvali-majze-70-naselenna/.
[98] Olena Mihachova. 2015. "Za shcho holoduvaly peredvisnyky nezalezhnosti?" *Ukrinform*, October 2. www.ukrinform.ua/rubric-polytics/1892139-za-scho-goloduvali-peredvisniki-nezalejnosti.html.
[99] Video footage of Mariia Burmaka's performance at the Chervona Ruta festival is available at: https://youtu.be/jJHOlRFsYAU.

the hunger strike. First, male leaders of the student strike envisioned men's frontline participation in the protest campaign. Given the fate of student hunger strikers in the People's Republic of China in 1989, Ukrainian students braced themselves for the worst.[100] In anticipation of their arrests, male activists planned to send groups of students to Kyiv in a sequence. Once the first group of striking students was arrested, the second group was supposed to replace it. Then the third group would step in and mobilize students inside and outside the Soviet republic. Female students were discouraged from joining the first group to reduce the risk of their immediate imprisonment. Concurrently, male activists claimed that they were emotionally and physically fit to spend several days in a detention center, especially in light of prior arrests of student activists in February 1990.[101] Following the departure of male members of the Student Brotherhood, Nataliia Klymovska, an undergraduate student at Lviv Polytechnic Institute, was supposed to deliver to the capital city a large blue-and-yellow flag. Once in Kyiv, Klymovska informed female members of the Student Brotherhood about the presence of Kyiv-based female students inside the encampment, which prompted the arrival of more female students from Lviv.[102]

Second, a set of rules drafted by male student leaders prohibited women's abstinence from food. Instead, female students were supposed to perform support tasks and, for example, distribute warm water among male hunger strikers. A few young men went on a dry hunger strike and refused to take any food or fluid. Anzhelika Rudnytska, an undergraduate student at Kyiv State University, recalled how she had taken on the responsibility of persuading such students to take a sip of warm water to sustain their physical well-being.[103] Yaryna Skurativska, freshman at Kyiv State University, joined the safety control service, monitoring the quality of beverages donated by Kyiv residents:

---

[100] Ukrainska Pravda. 2015. "Revoliuitsiia na hraniti: Nas mozhna nazvaty tsynikamy, iaki hotovi zahynuty za ideiu." October 2. www.istpravda.com.ua/articles/2015/10/2/148579/.

[101] In February 1990, the Ukrainian Student Union (USU) organized a strike, articulating a broad spectrum of political and economic demands. USU called for the provision of housing for all students and the payment of stipends that were not below the living minimum. Moreover, students demanded the removal of Marxism-Leninism from the curricula in institutions of higher education and the liquidation of the first departments (KGB representatives) inside universities. Approximately a dozen student activists were arrested and sentenced to an imprisonment, lasting from five to fifteen days. Under the pressure of striking students, however, most detainees were released prior to the completion of their sentences. This protest experience enhanced the organizational strength of USU and helped students overcome the fear of arrest.

[102] Halyna Tereshchuk. 2020. "30 rokiv tomu studenty rozpochaly v Kyevi Revoluitsiiu na hraniti." *Radio Svoboda*, October 2. www.radiosvoboda.org/a/rokiv-tomu-studenty-rozpochaly-u-kyyevi-revolyutsiyu-na-hraniti-/30868864.html.

[103] Informatsiino-vystavkovyi tsentr Muzeiu Maidanu. 2020. "Dyskusia 'Revoluitsiia na hraniti: de vzialys' i kudy podalys' ii tvortsi." October 9. www.facebook.com/infocentre.maidanmuseum/videos/3360728957381339/_so_=channel_tab&_rv_=all_videos_card.

For the first few days, when the supply of water from the nearby cafés was not centrally organized, we accepted water from nearly everyone. People brought a lot of drinking water. Among our tasks was quality control of this water. At first, we accepted any type of tea, then we started limiting it to sweetened water. We tasted these teas and waited for 30-40 minutes, and then passed on the water to boys and girls who were on hunger strike. I've heard about cases when water was poisonous, and people did not feel well.[104]

In addition, the student-run health services headed by Taras Semushchak placed a cap on the length of women's participation in a hunger strike. Female students who disregarded the initial recommendation of performing the so-called support tasks were supposed to abstain from food for no longer than five days. As Rudnytska put it, "Girls were highly protected" (*Divchat duzhe berehly*).[105] Some female students, however, defied dominant gender norms. Among hunger strikers were Yaryna Hrydko, Liudmila Hrudkovets, Viktoria Radchenko, and Rudnytska. Hrudkovets, a computer science student at Kyiv State University, explained why they refused to follow the rules:

We are Ukrainian girls ... if a girl made a decision, then no matter what others say, she would do it. And I was on a hunger strike for ten days ... There was a feeling that you were doing something important.[106]

Rudnytska shared the belief that it was incumbent upon everyone to take action:

There was a feeling of great transformations and a feeling that someone ought to realize these changes ... We wanted to revive Ukraine's statehood, Ukraine's independence ... It was a moment when you undergo the transformation from a child into an adult who assumes responsibility for the whole country, the country that we dreamt of, but which did not exist yet. That's why you ought to take action to create it.[107]

Hrudkovets invoked the idea of gender equality to remain on a hunger strike beyond the five-day cap:

Lads would come to our tent after the fifth day and say, "Girls, have a conscience." And we would reply, "Lads, have a conscience! Why is there such inequality?" When the sixth day [of her hunger strike] passed by, they let it go.[108]

Meanwhile, some female students who initially followed dominant gender norms subsequently decided to challenge them to enact their understanding of

---

[104] Ukrainian Institute of National Remembrance. 2020. "Studentska revoliutsiia na hraniti: Pohliad cherez 30 rokiv." October 2. www.facebook.com/332380996916541/videos/398139264510005/?
[105] Informatsiino-vystavkovyi tsentr Muzeiu Maidanu. "Dyskusia 'Revoluitsiia na hraniti.'"
[106] Radio Svoboda. 2020. "Revoluitsia na hraniti. Choho i iak domohlysia uchasnyky studentskoho holoduvannia u zhovtni 1990?" October 18. https://youtu.be/k_iDCuXzoco?t=1297.
[107] Informatsiino-vystavkovyi tsentr Muzeiu Maidanu. "Dyskusia 'Revoluitsiia na hraniti.'"
[108] Informatsiino-vystavkovyi tsentr Muzeiu Maidanu. 2020. "Revoluitsiia na hraniti: pershyi dosvid Maidanu." October 2. www.facebook.com/504709820032390/videos/333172731309062

women's agency. Radchenko, for example, felt discomfort that she had not participated in the hunger strike to the fullest.

> When we came to Maidan, girls were barred from going on hunger strike. We started helping, and we were wearing black bandanas. But we felt ill at ease. Everyone around us was on hunger strike, and we were stuffed. So we decided to enter the active phase [of the hunger strike].[109]

Based on participants' recollections of the hunger strike, this chapter identifies numerous cases of young women's contestation of dominant gender norms inside the encampment. Some female protesters, however, appeared to reinforce a hierarchy of nonviolent action by considering abstinence from food as the utmost form of student engagement in the strike. Furthermore, female students neither set up a women's group nor released a public statement to demand gender equality as a critical component of the liberation struggle.

Outcomes of the Student Strike

The student hunger strike culminated in a parliamentary vote, pledging to address students' demands. Masol resigned from the post. Nine months after the hunger strike, Verkhovna Rada adopted the Act of National Independence. Some striking students, however, felt that the political opposition betrayed their trust. According to Oles Donii, the student hunger strike was a "missed opportunity" for Ukrainians because parliamentarians who represented proindependence forces cut a deal with the Communist Party leadership and neglected the students' key demand to conduct multiparty elections in the spring of 1991.[110] As a result, many former party officials remained in positions of power and inhibited Ukraine's transition to democracy and a market economy in the early 1990s.

From the gender perspective, the collapse of communism heralded another shift in women's participation in the labor market and public affairs.[111] The introduction of market reforms entailed the growing socioeconomic inequality and the widening gender pay gap in the 1990s.[112] In the absence of gender

---

[109] Ukrainian Institute of National Remembrance. "Studentska revoliutsiia na hraniti".

[110] Yuliia Kapshuchenko. 2016. "Revoluitsia na hraniti – vtrachennyi shans dlia Ukrainy – Oles Donii." October 2. http://kapshuchenko.blogspot.com/2016/10/blog-post_3.html.

[111] On women's status during the transition from communism, see Mary Buckley, ed. 1997. *Post-Soviet Women: From the Baltic to Central Asia*. New York: Cambridge University Press; Daina Stukuls Eglitis. 2002. *Imagining the Nation: History, Modernity and Revolution in Latvia*. University Park: Pennsylvania State University Press; Susan Gal and Gail Kligman. 2000. *Reproducing Gender: Politics, Publics, and Everyday Life After Socialism*. Princeton: Princeton University Press; Marilyn Rueschemeyer, ed. 1994. *Women in the Politics of Postcommunist Eastern Europe*. New York: M. E. Sharpe.

[112] Ina Ganguli and Katherine Terrell. 2006. "Institutions, Markets and Men's and Women's Wage Inequality: Evidence from Ukraine." *Journal of Comparative Economics* 34 (1): 200–27.

quotas, women's representation in the national parliament, Verkhovna Rada, dropped from nearly 33 percent in the late 1980s to 5.3 percent in 2002.[113] Concurrently, women assumed a prominent role in the NGO sector, with a focus on various socioeconomic and cultural issues, and cultivated contacts with a global feminist movement.[114] Originally established as the Ukrainian Language Society named after Taras Shevchenko (*Tovarystvo ukrainskoi movy imeni Tarasa Shevchenka*) in 1989, the new civic organization was renamed into the Ukrainian Society "Prosvita" named after Taras Shevchenko (*Vseukrainske tovarystvo Prosvita imeni Tarasa Shevchenka*) in October 1991.[115] By December 1996, Prosvita had branches in each oblast (province), with a total membership of 650,000 people.[116] Women played an active role in advancing the organization's mission of strengthening Ukraine's statehood, promoting the use of the Ukrainian language in various domains, and fostering national consciousness in post-Soviet Ukraine.

THE 2004 ORANGE REVOLUTION

The 2004 presidential election was another watershed event in Ukrainian politics, since the two main contenders, Viktor Yushchenko and Viktor Yanukovych, advanced competing visions of Ukraine's political development.[117] Yushchenko emphasized the importance of deepening cooperation with the European Union and fostering the revival of Ukrainian culture.

---

[113] Inter-Parliamentary Union. 2021. *Historical Archive of Parliamentary Election Results*. http://archive.ipu.org/parline-e/reports/2331_arc.htm; Oleksandr Shakivskyi, ed. 2011. *V Ukrainy zhinoche oblychhia*. Kyiv: Publishing Center Giperion.

[114] Martha Bohachevsky-Chomiak. 2000. "Women's Organizations in Independent Ukraine." In *Ukraine: The Search for a National Identity*, eds. Sharon Wolchik and Volodymyr Zviglyanich. Lanham: Rowman and Littlefield, pp. 265–84; Alexandra Hrycak. 2001. "The Dilemmas of Civic Revival: Ukrainian Women Since Independence." *Journal of Ukrainian Studies* 26: 135–58; Alexandra Hrycak. 2007. "From Global to Local Feminisms: Transnationalism, Foreign Aid and the Women's Movement in Ukraine." *Advances in Gender Research* 11: 75–93; Sarah Phillips. 2000. "NGOs in Ukraine: The Makings of a '"Woman's Space"'?" *Anthropology of East Europe Review* 18 (2): 23–28.

[115] Ukrainian Institute of National Remembrance. n.d. "1989, utvorennia Tovarystva ukrainskoi movy imeni Tarasa Shevchenka." https://uinp.gov.ua/istorychnyy-kalendar/lyutyy/11/1989-utvorennya-tovarystva-ukrayinskoyi-movy-imeni-tarasa-shevchenka.

[116] Vasyl Shvydkyi and Olha Maliuta. 2012. "Prosvita, Vseukrainske tovarystvo Prosvita imeni Tarasa Shevchenka." In *Entsiklopedia istorii Ukrainy*, volume 9, eds. Valerii Smolii, et al. Kyiv: Naukova Dumka and the Institute of Ukrainian History, National Academy of Sciences of Ukraine, pp. 35–36.

[117] For details, see David Marples. 2011. "The Yanukovych Election Campaigns in Ukraine, 2004 and 2006: An Analysis." *Journal of Ukrainian Studies* 35–36: 265–80; Lyudmyla Pavlyuk. 2005. "Extreme Rhetoric in the 2004 Presidential Campaign: Images of Geopolitical and Regional Division." *Canadian Slavonic Papers* 47 (3–4): 293–316; Olena Yatsunska. 2006. "Mythmaking and Its Discontents in the 2004 Ukrainian Presidential Campaign." *Demokratizatsiya: Journal of Post-Soviet Democratization* 14 (4): 519–33.

In contrast, being a leader of the Party of Regions, Yanukovych campaigned on the promise of cultivating closer economic ties with Russia. Moreover, given his track record as a governor of Donetsk oblast, there were widespread concerns about democratic backsliding in case of Yanukovych's electoral victory.[118]

A high level of electoral malpractices during the 2004 presidential election caused public outrage. According to the official results released by the Central Election Commission on November 24, 2004, Yanukovych received 49.5 percent of the vote and Yushchenko came second with 46.6 percent of the vote.[119] Concurrently, the results of an exit poll conducted by the Kyiv International Institute of Sociology and the Razumkov Center indicated that 52.9 percent of voters cast the ballot for Yushchenko and 44.2 percent voted for Yanukovych.[120] In response, thousands of people joined postelection protests. Opinion polls suggest that nearly one-fifth of the country's thirty seven million voting-age population participated in the Orange Revolution.[121] Specifically, 3 percent of women and 6 percent of men joined postelection protests in Kyiv. 11 percent of women and 15.5 percent of men reported their participation in postelection protests outside the capital city.

A protest sign made by two men, Anatolii and Yuri, conveyed the idea that everyone, including women, joined the Orange Revolution by citing a few lines from Shevchenko's poem *Haidamaky* (1841). "There's no one left, only the dogs and groups of children roam – the women, too, took oven-prongs, and Haidamaky joined," wrote the famous Ukrainian poet, depicting a popular uprising against the socioeconomic and religious oppression in eighteenth-century Right-Bank Ukraine under the Polish rule.[122] Participants in postelection protests, however, employed nonviolent methods of resistance. "Unlike

---

[118] On politics and culture in Donbas, see Hiroaki Kuromiya. 2008. "The Donbas – The Last Frontier of Europe?" In *Europe's Last Frontier?*, eds. Oliver Schmidtke and Serhy Yekelchyk. New York: Palgrave Macmillan, pp. 97–114; Heiko Pleines. 2009. "The Political Role of the Oligarchs." In *Ukraine on Its Way to Europe: Interim Results of the Orange Revolution*, ed. Juliane Besters-Dilger. Frankfurt am Main: Peter Lang, pp. 103–20.

[119] For an overview of electoral irregularities, see Organization for Security and Cooperation in Europe. 2004. *Presidential Election (Second Round) Ukraine, 21 November 2004: Statement of Preliminary Findings and Conclusions*. Warsaw: Office for Democratic Institutions and Human Rights.

[120] Natalia Kharchenko and Volodymyr Paniotto. 2010. "Exit Polling in an Emerging Democracy: The Complex Case of Ukraine." *Survey Research Methods* 4: 31–42, 36.

[121] Mark Beissinger. 2013. "The Semblance of Democratic Revolution: Coalitions in Ukraine's Orange Revolution." *American Political Science Review* 107 (3): 574–92, 579; Viktor Stepanenko. 2005. "How Ukrainians View Their Orange Revolution: Public Opinion and the National Peculiarities of Citizenry Political Attitudes." *Demokratizatsiya: Journal of Post-Soviet Democratization* 13 (4): 595–616, 609.

[122] The English-language translation of the poem is quoted from Taras Shevchenko. 1977. *Selected Poetry*, trans. John Weir. Kyiv: Dnipro Publishers.

our ancestors, we are fighting via peaceful means, and we will achieve a happy future for Ukraine," Anatolii and Yuri said.[123]

Women on Maidan

The data from a nationally representative survey conducted by the Institute of Sociology, the National Academy of Sciences of Ukraine, reveals some gender differences in protest participation.[124] As shown in Table 2.3, the plurality of protesters were aged between thirty and fifty-four. Meanwhile, 42.9 percent of male protesters and 25.8 percent of female protesters in the capital city were under thirty. Another noteworthy finding is that Kyiv-based male protesters had, on average, lower levels of educational attainment than female protesters. Thirty-five percent of female and 16 percent of male participants in Kyiv-based protests had a university degree. One-third of men on Kyiv's Maidan were blue-collar workers. These gender differences shaped women's engagement in the Orange Revolution.

A wide range of political, socioeconomic, and cultural grievances served as a catalyst for women's engagement in the Orange Revolution, including (1) motherhood, (2) solidarity with protesters, and (3) dissatisfaction with the quality of governance. Motherhood was oft cited as a motivation for protest participation. In a media interview, for example, "a woman of post-Balzac's age" laconically stated, "I am a mother of two. That's why [I am here]."[125] In a *vox pop* by the Kyiv-based newspaper *Vechirnii Kyiv*,[126] women of different ages shared their concerns about the future of their country and their (grand)children:

> Everyone – our faculty and students – is on Khreshchatyk Street [a street leading to Independence Square]. The Institute's doors are locked, and there is not a single soul inside. Because today a nation is born. One cannot miss such a lesson. (Tetiana Miroshnychenko, undergraduate student, Kyiv Polytechnic Institute)

> I came here to say one more time, "No – to lies! Death or freedom!" I have seen a lot in my lifetime. I know Ukraine from the west to the east. Now it is torn into regions. One should not let it happen. (Olha Krysiuk, pensioner, Lviv oblast)

> My daughter and my grandchildren came here. And today I brought food for boys so that they can persevere and defeat bandits. So that my grandchildren will have a better

---

[123] Taras Briazhunov. 2004. "Holovposhtamt iak karta Ukrainy." *Vechirnii Kyiv*, December 4.
[124] A total of 1,800 respondents, including 798 men and 1,002 women, were surveyed in March 2005. For details, see Natalia Panina, ed. 2005. *Ukrainske suspilstvo 1994–2005: Sotsiolohichnyi monitorinh*. Kyiv: Institute of Sociology, National Academy of Sciences of Ukraine.
[125] Liudmyla Kokhanets. 2004. "Pomarancheva nich Khreshchatyka." *Holos Ukrainy*, November 24.
[126] Kostiantyn Koval and Roman Chabak. 2004. "Tut narodzhuetsia natsiia." *Vechirnii Kyiv*, November 25.

TABLE 2.3 *Participants in the 2004 postelection protests*

	Kyiv		Outside the capital city	
	Men	Women	Men	Women
Age				
18–29	42.9	25.8	29.8	29.9
30–54	48.2	51.6	50.0	45.8
≥55	8.9	22.6	20.1	24.3
Higher education	16.1	35.5	16.9	10.3
Occupation				
White-collar professional	14.9	35.5	11.5	12.2
Entrepreneur	11.1	9.7	8.2	2.8
Blue-collar worker	35.2	16.1	30.3	17.7
Farmer/agricultural worker	3.7	3.2	4.9	0.9
Ethnic Ukrainian	85.7	96.8	91.9	95.3
Language spoken at home				
Mostly Ukrainian	55.4	64.5	70.2	73.8
Mostly Russian	26.8	12.9	16.1	9.3
Both Ukrainian and Russian	16.1	22.6	13.7	16.8
Number of respondents	56	31	124	107

Note: Percentages are displayed in the table.
Source: Institute of Sociology, the National Academy of Sciences of Ukraine, *Ukrainian Society-2005: Social Monitoring*.

life. So that they can study tuition-free and will not have to work abroad. (Mariia Petrivna, pensioner, Kyiv)

Solidarity with protesters was another motivation for women's involvement in postelection protests. In many cases, the whole households participated in the Orange Revolution. A woman from Luhansk, for example, arrived in Kyiv with her spouse and two sons to defend their stolen votes.[127] Similarly, the Ukrainian novelist Tetiana Maliarchuk described the significance of romantic relationships in stimulating women's activism:

Women go to the barricades against their volition so that they can be near their irrational spouses who are eager to be heroes for some reason. There were a lot of men like this on Maidan. Journalists, poets, artists, photographers, university professors. Next to them stood young women and wives – revolutionaries under cover. And I am convinced that they are more dangerous in their anger [than men] because they protect the back of their spouses, rather than elusive, worthless political slogans.[128]

---

[127] Roman Chabak. 2004. "Narod, iakoho pravdy syla nikum." *Vechirnii Kyiv*, November 30.
[128] Tania Maliarchuk. 2009. "Isty i pyty." In *Zhinky v dobu zmin, 1989–2009: Polshcha, Cheska respublika, Skhidna Nimechchyna ta Ukraina*, ed. Agnieszka Grzybek. Kyiv: Boell Foundation, pp. 115–21, 119.

Another motivation for women's engagement in the Orange Revolution derived from their long-term dissatisfaction with the quality of governance and the government's encroachment on human rights. As noted in the popular song "Together We Are Many," protesters reasserted the idea that state authorities should not treat citizens as cattle (*bydlo*). Halyna Sheshenia, head of a farmers' association in Skadovsk district in Kherson oblast, explained it as follows:

Unfortunately, not only the results of the presidential elections were falsified, but also our lives. So much lawlessness in the economic realm, such nonsense was happening last summer in Skadovsk. In addition to the overt harassment of farmers, the government tried to paralyze our will to resist, our sense of human dignity and foment fear. I resisted it, and I urged my colleagues [to do the same], although I was subject to intimidation and blackmail.[129]

The youth movement Pora (It's Time) played a prominent role in mobilizing the population in favor of political change.[130] In March 2004, a group of youth activists launched an information campaign "What is Kuchmism?" to raise public awareness of the shortcomings of the current regime. The next month, another group of civic activists announced in the town of Mukachevo that they would carry out a voter mobilization and voter education campaign named Pora. Based on the primary colors of their print material, these two initiatives became informally known as black Pora and yellow Pora. Yet, despite some tensions among movement leaders, rank-and-file youth activists jointly worked toward the common goal of bringing about political change in the country. Within each movement, there was a division of labor in the main office, wherein activists were responsible for different tasks, including public relations, finance, and logistics. Anastasiia Bezverkha, for example, was a spokesperson for yellow Pora. Within black Pora, Tetiana Boyko worked in the finance department, Olha Salo was a designer of Pora's print material, and Yaryna Yasynevych dealt with logistics.

Prior membership in Moloda Prosvita (Young Enlightenment) was a common denominator of many female activists. Liubov Yeremycheva, for example, was a member of Moloda Prosvita's chapter in Kherson, while Olha Aivazovska headed Moloda Prosvita's chapter in Cherkasy. Before assuming a leadership position in Pora, Yasynevych was an active member of Moloda Prosvita in Lviv. Banned for nearly half a century in the Soviet Union, Prosvita reemerged in Ukraine in the late 1980s and gradually rebuilt a network of its chapters nationwide.[131] Thousands of university students joined Moloda

---

[129] Hanna Kulaha. 2004. "Iz nametiv – po domivkakh." *Vechirnii Kyiv*, December 10.

[130] For an overview, see Olena Nikolayenko. 2017. *Youth Movements and Elections in Eastern Europe*. New York: Cambridge University Press.

[131] On the history of Moloda Prosvita, see Evhen Buket. 2004. *Visimdesiat rokiv dialnosti Molodoi Prosvity*. Kyiv: O.V. Puhach.

Prosvita to foster Ukrainian culture in the post-Soviet period. In 2001, for example, the Kyiv chapter of Moloda Prosvita adopted the slogan "Ukrainian youth speaks Ukrainian" to promote the daily use of the Ukrainian language among youth. In December 2003, delegates to Moloda Prosvita's national convention elected an executive board, including two women and three men.[132]

The rise of a female politician within the political opposition camp was a salient feature of the Orange Revolution. Having made a fortune in the energy sector, Yuliia Tymoshenko set up the political party *Batkivshchyna* (Fatherland) and secured key positions in the national government.[133] In exchange for political favors, Tymoshenko backed Yushchenko's candidacy during the 2004 presidential election. Along with Yushchenko and Oleksandr Moroz, another presidential contender, Tymoshenko regularly appeared on the main stage erected on Kyiv's Independence Square and addressed the electorate. Showing off her feminine side, Tymoshenko, for example, urged people to make a political statement by wearing orange, Yushchenko's campaign color.[134] Concurrently, Tymoshenko delivered feisty speeches, calling for such radical action as the blockade of government buildings. Yet, the female politician stopped short of articulating a feminist agenda. As noted by Oksana Kis, Tymoshenko positioned herself as both "a virtuous mother of her nation" and "a national sex symbol."[135]

Forms of Women's Participation in the Orange Revolution

Women's involvement in the Orange Revolution took multiple forms, including street actions, public relations, production of art, provision of food and first aid, and distribution of warm clothes. Most protesters matched their involvement in the protest movement with their professional skills. For example, trained as a journalist, Zoriana Ilenko volunteered in the movement's press center. She daily handled up to 150 requests for information from ordinary citizens and foreign journalists.[136] Similarly, street medics daily saw around 100 patients, mostly with a cold or a sore throat. Food provision was another

---

[132] The executive board had representatives from different parts of Ukraine: Lesia Nepiiko (center), Yuliia Suchak (north), Taras Perehinchuk (south), Ihor Velyhan (west), and Mykhailo Diuzhenko (east). For details, see Buket. 2004. *Visimdesiat rokiv dialnosti Molodoi Prosvity*.

[133] Tatiana Zhurzhenko. 2014. "Julia Tymoshenko's Two Bodies." In *Women in Politics and Media: Perspectives from Nations in Transition*, eds. Maria Raicheva-Stover and Elza Ibroscheva. London: Bloomsbury Academic.

[134] Bohdan Hdal. 2004. "Nezalezhnist zhovtohariachoho koloru." *Slovo Prosvity*, 46 (November 11–17): 3.

[135] Oksana Kis. 2007. "Beauty Will Save the World! Feminine Strategies in Ukrainian Politics and the Case of Yulia Tymoshenko." *Spaces of Identity* 7 (2): 31–75. www.yorku.ca/soi/_Vol_7_2/_HTML/Kis.html.

[136] Halyna Kryvenko. 2004. "Naperedodni. Hruden-2004 (khronika)." *Molod Ukrainy*, December 3.

nontrivial task. In early December, the encampment provided meals for 8,000 people per day.[137] Some women did not permanently stay on Maidan, but they did their bit to sustain the protest movement. Maia Chuiko and Lidiia Pohribna, for example, daily cooked meals for one hundred protesters, which was a product of collaboration between their employer (a publishing house) and a local supermarket. "Let our Ukrainian borscht work toward victory," the women said.[138]

Many female artists, musicians, and writers showed their support for the revolutionary cause through their creative work. Among the performers on Maidan's main stage were Mariia Burmaka, Katia Chilly, Nina Matvienko, and Ruslana.[139] Likewise, artists organized exhibits and drew paintings in the heart of the encampment. "We cannot sit inside our art galleries right now," said Iryna, owner of a Kyiv art gallery. "Every artist aspires to be useful, be with the people."[140] For example, the professional photographer Tetiana Tiryshkina chronicled protest events with the help of a camera, which later resulted in the publication of a photo book on the topic.[141]

An abundance of media reports also shows that women from different socioeconomic backgrounds donated money, food, and medicine to the protest movement. Despite their meager pensions, grannies (*babusi*) brought homemade pastries and donated money.[142] Meanwhile, well-off women purchased socks and medical supplies for protesters in a nearby shopping center.[143] Given subfreezing temperatures, warm clothes were in high demand inside the encampment.[144]

As a mode of civic activism, the knitting of an orange scarf for Yushchenko received considerable media attention. Polish students conceived the idea and asked the winner of the 2004 Eurovision singing contest Ruslana to slip the first stitch during her visit to Warsaw. As a symbol of Polish solidarity with Ukraine's struggle for democracy, the scarf traveled from one Polish city to another until it reached Kyiv. In Ternopil, for example, Polish students held a street action, titled "Gnomes Are Coming to Ukraine," drawing a symbolic

---

[137] Natalia Dolyna. 2004. "Likari vpevneni: Meninhitu na Maidani nemae." *Robitnycha hazeta*, December 3.
[138] Mykola Tsyvirko. 2004. "Shchedryi borsch i zapashnyi chai." *Vechirnii Kyiv*, December 2.
[139] Svitlana Bozhko. 2004. "Chy movchat muzy, koly mitynhue narod?" *Robitnycha hazeta*, December 8; Olha Shrek. 2004. "Muzykanty – za Yushchenka!" *Vechirnii Kyiv*, November 27.
[140] Valentyna Briazhunova. 2004. "A zavtra namaliue usmikhnenu Ukrainu." *Vechirnii Kyiv*, December 2.
[141] Tetyana Tiryshkina. 2007. *The Orange Revolution in Ukraine – A Step to Freedom*. Morrisville: Lulu Press.
[142] Valentyna Briazhunova. 2004. "Nache sestry i braty." *Vechirnii Kyiv*, December 4.
[143] Tetiana Fedorenko. 2004. "Tak osviachuetsia natsiia." *Vechirnii Kyiv*, November 26.
[144] On this point, see, for example, Taras Briazhunov. 2004. "Moralnyi dukh moroz ne vbe." *Vechirnii Kyiv*, December 1.

connection between the Orange Alternative (*Pomaranczowa Alternatywa*) and the Orange Revolution.[145] Furthermore, the knitting initiative bound together people from different parts of the country. "I am proud that I joined this action," said Liubomyra Kotsko who was taking a professional development course in the capital city. "Whenever there is a free minute, I rush to Maidan. Tomorrow I am going home – I'll have something to tell my compatriots."[146]

In contrast, the deployment of direct action and the provision of public safety were framed as a men's domain. At a protest rally on November 23, men were asked to stay on patrol and women were told to go home and get warm.[147] Not all the women agreed with this idea, claiming that women's departure might increase the likelihood of police violence against protesters. Media reports also suggest that many out-of-town men stayed overnight in the encampment, while the provision of temporary housing was prioritized for women.[148] These measures signify the prevalence of certain gender norms within the protest movement.

Overall, women actively participated in the Orange Revolution. Based on the fieldwork and in-depth interviews with three women activists, Hrycak concludes that women displayed "support by performing care work for the activists who constitute the visible vanguard of a protest."[149] Meanwhile, numerous media reports demonstrate that women's activism was not limited to the provision of food and first aid. Most women, however, refrained from explicit calls for the advancement of gender equality and toiled toward the common cause of averting Ukraine's slide into authoritarianism.

Outcomes of the Orange Revolution

The 2004 protests culminated in the unprecedented annulment of the official results of the second round of the presidential elections and Yushchenko's victory in a rerun on December 26. Under Yushchenko's

---

[145] The Orange Alternative was a Polish social movement that ridiculed the absurdity of the communist system in the 1980s. On the movement's history, see Elçin Marasli Ball. 2015. "The Orange Alternative: There Is No Freedom without Dwarfs." *Culture.pl*, December 22. https://culture.pl/en/article/the-orange-alternative-there-is-no-freedom-without-dwarfs.
On street happenings in Ukraine, see 20 khvylyn. 2004. "Aktsiiu na pidtrymku 'pomaranchevoi' revoliutsii vlashtuvaly polski studenty z Varshavy." December 24. https://te.20minut.ua/Podii/aktsiyu-na-pidtrymku-pomaranchevoyi-revolyutsiyi-vlashtuvali-polski-st-19646.html; Lvivskii Portal. 2004. "Yushchenko ta Yanukovycha mozhna bylo skushtyvaty na smak." December 20. https://portal.lviv.ua/news/2004/12/20/183017.
[146] Valentyna Briazhunova. 2004. "Sharfik dlia prezydenta." *Vechirnii Kyiv*, December 28.
[147] Liudmyla Kohanets. 2004. "Khryzantemy proty vodometiv." *Holos Ukrainy*, November 25.
[148] Svitlana Kovalenko. 2004. "Aktsiia Pomyisia! Tut usi rivni." *Vechirnii Kyiv*, December 7.
[149] Alexandra Hrycak. 2007. "Seeing Orange: Women's Activism and Ukraine's Orange Revolution." *Women's Studies Quarterly* 35 (Fall–Winter): 208–25, 216.

presidency, the Ukrainian government adopted some policies in favor of gender equality.[150] Yet, Tymoshenko refrained from using her political clout to become an outspoken critic of gender inequality in Ukrainian society. Women remained under-represented in high-level positions,[151] which contributed to the persistence of gender inequality and a need for another revolution to raise a feminist voice.

CONCLUSION

This chapter has explored patterns of women's participation in the national liberation struggle at three pivotal moments in Ukrainian history: the 1917–1921 Revolution, the 1990 Revolution on Granite, and the 2004 Orange Revolution. An examination of women's activism suggests that women gradually gained greater visibility during a period of mass mobilization. Many women who were involved in state-building processes in the UNR remained in the background, tirelessly working to advance the development of Ukrainian education, science, and art. Over the course of the 1990 Revolution on Granite, some female students articulated their right to participate in the hunger strike on an equal footing with male students and challenged a gender-based division of labor inside the encampment. By the time of the Orange Revolution, a female politician became a leader of postelection protests.

A recurrent trend across these episodes of contention is the importance of educational and student organizations in stimulating women's activism. Prosvita served as a platform for raising a generation of young women in support of Ukrainian culture and statehood in the early twentieth century. Similarly, Moloda Prosvita was vital to the upbringing of youth activists in the post-Soviet period. In addition, independent student unions and student organizations were instrumental in facilitating the coordination of student actions against the ruling elite.

Another recurrent trend is an incomplete realization of the main goals pursued by the protest movement. Despite mass mobilization in favor of regime change, participants in revolutionary events were unable to achieve their utmost goal of enacting irreversible political and economic reforms to safeguard national independence and sustain democratic development in the

---

[150] Alexandra Hrycak. 2010. "Orange Harvest? Women's Activism and Civil Society in Ukraine, Belarus and Russia Since 2004." *Canadian-American Slavic Studies* 44 (June): 151–77.

[151] For an overview, see Tamara Martsenyuk. 2015. "Women's Top-Level Political Participation: Failures and Hopes of Ukrainian Gender Politics." In *New Imaginaries: Youthful Reinvention of Ukraine's Cultural Paradigm*, ed. Marian J. Rubchak. New York: Berghahn Books, pp. 33–52.

Conclusion

country. Signifying mass discontent with the sluggish pace of reforms in the wake of the Orange Revolution, Burmaka declared in a song, "I am tired of such revolutions that are not revolutions at all."[152] The prevailing view was that a wider range of drastic political, socioeconomic, and cultural reforms should be implemented to transform Ukraine into a democratic and prosperous country.

---

[152] Mariia Kovalenko. 2006. "Mariia Burmaka: Te, shcho zaraz vidbuvaetsia v parlamenti ne vpysuetsia v moi moralni ramky." *Ukrainska Pravda*, December 27. www.pravda.com.ua/rus/articles/2006/12/27/4410954.

3

Drivers of Women's Participation in the Revolution of Dignity

Women's participation in contentious politics can be attributed to a wide range of factors. In line with an egalitarian model of women's participation in a revolution, the assertion of women's rights might provide a catalyst for women's action.[1] However, women's involvement in national liberation struggles "often emerges without any direct identification with feminism."[2] Instead, consistent with a patriarchal model, the maternal identity is frequently invoked as an incentive for women's activism. The Mothers of the Plaza de Mayo is a prime example of a women-led human rights movement in a military dictatorship. For several decades, Argentinian women in white headscarves held weekly marches near the presidential palace to demand the prosecution of military officers responsible for the kidnapping, torture, and murder of thousands of people in 1976–1983.[3] More recently, a group of women known as the Saturday Mothers weekly gathered in Istanbul to protest the disappearance of their relatives in the wake of the 1980 coup.[4] A growing body of scholarship also indicates that women might be drawn into contentious politics

---

[1] For an overview, see Myra Marx Ferree and Carol McClurg Mueller. 2004. "Feminism and the Women's Movement: A Global Perspective." In *The Blackwell Companion to Social Movements*, eds. David Snow, Sarah Soule, and Hanspeter Kriesi. Malden: Blackwell, pp. 576–607.
[2] Jennifer Leigh Disney. 2008. *Women's Activism and Feminist Agency in Mozambique and Nicaragua*. Philadelphia: Temple University Press, p. 2.
[3] Marguerite Guzman Bouvard. 2002. *Revolutionizing Motherhood: The Mothers of the Plaza de Mayo*. Lanham: Rowman and Littlefield.
[4] Gülsüm Baydar and Berfin İvegen. 2006. "Territories, Identities, and Thresholds: The Saturday Mothers Phenomenon in İstanbul." *Signs: Journal of Women in Culture and Society* 31 (3): 689–715; Başak Can. 2022. "How Does a Protest Last? Rituals of Visibility, Disappearances under Custody, and the Saturday Mothers in Turkey." *American Anthropologist* 124 (3): 467–78.

Findings from On-Site Surveys of Protesters

via social networks and social media.[5] Research, for example, suggests that Facebook was an effective tool for spreading feminist ideas and mobilizing public opinion during the Tunisian Revolution.[6] Nonetheless, it is puzzling why women would put their lives at risk by joining a revolution. The case of the Revolution of Dignity provides us with a superb opportunity to explore factors associated with women's engagement in a revolution.

The empirical analysis presented in this chapter illustrates a hybrid model of women's participation in a contemporary revolution. First, this chapter examines a variety of motivations for citizens' engagement in anti-government protests, using data from on-site surveys of protesters. Next, drawing on data from oral history projects, this chapter sheds additional light on the multiplicity of women's motivations for joining the protest movement. This study also highlights various mobilizing structures that galvanized women into action, including friendship networks, professional associations, and civic organizations. Finally, the empirical analysis explores how parenthood influenced women's participation in the protest movement. Taken as a whole, this chapter demonstrates that women from diverse backgrounds became involved in the revolution.

FINDINGS FROM ON-SITE SURVEYS OF PROTESTERS

Over the course of mass mobilization, a team of Ukrainian sociologists conducted three on-site surveys of protesters on Kyiv's Independence Square and prompted survey respondents to choose from an eleven-item list three main reasons for their participation in the protest movement.[7] Table 3.1 summarizes the main motivations for citizens' participation in Kyiv-based protests. The most cited motivation for protest engagement was outrage over state repression and in particular police violence against peaceful protesters on November 30. For example, 68.6 percent of men and 70.8 percent of women cited state repression as a primary motivation for their participation in protest rallies in early December 2013. The incumbent's refusal to sign an Association Agreement with the EU came second. Approximately half of the protesters mentioned the Association Agreement as a catalyst for protest participation.

---

[5] Ahmed Al-Rawi. 2020. *Women's Activism and New Media in the Arab World*. Albany: State University of New York; Hend T. Alsudairy. 2020. *The Role of the Social Media in Empowering Saudi Women's Expression*. Newcastle upon Tyne: Cambridge Academic Publishers; Elham Gheytanchi. 2015. "Gender Roles in the Social Media World of Iranian Women." In *Social Media in Iran: Politics and Society After 2009*, eds.David Faris and Babak Rahimi. Albany: State University of New York, pp. 41–56; Asuman Özgür Keysan. 2019. *Activism and Women's NGOs in Turkey: Civil Society, Feminism and Politics*. London: Bloomsbury Publishing.

[6] Sami Zlitni and Zeineb Touati. 2012. "Social Networks and Women's Mobilization in Tunisia." *Journal of International Women's Studies* 13 (5): 46–58.

[7] Survey respondents could select "other" as a response option if the list of various motivations for protesting did not cover their own motivation for action.

TABLE 3.1 *Motivations for participation in Kyiv-based protests: findings from on-site surveys*

Motivation	Date of the survey					
	December 7–8, 2013		December 20, 2013		February 3, 2014	
	Men	Women	Men	Women	Men	Women
Yanukovych's refusal to sign an Association Agreement with the EU	53.7	53.3	37.7	53.1	45.7	56.6
The ruthless beating of protesters on November 30; state repression against protesters	68.6	70.8	67.6	77.2	60.5	67.1
Calls for action by opposition politicians	6.7	3.9	6.8	6.4	2.9	1.3
Aspirations to bring about the turnover of power	40.9	36.7	39.1	37.9	45.8	44.1
Aspirations to change life in Ukraine for the better	47.2	53.3	36.3	36.1	51.9	44.4
Solidarity with friends, colleagues, and relatives on Maidan	6.9	5.3	4.1	4.3	3.3	6.9
Democratic regression, the threat of dictatorship	16.3	22.3	13.5	14.9	17.2	19.9
It is fun and interesting to be on Maidan.	1.9	2.6	1.4	0	0.5	0
Taking revenge on the government	6.4	3.7	9.5	10.3	10.6	4.5
The threat of Ukraine's membership in the Customs Union and the Russian influence	17.1	16.6	13.9	17.8	18.3	33.1
Money for protest participation	0.2	0.5	0.2	0	0	0
Other	4.7	1.6	8.9	4.1	5.2	0
Number of respondents	584	453	438	77	443	59

Note: Percentages are reported in the table. The three-wave survey Student Maidan (N = 1,037), Maidan Tabir (N = 515), and Maidan Sich (N = 502) was conducted by the Ilko Kucheriv Democratic Initiatives Foundation and the Kyiv International Institute of Sociology.

Aspirations for a better quality of life in their home country were the third-most cited reason for joining anti-government protests in early December. A related motivation for protest engagement was citizens' yearning for the turnover of power. In February 2014, for example, 51.9 percent of male and 44.4 percent of female protesters were driven by the resolve to remove the incumbent from office. Concurrently, the survey results indicate that opposition politicians played a marginal role in mobilizing the population against the ruling elite. Only 6 percent of protesters reported that the opposition's call for action was a primary reason for their engagement in civil resistance.

The results of on-site surveys suggest that there were slight gender differences in motivations for protest engagement. Taking revenge on the incumbent government for all the wrongdoings appeared to be more salient among men at the beginning and at the end of mass mobilization. In February 2014, for example, twice as many men (10.6 percent vs. 4.5 percent) mentioned revenge as a major motivation for their involvement in the protest movement. Meanwhile, the threat of Ukraine's membership in the Moscow-led Customs Union and the persistence of Russian interference in Ukraine's domestic politics emerged as a major catalyst for protest engagement for 33.1 percent of women and 18.1 percent of men in February 2014.

The bivariate analysis explores how age and education shaped women's and men's motivations for protesting. Among all the respondents, university students were most likely to cite the incumbent's rejection of the EU treaty as a top reason for protest participation. Meanwhile, there are gender differences in the impact of age on the significance of police violence as a catalyst for action. As seen in Figure 3.1, 73 percent of young men, compared to 58 percent of those over 54, cited police violence as a primary motivation for protesting. Among female protesters, however, there were negligible age differences in terms of mentioning police violence as an incentive for protesting. Another finding is that young women were more likely than older women to cite the quality of life in Ukraine as a motivation for protesting. As shown in Figure 3.1, 57.2 percent of eighteen–twenty nine-year-old female protesters, compared to 47.3 percent of female protesters over 54, were driven by concerns about the quality of life in the country. A related finding is that a sizeable proportion of young women enrolled in tertiary education cited the quality of life as a motivation for protesting.

Moreover, given cultural divides in the country, additional analysis (not displayed in Figure 3.1) examines the impact of language use on the salience of certain motivations for protesting. Using language spoken at home as a marker of identity, the analysis compares and contrasts the frequency of citing the EU treaty and the quality of life in Ukraine as incentives for protest engagement. As expected, Ukrainian-language speakers mentioned the EU treaty more frequently than Russian-language speakers. For example, 57.8 percent of Ukrainian-language female protesters, compared to 49.6 percent of Russian-language female protesters, cited the incumbent's rejection of the EU treaty as a reason for protesting. Meanwhile, the quality of life was more frequently mentioned by Russian-language speakers. Among male protesters, for example, 52.1 percent of Russian-language speakers, as well as 46.6 percent of Ukrainian-language speakers, cited concerns about the quality of life as a

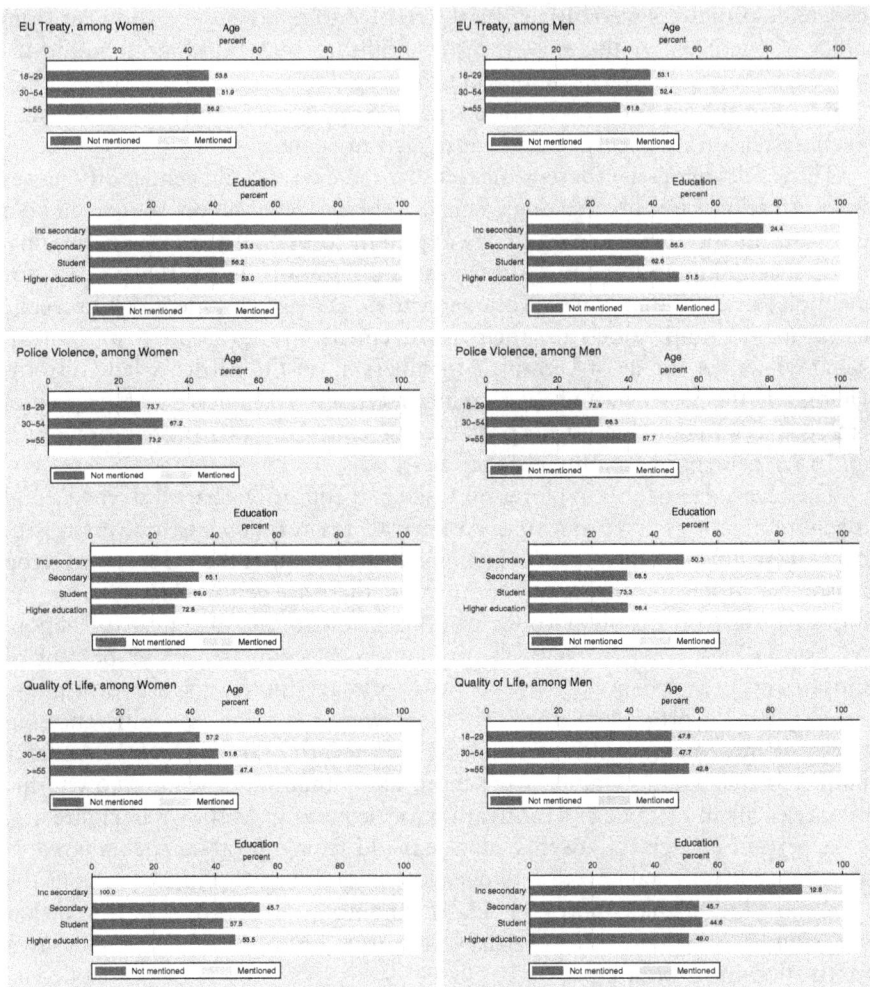

FIGURE 3.1 Motivations for protesting by age and education.
The percentage of respondents who mentioned a specific motivation for protesting is listed in the figure (N = 1,037).

The survey Student Maidan conducted by the Ilko Kucheriv Democratic Initiatives Foundation and the Kyiv International Institute of Sociology.

reason for getting involved in anti-government protests. These findings suggest that citizens from various regions of the country differed in their rankings of the importance of certain cultural and socioeconomic challenges that Ukraine faced.

Table 3.2 displays the results of the logistic regression analysis, with the top three motivations for protesting as a dependent variable. The multivariate

TABLE 3.2 *Determinants of motivations for protesting*

Variables	Model 1 EU treaty	Model 2 Police violence	Model 3 Quality of life
Gender (female = 1)	1.040	1.097	1.192
	(0.149)	(0.172)	(0.170)
Age	1.021	1.021	0.988
	(0.027)	(0.029)	(0.026)
Age squared	1.000	1.000	1.000
	(0.0003)	(0.0003)	(0.0003)
Higher education	0.993	1.158	1.186
	(0.167)	(0.206)	(0.200)
Ukrainian language	1.320**	1.104	0.963
	(0.185)	(0.166)	(0.134)
Party membership	0.728	0.650	0.727
	(0.243)	(0.218)	(0.249)
Civic organization	1.285	0.790	0.768
	(0.465)	(0.297)	(0.277)
Civic movement	0.674	1.506	1.825
	(0.391)	(0.969)	(1.121)
Log-likelihood	-704.012	-626.873	-706.041
Pseudo R-square	0.005	0.005	0.006
Observations	1,023	1,023	1,023

Note: Odds ratios, with robust standard errors in parentheses, are reported in the table.
*p < 0.1; **p < 0.05; ***p < 0.01.
Source: The survey Student Maidan conducted by the Ilko Kucheriv Democratic Initiatives Foundation and the Kyiv International Institute of Sociology on December 7–8, 2013.

analysis reaffirms the significance of the Ukrainian-language use as a determinant of support for the EU treaty as a motive for protest engagement. However, the significance of the language spoken at home seems to diminish when it comes to such grievances as police violence and quality of life. A set of basic sociodemographic variables appears to be insufficient to explain the salience of a particular motive for civil resistance. Analysis of qualitative data from oral history projects will shed additional light on women's motivations for activism and their networks of contention.

WOMEN'S MOTIVATIONS FOR PARTICIPATION IN THE REVOLUTION OF DIGNITY

Data from oral history projects reveal a variety of motivations for women's engagement in the Revolution of Dignity, ranging from the disapproval of the incumbent's refusal to sign an Association Agreement with the EU and outrage over police violence to dissatisfaction with the quality of governance and solidarity with protesters. These findings are consistent with the results of on-site surveys of protesters conducted by the Ilko Kucheriv Democratic Initiatives Foundation and the Kyiv International Institute of Sociology. In addition, qualitative data show that professional service was a catalyst for women's activism. Some female interviewees also invoked the notion of motherhood to explain their involvement in the revolution. Meanwhile, few women cited feminism as a primary reason for their engagement in the protest movement. The main motivations for women's activism are summarized in Table 3.3 and discussed in this section.

EU Integration

Popular aspirations for EU membership, especially among Ukrainian youth and the middle class, served as an incentive for the onset of anti-government protests in November 2013. Many university students viewed EU membership as a gateway to international travel and career mobility. The number of Ukrainians studying abroad has increased from 26,259 people during the 2008–2009 academic year to 46,591 people during the 2013–2014 academic year.[8] Poland has become the most popular destination for young Ukrainians, with the number of Ukrainian students at Polish universities rising from 2,831 people in 2008 to 14,951 people in 2013. Germany was the second most popular country for studying, with 9,212 Ukrainian students in 2013. Only 13 percent of Ukrainians who studied abroad (6,029 people) headed for Russia that year. These statistics suggest that most young people in independent Ukraine did not consider the former capital of the Soviet Union as the main destination for education attainment, and fluency in Russian was no longer viewed as an essential tool for accessing cutting-edge knowledge in science. Instead, Ukrainian youth learned Germanic languages to study in the West. Since its opening in 1993, the Goethe-Institut Ukraine saw a significant increase in the number of applicants for its German-language courses.[9] Given expanding opportunities for international travel and studying in the West, most Ukrainian youths favored the idea of European integration. Against this backdrop, the government's rejection of the EU–Ukraine agreement was seen as a brazen subversion of youth's future orientation. For example, Sofiia Borysko, an undergraduate student at the Taras Shevchenko National University, felt a sense of injustice.

When there looms a chance for a better future, when new opportunities – the European vector of development – open up, and then suddenly you are told, "No, it is not going to

---

[8] Ehor Stadnyi, ed. 2016. *Osvita v Ukraini-2015*. Kyiv: CEDOS. https://cedos.org.ua/data/pdfs/osvitaua_250416_updated.pdf.

[9] Olha Vesnianka. 2013. "Iuvilei Gete-Instytutu v Ukraini." *Deutsche Welle*, July 19. https://p.dw.com/p/19ASr.

TABLE 3.3 *Women's motivations for participation in a revolution: insights from oral history projects*

Motivation	Illustrative interview quotes
EU integration/ National independence	I realized that I definitely did not want to be under Russia so the EU might be a better option. But in general, I wanted to show that Ukrainians have their aspirations and their vision of the future (Anastasiia Makarenko, twenty-three, student).
Police violence	When I saw the footage [of police violence], it was such a blow for me. It was something absolutely unacceptable for me – something that did not fit into my worldview. I did not understand how it was possible to beat children so savagely (Anastasiia Dmytruk, twenty-three, student).
Quality of governance	The more developed the country, the greater respect for the individual. The less developed the country, the greater respect for money. There was colossal respect for money and disrespect for the individual [under Yanukovych]. The government that originated from Donetsk got used to treating people with contempt and impudence (Nelia Vterkovska, thirty, journalist).
Human dignity	Dignity is such a thing that you daily turn to. And I think that it is the crux of the issue: Yanukovych simply showed [us] that he viewed us as nobody and nothing, but we considered ourselves as human beings (Nataliia Sokolenko, thirty-nine, journalist).
Civic duty	I love my country very much. The phrase "Ukraine above all" (*Ukraina ponad use!*) really means "above all" to me (Olha Streltsova, forty-two, doctor).
Motherhood	The first thought that I had at that moment was that if I do not do anything right now, then sooner or later my children will do it. Having a daughter, I did not want her to go through the same phase in her life as her parents. I wanted my child to live in a bright future and not to deal with the same issues (Mariia Burdun, thirty, executive producer at a radio station).
Professional service	On January 19, my friend and I found white T-shirts, drew crosses on them, and went to Hrushevska [street]. There was a medical station at Hrushevska 4, and we worked there through the night. We put bandages and sent people to hospitals (Oksana Syvak, forty, doctor).

happen. We are turning 90 degrees and moving in another direction." I think that the driving force [behind civil resistance] was above all this feeling of injustice.[10]

Meanwhile, older movement participants primarily considered the EU as a check on the national government and a mechanism for upholding the rule of

---

[10] UINP interview with Sofiia Borysko, August 19, 2014.

law. The ruling elite was notorious for its reluctance to create a level playing field for political competition and entrepreneurship. Yet, in accordance with the EU's Copenhagen criteria for accession, state authorities were expected to implement reforms aimed at "stability of institutions guaranteeing democracy, the rule of law, human rights, and respect for and protection of minorities."[11] Having run a small business in Ternopil, Tetiana Movchan visited several European countries and developed a more nuanced understanding of European societies than young people without such international experience. She realized that ordinary citizens in Europe also grappled with various policy challenges. Nonetheless, Movchan placed a high value on the EU's oversight functions.

Having traveled [across Europe], I met with ordinary people and saw that not everything was as deceptively beautiful as young people imagined it. For me, Europe was primarily important in terms of its oversight because if the EU was going to invest its money [in Ukraine], then it would act as a manager and would oversee how the money is spent.[12]

What becomes clear from the oral history data is that there existed differences in public understanding of the notion of Europe. Yet, there was a consensus within the protest movement that the EU offered a more attractive model of political and socioeconomic development than the Moscow-led Customs Union.

Police Violence and the Denigration of Human Dignity

The brutal dispersal of peaceful protesters on November 30 triggered the transformation of the protest movement. Euromaidan, with its primary focus on EU integration, has evolved into the Revolution of Dignity marked by a wider range of grievances against the incumbent government. Furthermore, the size of the protest movement ballooned because thousands of people, including Europhiles and Eurosceptics, joined the protest movement to demand the government's adherence to the rule of law and respect for human dignity. For example, the entrepreneur Olha Hodovanets harbored some skepticism about the benefits of European integration, but she unequivocally disapproved of state violence against regime opponents.

In principle, I think that Ukraine does not need to be a part of the European Union. Ukraine has already been a part of the [Soviet] Union, and nothing good came out of it. That's why the first week [of protests] for me was more about meeting people whom I had not seen for a while, rather than [defending] the idea of joining the European Union. But after the beating of youth on the night of November 29th to 30th, it became a

---

[11] For a full list of the Copenhagen criteria, visit the webpage of EUR-Lex, https://eur-lex.europa.eu/EN/legal-content/glossary/accession-criteria-copenhagen-criteria.html.
[12] UINP interview with Tetiana Movchan, August 20, 2014.

matter of honor and dignity. Afterward, Maidan ceased to be about the EU for me, it became a matter of history and the return to our traditions.[13]

Similarly, Iryna Kyselova viewed November 30th as a watershed event in Ukrainian society. She carried on with her life as usual during the first week of protests, but her attitude toward mass protests changed on November 30. The next day, she traveled from Bila Tserkva, a town located 56 miles from Kyiv, to the capital city to attend a protest rally.

When the student-led Euromaidan started in November, it did not profoundly affect me. Kudos to students for standing up, it is necessary to stand up for one's rights. But I was at home, minding my own business, and it did not occur to me to come to Maidan. But after the events of November 30, I woke up in another country. How could such things happen in our country? How is it possible to live in such a country? On December 1, I was already in Kyiv.[14]

The data from the oral history projects demonstrate that police brutality might cause a backlash and engender the growth of the social movement. According to the Ukrainian sociologist Iryna Bekeshkina, "Ukrainians are a remarkable nation. When they are being beaten, they run to the site of violence, they do not run away. They run to defend those who are being beaten."[15] Yanukovych, along with the Kremlin, miscalculated public response to state repression.[16] In defiance of the ruling elite, ordinary citizens persevered in their struggle to live in a free country.

Quality of Governance

A related set of grievances that came to the forefront in the post-November phase of mass mobilization tapped into the long-seated dissatisfaction with the quality of governance under Yanukovych. An opinion poll conducted by the Kyiv International Institute of Sociology in February 2012 found that 73 percent of Ukrainians did not trust the national parliament, 66 percent of survey respondents did not trust the incumbent president, and 63 percent distrusted the police.[17] In 2013, half of the adult population shared the view that the

---

[13] UINP interview with Olha Hodovanets, August 27, 2015.
[14] UINP interview with Iryna Kyselova, March 7, 2017.
[15] UINP interview with Iryna Bekeshkina, March 3, 2014.
[16] Following anti-government protests against electoral malpractices during the 2011 parliamentary elections and Putin's reelection for a third term in office in March 2012, the Russian government arrested main opposition politicians and introduced new restrictions on the freedom of assembly, which entailed a decline in protest activism. See, for example, Ellen Barry. 2013. "As Putin's Grip Gets Tighter, a Time of Protest Fades in Russia." *The New York Times*, January 5. www.nytimes.com/2013/01/06/world/europe/in-russia-a-trendy-activism-against-putin-loses-its-moment.html.
[17] Kyiv International Institute of Sociology. 2012. "Dovira ukraintsiv do sotsialnykh instytutsii." [Press Release], April 18. https://kiis.com.ua/?lang=ukr&cat=reports&id=81. The survey was conducted on February 10–19, 2012. N = 2,029.

police and the judiciary did not uphold the rule of law and served whoever paid a higher price.[18] Furthermore, the results of Round 6 of the European Social Survey (2012–2013) indicate that Ukrainians were among the least satisfied with the functioning of democratic institutions in their home country in the summer of 2013.[19] Broadly speaking, participants in the Revolution of Dignity were discontent with the government's unfulfilled promises and the incumbent's deceitful claims. Nelia Vterkovska, for example, felt that the incumbent president displayed utmost disrespect for citizens and betrayed people's hopes for the European future.

I was not so bothered by the potholes in the roads – although when you drive a car, it feels unpleasant – I was bothered by the lack of respect for the person ... From the very first day, when Yanukovych expressed his refusal to sign an Association Agreement with the European Union, I wrote an unobtrusive post on Facebook. Like, well, it's such a humiliation, such a spat in the face – they promise, and then ... They just lied, deceived us.[20]

In particular, movement participants were dissatisfied with the high incidence of corruption and the low quality of living standards in the country. The quality of life in Ukraine was seen in a negative light, especially in comparison with the neighboring European countries. In 2012, for example, the gross domestic product per capita (ppp) was approximately 2.5 times lower in Ukraine ($9,705) than in Hungary ($24,556) or Poland ($23,589).[21] Additionally, small- and medium-size businesses in Ukraine encountered a litany of problems in their dealings with government agencies. Based upon a battery of indicators measuring the strength of legal institutions relevant to business regulation and the complexity and cost of regulatory processes, the 2013 Ease of Doing Index compiled by the World Bank ranked Ukraine 137th of 185 economies, placing it between Lesotho and the Philippines. For comparison, the Republic of Georgia that underwent a series of structural reforms in the wake of the 2003 Rose Revolution was ranked ninth that year in terms of the ease of doing business.[22] In light of these economic

---

[18] Valerii Vorona and Mykola Shulha, eds. 2013. *Ukrainske suspilstvo 1992–2013: Stan ta dynamika zmin. Sotsiolohichny monitorinh*. Kyiv: Institute of Sociology, National Academy of Science of Ukraine, pp. 453–54. https://i-soc.com.ua/assets/files/monitoring/soc-mon-2013.pdf.

[19] Round 6 of ESS was conducted in twenty-nine countries. The survey was administered in Ukraine between August 11, 2013, and September 9, 2013. For an overview, see Monica Ferrin and Hanspeter Kriesi. 2014. *European's Understandings and Evaluations of Democracy: Topline Results from Round 6 of the European Social Survey*. London: City University London, p. 14.

[20] UINP interview with Nelia Vterkovska, September 21, 2015.

[21] Gross domestic product (GDP) per capita (ppp) provides per capita values for GDP expressed in current international dollars converted by purchasing power parity (PPP) conversion factor. Data are retrieved from the World Development Indicators database constructed by the World Bank, https://databank.worldbank.org/source/world-development-indicators#

[22] The World Bank. 2012. *Doing Business 2013: Smarter Regulations for Small and Medium-Size Enterprises*. Washington, DC: The World Bank. https://archive.doingbusiness.org/en/reports/global-reports/doing-business-2013.

trends, Yaryna Kvitka and her spouse who travelled by bicycle around the world with a cultural project named Two-Wheeled Chronicles felt discontent with a high incidence of corruption and poverty in their home country.

> Everything was building up for the past two years ...We saw how people there [overseas] live and we did not understand why it was like this. Why do we have such good-natured, smart, and hard-working people, but we live so poorly? There is so much corruption, politicians do not respect ordinary citizens ... When Maidan started, I found out about it on November 22, and we went there right away. There was some hope, hope that something better might come out of it and that you can make a difference.[23]

The deployment of police violence against protesters in November 2013 might have been the last straw that broke people's patience. Being a student and an activist of the Youth Nationalist Congress, Rada Kishka joined Euromaidan in the fall.[24] "Those who planned to build their future in a European country turned out during Euromaidan," Kishka said. "People mostly chanted such slogans as European integration (*Evrointehratsiia*) and the European Union."[25] Protest chants, however, changed in December.

> The phrases "European integration" and the "European Union" were put aside. People began to speak about dictatorship, state terror, power, nepotism, bribery. All the issues that state authorities covered up with the help of other fake problems.[26]

These findings illustrate how mass support for European integration was related to widespread dissatisfaction with the quality of governance. For many participants in the revolution, it was clear that EU membership was a viable mechanism for an improvement in the quality of life. Additionally, European integration was viewed as a shield against Russian imperialism.

Civic Duty

Patriotism was another key motivation for women's engagement in the revolution. For many participants in the Revolution of Dignity, it was the second Maidan. Kateryna Chepura, for example, joined the youth movement Pora and participated in the 2004 Orange Revolution. In 2013, Chepura again came to Independence Square. "We did it out of civic duty," Chepura explained. "It is very difficult to do nothing when something is happening [to your country] and you understand that you can help."[27] Attachment to the political community was closely intertwined with solidarity with compatriots. For example, Tetiana Udovytska, a nurse from Kyiv, described her feelings as follows:

---

[23] UINP interview with Yaryna Kvitka.
[24] The Youth Nationalist Congress was formed in February 2001 upon the initiative of the Organization of Ukrainian Nationalists-R. For an overview of its activities, visit the webpage https://mnk.org.ua/nasha-istoriya.
[25] UINP interview with Rada Kishka.   [26] Ibid.
[27] UINP interview with Kateryna Chepura, June 12, 2014.

I went to Maidan following people, for the sake of people. I was yearning to be in a place where people were making history not for their own sake, but for the sake of a better future ... I could not let them down, I should be with them. The thing is that my faith in people remained, but my faith in government was gone.[28]

Professional Service

Professional experience, along with educational training, was another driving force behind women's engagement in the revolution. Medical personnel, human rights defenders, and journalists felt that they could not stand on the sidelines when the protest movement was in high need of their professional skills. For example, Nataliia Sholoiko, professor of pharmacology at the Bohomolets National Medical University, put her medical knowledge to use by getting involved in the movement's medical services. Many of her colleagues and, in particular, surgeons volunteered to provide medical care for protesters when the police started using live ammunition against regime opponents.

I came to Maidan not entirely by chance, I saw that a lot of medicine had been brought there and dumped in a pile. Therefore, there was a need for professionals who could organize all this and help doctors. That's why I came to do my job.[29]

Likewise, lawyers' participation in the revolution was driven by the need to defend the interests of detained protesters in court. When the first wave of arrests began, lawyers started coming to the Shevchenko district court in Kyiv to provide pro bono legal services for the detained. The lawyer Olena Nozhovnik, for example, volunteered to defend the interests of several AutoMaidan activists in court.[30] In many cases, the traffic police claimed that AutoMaidan activists failed to obey the police order to stop, and protesters were threatened with the revocation of their driving licenses for several months.

The salience of professional service as a motivating factor arises, in part, from the fact that many participants in the Revolution of Dignity represented the middle class. College-educated women sought to maximize their contributions to civil resistance by drawing on their toolkit of professional skills.

Parenthood

Motherhood is frequently seen as a catalyst for women's activism. Consistent with this perspective, concerns over their children's well-being and prospects for youth's self-realization in the home country influenced women's decision to get involved in the Revolution of Dignity. Working as a pediatrician, Kateryna

---

[28] NaUKMA interview with Tetiana Udovytska. Qtd. *from Maidan. Svidchennia. Kyiv, 2013–2014 roky*, p. 658.
[29] UINP interview with Nataliia Sholoiko, December 4, 2014.
[30] UINP interview with Olena Nozhovnik, September 22, 2015.

Korniiko regularly met with parents of little children and aspired to live in "a stable, economically viable country, with certain cultural values. It is the universe in which we would like our children, grandchildren, and great-grandchildren to be born. That's what we would like to bequeath to our next generations."[31] Likewise, Svitlana Umeliukh, a mother of two children, pointed out that she wanted her children to live in a free country.[32]

Some women construed citizens' willingness to risk their lives and make sacrifices for the sake of their children as an innate trait of Ukrainians. As a mother of two sons, Nataliia Koltsova felt that the incumbent government miscalculated the society's response to police violence against youthful protesters.

I do not know who was in charge and how they made such decisions [about the use of force], but one should have known the mentality of Ukrainians. A Ukrainian would do anything for the sake of their child. Had they [the police] not beaten up our children, then I am not sure whether everyone would have risen up. Our children were beaten up, and children are the most precious treasure that Ukrainians have.[33]

It should be noted that parenthood also influenced men's decision to join civil resistance. In describing their motives for activism, some male protesters emphasized the importance of building a more democratic and prosperous country for the sake of their children. For example, Serhii Halchyk, a member of the Afghan *sotnia*, stated, "We and our children are going to live in this country. Nobody except ourselves will change it."[34] Another man who lost an eye after being hit by the police reassured his girlfriend that it was not in vain. "It is for the freedom of our future children," he said after his visit to the ophthalmologist.[35]

A short dialog between two men, a protester and a government official, illustrates how parenthood might have divergent effects on protest behavior. Andrii Humeniuk, an artist from Lviv, participated in the lying-down protest near the entrance to the Prosecutor's Office.[36] Movement participants pressured state employees into signing a petition to release detained protesters. When a government official tried to get through the crowd and enter the building, Humeniuk urged him to sign the petition first. "I cannot do it. I have two children," the government official meekly said. "So what? I also have two

---

[31] UINP interview with Kateryna Korniiko, September 24, 2015.
[32] NaUKMA interview with Svitlana Umeliukh. Qtd. *from Maidan. Svidchennia. Kyiv, 2013–2014 roky*, p. 304.
[33] UINP interview with Nataliia Koltsova, August 11, 2015.
[34] NaUKMA interview with Serhii Halchyk. Qtd. from *Maidan. Svidchennia. Kyiv, 2013–2014 roky*, p. 565.
[35] This vignette is retrieved from the NaUKMA interview with Oleksii Soloviov. Qtd. from *Maidan. Svidchennia. Kyiv, 2013–2014 roky*, p. 642.
[36] This vignette is retrieved from the NaUKMA interview with Andrii Humeniuk. Qtd. from *Maidan. Svidchennia. Kyiv, 2013–2014 roky*, p. 226.

children. I am lying down here, and you are afraid to sign it." After some hesitation, the man did sign the petition, overcoming his fear of state reprisal. In many cases, women and men alike were willing to take risks to secure a better future for their families.

Feminism

Feminism is rarely cited as a primary motivation for women's engagement in the Revolution of Dignity. Nonetheless, feminists represented a significant fraction of the protest movement. To make women's presence more visible and advance their demands for gender equality, the Ukrainian anthropologist and film director Nadia Parfan set up the Facebook group Half of Maidan – Women's Voice of Protest (*Polovyna Maidanu – Zhinochyi holos protestu*).[37] "Women came forward in support of the European future, and they considered the European future as equality," Parfan stated.[38] To broaden the scope of women's participation in the revolution, a group of activists, including Anna Dovhopol and Nina Potarska, established a self-defense unit named after Olha Kobylianska, a well-known Ukrainian writer and a leading figure in the nineteenth-century women's movement in Bukovyna. Many women felt outraged by the chasm between women's diverse roles within the protest movement and the dominant portrayal of women as caretakers. "[Women's participation in] Maidan does not boil down to making sandwiches," summed up Potarska.[39] Specifically, the emergence of the women's unit was triggered by women's exclusion from the barricades during an escalation in police violence. "Our sotnia came about because women were not allowed to enter the scene of clashes at Hrushevskoho Street because they were women," said Ruslana Panukhnyk, director of the NGO KyivPride.[40]

Women activists also tried to articulate feminist ideas on Maidan through the organization of street actions and the display of protest signs in favor of gender equality. In response to women's exclusion from the barricades, feminists organized the Night of Women's Solidarity on December 12. Women insisted on their right to decide whether they should take a risk and remain on Maidan during a police assault. "To take care does not mean to impose constraints on someone. To take care means to help me and respect my choice,"

---

[37] On the mission of the Facebook group, see www.facebook.com/groups/255422234633303/about.
[38] Vikna. 2014. "Tamara Zlobina: 'Cholovik – dyvytsia, zhinka – sebe pokazue'." April 14. https://vikna.if.ua/news/category/articles/2014/04/14/17470/view.
[39] NaUKMA interview with Nina Potarska. Qtd. from *Maidan. Svidchennia. Kyiv, 2013–2014 roky*, p. 478.
[40] Nataliya Trach. 2014. "EuroMaidan Women Warriors Eager to Fight Injustice, Sex Discrimination." *Kyiv Post*, February 13. https://archive.kyivpost.com/ukraine-politics/euromaidan-women-warriors-eager-to-fight-injustice-sex-discrimination-336806.html.

stated Mariia Berlinska.[41] Standing on Maidan's stage, Berlinska urged all the revolutionaries to uphold the principle of gender equality in their daily interactions with each other. "Whenever possible, in response to the greeting 'Glory to Ukraine!' let's try to reply not only with 'Glory to Heroes!' but also with 'Glory to Heroines!'"[42]

Yet, public calls for gender equality and social justice were met with violence on the part of some right-wing groups. On November 27, 2013, feminists and left-wing activists gathered on Kyiv's Independence Square with protest signs such as "Freedom, Equality, Sisterhood" and "Europe Is Equality." However, members of some far-right groups assaulted left-wing activists and took away their protest signs.[43] The next day, participants in a protest rally under such slogans as "European Wages for Ukrainian Women" and "Europe is a Paid Maternity Leave" came under another attack from a right-wing group. These violent attacks suggest that movement participants differed in their understanding of European integration and the implications of EU membership for gender equality in Ukraine.

NETWORKS OF CONTENTION

Social scientists have long investigated the significance of various mobilizing structures in fostering contentious collective action.[44] Historically, political parties, labor unions, and religious institutions were influential in bringing people together. In recent years, social media emerged as a powerful platform for building a cross-cutting coalition of regime opponents and confronting the ruling elite. A major advantage of using social media is the creation of "a networked space for the exchange of information that is not geographically bounded" and the breakdown of hierarchies inherent in traditional media environments.[45] Furthermore, some social movements adopt a hierarchical organizational structure, while others seek to build a horizontal organizational

---

[41] UINP interview with Mariia Berlinska, July 20, 2015.
[42] Ibid. The slogan "Glory to Ukraine" has been used by Ukrainians for several centuries, signifying their attachment to the political community. This secular salutation might have emerged as an alternative to the religious salutation Glory to Jesus Christ. The salutation Glory to Ukraine was used by Ukrainian students in Kharkiv in the late nineteenth century. The slogan was also adopted by Ukrainians during the 1917 Revolutions in the Russian Empire. On this point, see Yuriy Yuzych. 2018. "'Glory to Ukraine!': Who and When Created the Slogan?" *Istorychna Pravda*, October 4. www.istpravda.com.ua/eng/articles/2018/10/4/153036/.
[43] Yustyna Kravchuk. 2013. "On Those Who 'Sow Discord' on Maidan." *Krytyka* [blog entry], December. https://krytyka.com/ua/articles/pro-tykh-khto-siie-rozbrat-na-maydani.
[44] On the conceptualization of mobilizing structures, see Doug McAdam, John D. McCarthy, and Mayer N. Zald, eds. 1996. *Comparative Perspectives on Social Movements: Political Opportunities, Mobilizing Structures, and Cultural Framings*. New York: Cambridge University Press.
[45] Megan MacDuffee Metzger and Joshua A. Tucker. 2017. "Social Media and EuroMaidan: A Review Essay." *Slavic Review* 76 (1): 169–91, 171.

structure. A closer look at the networks of contention during Euromaidan speaks to this growing body of literature by illustrating how citizens from different backgrounds join a revolution and form a united front against the incumbent government.

Data from oral history projects demonstrate the diversity of mobilizing structures conducive to women's engagement in the Revolution of Dignity. The analysis shows how such institutions as social media, friendship networks, family, civic organizations, professional associations, religious institutions, and universities influenced women's decision to join the protest movement and shaped modes of their participation in the revolution. In contrast, opposition political parties reportedly had a weak impact on mass mobilization in Ukraine.

Social Media

Over the past several decades, Internet use has experienced exponential growth in Ukraine. The percentage of regular Internet users increased from 12 percent in 2004 to 56 percent in 2013.[46] In particular, 77 percent of eighteen–twenty nine-year-old Ukrainians and 70 percent of thirty–thirty nine-year-olds reported using the Internet in September 2013.[47] A related trend is the increasing use of social media. Facebook became the main platform for the cultivation of professional ties and the discussion of politics within the middle class in the 2010s. According to some estimates, the number of Facebook users in Ukraine increased forty-eight times within four years, rising from 63,000 users in 2009 to over three million users in 2013.[48] As mentioned in Chapter 1, the first protest rally on Independence Square began with a Facebook post by Mustafa Nayyem on November 21. Nayyem urged people to gather on the city's main square, rather than merely "like" his post.[49] Hundreds of people, including civic activists and journalists, acted upon his call for action.

An abundance of empirical evidence indicates that Facebook served as an important hub for the dissemination of information and the distribution of resources, sustaining the viability of the protest movement. The civic initiative Hospital Guard (*Varta v likarni*), for example, created a Facebook account to recruit volunteers and take care of the injured protesters at local hospitals.[50]

---

[46] The Ukrainian marketing research company Falcum Group defined regular Internet users as those who used the Internet at least once a month. For details, see online reports of the Ukrainian Internet Association, https://inau.ua/proekty/doslidzhennya-internet-audytoriyi.

[47] Kyiv International Institute of Sociology. 2013. "Dynamika vykorystannia Internet v Ukraini." October 28. www.kiis.com.ua/?lang=ukr&cat=reports&id=199&page=2&y=2013.

[48] Olha Minchenko. 2013. "Vzhe 3 miliony ukraintsiv korystuuitsia Facebook." *Watcher*, October 25. http://watcher.com.ua/2013/10/25/vzhe-3-milyony-ukrayintsiv-korystuyutsya-facebook/.

[49] Nayyem,. 2014. "Uprising in Ukraine: How It All Began."

[50] Anton Polishchuk. 2014. "Nichna varta v likarni: protestuvalnyka bez nasylstva zabraly u militsii (Reportazh uchasnyka)." *Texty*, January 25. https://texty.org.ua/fragments/51257/Nichna_varta_v_likarni_protestuvalnyka_bez_nasylstva-51257.

Networks of Contention

Another civic initiative named AutoMaidan set up a Facebook account to spread the news and raise funds to buy petrol and video equipment for car drivers.[51]

The mobilizing effect of social media might have been the strongest among those protesters whose family and friends did not support the ideals of Euromaidan. Raised in Odesa oblast, thirty-four-year-old Larysa Yushkevych encountered indifference or antipathy toward the protest movement in her social circle. However, given her opposition to the incumbent government and prior medical training, she responded to a Facebook post, recruiting volunteers for the movement's medical services.

> I read on Facebook that there was a need for medics and anyone who was not afraid of blood and could do night shifts and patrol Maidan. I called [them]. It was inside St. Michael's Cathedral. I came, and they gave me a vest and a first aid kit and sent me forward.[52]

Social media was also used as a method for the recruitment of revolutionaries outside a person's social circle. The psychologist Halyna Tsyhanenko, for example, observed a great deal of anxiety about personal safety among movement participants. It dawned on her that men with prior combat experience might be well positioned to guard the encampment, and she called a veteran of the Soviet–Afghan war (1979–1989).[53]

> He said, "We have a forum on the net, find its address and post there whatever you want. Maybe, someone will reply." And I wrote this post, saying that you could take it with a grain of salt, but I was doing what I believed was necessary. I was not the only one who had this idea. Because there appeared shifts [staffed with war veterans], sooner or later.[54]

The data from oral history projects provide insights into the mobilizing potential of social media. Facebook facilitated the cultivation of contacts among people with diverse backgrounds.

Family and Friendship Networks

Oftentimes, the whole household got involved in the revolution. Evheniia Yanchenko, for example, had some medical knowledge so she became the head

---

[51] Liubov Velychko. 2013. "Kavaleriia revoluitsii. Odyn den z zhyttia Avtomaidanu (reportazh)." *Texty*, January 15. https://texty.org.ua/articles/51046/Kavalerija_revoluciji_Odyn_den_z_zhytta_Avtomajdanu-51046.

[52] UINP interview with Larysa Yushkevych, October 28, 2014.

[53] Tens of thousands of Ukrainian soldiers fought in the Soviet–Afghan war. The Ukrainian Union of Veterans of the Soviet–Afghan war (*Ukrainska spilka veteraniv Afhanistanu*) was a civic organization that advocated the veterans' rights in Ukraine. For the union's activities, visit the webpage www.usva.org.ua.

[54] UINP interview with Halyna Tsyhanenko, October 30, 2015.

of the medical services in a self-defense unit. Meanwhile, given his military training, Evheniia's spouse, Andrii, assumed a leadership position in the self-defense unit Lvivska Brama. "We were on Maidan from the very beginning," twenty-nine-year-old Yanchenko said. "We do not have children."[55]

Participation in the Revolution of Dignity was a multigenerational phenomenon. Olha Zhyzhko's father, for example, joined a self-defense unit, her mother welcomed out-of-town protesters into their home, and her grandmother attended protest rallies and treated Euromaidan activists to homemade pancakes.[56] Some young people took the lead in attending protests and drew their parents into civil resistance. Svitlana Abaeva, for example, began volunteering at a medical station upon learning of her twenty-seven year old son's service in a self-defense unit.[57] In many cases, participants in the 2004 postelection protests became involved in the Revolution of Dignity and brought their families to Kyiv's Independence Square. In 2004, Olha Streltsova participated in the Orange Revolution, while her little daughter stayed at home. In 2013, Olha's daughter was the first to join Euromaidan, and Olha emulated her child's example.

In 2004, our entire company [group of friends] was on Maidan, and our children (my child was very young at the time), everyone stayed at my house, in one place, so that they would not be scared to spend a night alone. And when we got home, the children were still awake, watching *Channel 5* and shouting *Yushchenko!*, all adorned with ribbons ... Now my daughter was the first to run to Maidan, and my husband and I followed her. Seriozha joined Samooborona, I went to the medical headquarters, and we started to take shifts there [inside the encampment] during off-hours at work.[58]

Opinion polls indicate that Ukrainians place a high level of trust in friends.[59] Against this backdrop, it is not surprising that many participants in the revolution came to the protest site with a group of friends. Many interviewees mentioned that they found out about a protest rally via Facebook and came to Independence Square with a friend. Yuliia Tychkivska, for example, saw Nayyem's post on Facebook and called her friend who lived nearby to drive together to the protest site.[60] Being a professor at the Kyiv School of Economics

---

[55] NaUKMA interview with Evheniia Yanchenko. Qtd. from *Maidan. Svidchennia. Kyiv, 2013–2014 roky*, p. 261.
[56] NaUKMA interview with Olha Zhyzhko. Qtd. from *Maidan. Svidchennia. Kyiv, 2013–2014 roky*, p. 285.
[57] NaUKMA interview with Svitlana Abaeva. Qtd. from *Maidan. Svidchennia. Kyiv, 2013–2014 roky*, p. 635.
[58] NaUKMA interview with Olha Streltsova. Qtd. from *Maidan. Svidchennia. Kyiv, 2013–2014 roky*, p. 41.
[59] On this point, see Volodymyr Paniotto and Natalia Kharchenko. 2012. "Dovira sotsialnym instytutam." *KMIS Review* 4: 3–8. www.kiis.com.ua/materials/KMIS-Review/04(06-2012)/ds.php?file=04_KR_2_Analit1.pdf.
[60] UINP interview with Yuliia Tychkivska, April 28, 2015.

and a NaUKMA alumna, Tychkivska frequently visited the encampment with her colleagues and friends.

Universities

Universities have long been known as "hotbeds of activism" in Ukrainian society. Since the Soviet demise, institutions of higher education gradually revised their curriculum and deepened students' knowledge of the liberation struggle. For example, Yelyzaveta Hrynenko believed that her undergraduate education instilled in her "a greater sense of patriotism."[61] As a student at the Vinnytsia Mykhailo Kotsiubynskyi State Pedagogical University, she learned in her history courses about the oppression of Ukrainians under foreign rule and the Cossacks, freedom-loving people who fled serfdom and mostly professed the Orthodox faith. Similarly, the artist Nataliia Kadyn-Feseniuk deepened her appreciation of Ukrainian decorative painting through her coursework at the Kyiv Polytechnic University (KPI).[62] Educated in the post-Soviet period, the young generation could gain more systematic knowledge about the Ukrainian struggle for national independence and cultural heritage than older generations socialized in the Soviet Union.

Founded in the seventeenth century and modeled on Jesuit colleges in terms of its curriculum and teaching methods,[63] the Kyiv-Mohyla Academy was closed down by the Bolsheviks and reemerged as a leading institution of higher education in postcommunist Ukraine.[64] In line with its mission to contribute to the development of an open society in Ukraine, the university emphasized such values as active citizenship, democracy, humanism, and national consciousness.[65] NaUKMA adopted English and Ukrainian as languages of instruction, which facilitated the cultivation of international partnerships with Western universities. Moreover, several student organizations at NaUKMA were known for their efforts to promote Ukrainian culture and encourage the use of the Ukrainian language among the young generation.[66] The Student Brotherhood

---

[61] UINP interview with Yelyzaveta Hrynenko, March 5, 2014.
[62] UINP interview with Nataliia Kadyn-Feseniuk, June 27, 2014.
[63] On the history of the Kyiv-Mohyla Academy, see Alexander Sydorenko. 1977. *The Kievan Academy in the Seventeenth Century*. Ottawa: University of Ottawa Press.
[64] For an overview of educational changes in contemporary Ukraine, see Serhiy Kvit. 2020. "Higher Education in Ukraine in the Time of Independence: Between Brownian Motion and Revolutionary Reform." *Kyiv-Mohyla Humanities Journal* 7: 141–59. https://doi.org/10.18523/kmhj219666.2020-7.141-159; Volodymyr Panchenko. 2015. Viacheslav Briukhovetsky: "The Idea of the Rebirth of the Kyiv-Mohyla Academy Came to Me a Year before the Breakup of the USSR..." *Kyiv-Mohyla Humanities Journal* 2: 1–10. https://doi.org/10.18523/kmhj51010.2015-2.1-10.
[65] For a full list of NaUKMA values and its mission statement, visit the webpage of the NaUKMA, www.ukma.edu.ua/eng/index.php/about-us/today.
[66] UINP interview with Olena Hrechaniuk, November 10, 2014.

of NaUKMA (*Spudeiske bratstvo NaUKMA*), for example, organized St. Andrew's party (*andriivski vechornytsi*) and theatrical plays with a nativity scene (*vertep*).[67] In keeping with the university's mission, NaUKMA students actively participated in the Orange Revolution and organized protests against the Yanukovych government in the early 2010s. The data from the oral history projects reveal that many NaUKMA students or alumni, including Mariia Berlinska, Liubov Halan, Olena Hrechaniuk, Tamara Martsenyuk, Anna Prokhorova, and Yuliia Tychkivska, participated in the Revolution of Dignity. Associate professor of sociology Tamara Martsenyuk underscored the university's importance in fostering civic activism. "In part, my decision to get involved was influenced by the university's engagement," Martsenyuk said. "I strongly self-identify with my university."[68]

The faculty and students from other Ukrainian universities also visited the encampment in groups. Some undergraduate students from the Taras Shevchenko National University, for example, came to Independence Square as a group.[69] In November 2013, Kyiv-based students organized a march to signal their intent to go on a strike, demanding the incumbent's signing of the Association Agreement with the EU. KPI students marched in a column, carrying the university flags. "We walked with Ukrainian flags, with our university flags," recalled Tetiana Motsak, an undergraduate student at KPI and a Vidsich (Rebuff) activist. "Our eyes were shining. It was a time of incredible effervescence."[70]

It should be noted, however, that the administration at some institutions of higher education tried to induce political conformity among students by threatening participants in protest events with expulsion from the university. Vitalii Moskalenko, rector of the Bohomolets National Medical University, obstructed students' participation in Euromaidan.[71] In response, Vidsich activists tried to block entry to some universities so that students had an opportunity to attend protests instead of classes. "That's how Pora [youth movement] did it during the Orange Revolution," pointed out Vidsich activist Yaryna Chornohuz. "A file of students gathered near an entry to the university building, formed a human chain, and told students that they would not attend classes today, they should go to Maidan."[72] Furthermore, Vidsich called for the establishment of a

---

[67] St. Andrew's Day commemorates Andrew the Apostle. In addition, drawing on some pagan traditions, the day is marked by a party for single men and women, making a traditional bread, and fortune telling. On the Ukrainian traditions associated with St. Andrew's Day, see Maryna Chorna. 2020. "Andriivski vechornytsi: tradytsii sviatkuvannia." *Plast*, December 12. www.plast.org.ua/blog-ukrayinski-tradytsiyi-andriyivski-vechornytsi.
[68] UINP interview with Tamara Martsenyuk, November 11, 2014.
[69] UINP interview with Maryna Mirzaeva, June 23, 2015.
[70] UINP interview with Tetiana Motsak, March 24, 2015.
[71] Olha Skrypnyk and Oleksii Sova. 2014. "Rektor v ekzyli." *Dzerkalo tyzhnia*, March 21. https://zn.ua/ukr/EDUCATION/rektor-v-ekzili-_.html.
[72] UINP interview with Yaryna Chornohuz, August 10, 2014.

Student Squad (*Studentska sotnia*) to mobilize a significant fraction of the student population.[73]

Civic Organizations

Membership in civic organizations and involvement in various civic initiatives provided a foundation for mass mobilization against the regime. A mix of left-wing and right-wing groups participated in the Revolution of Dignity. Drawing on her ethnographic work, Emily Channell-Justice demonstrates how left-wing activists participated in the Revolution of Dignity and emphasized the importance of nonviolent action.[74] Specifically, the student union *Priama diia* (Direct Action) sought to build a leftist community among young Ukrainians. In addition, the data from the oral history projects used in this book reveal the role of such organizations as the Youth Nationalist Congress (*Molodizhnyi natsionalistychnyi kongres*) and the National Alliance (*Natsionalnyi alians*) in mobilizing youth in favor of the political change. Reflecting on the timing of the 2013 protests (coinciding with the eightieth anniversary of the man-made famine *Holodomor*), a twenty-five-year-old activist of the National Alliance Maiia Moskvych said, "Back then, they took away our freedom and our bread. Now we should not let them take away our freedom."[75]

The civic initiative *Vilni Liudy* (Free People) launched the public campaign *Evronastup* (Movement to Europe) in the fall of 2013 to collect signatures in support of Ukraine's integration into the European community. As noted by Rada Kishka, activists affiliated with the Youth Nationalist Congress planned to organize a street action on November 24, but events took a surprising turn with Nayyem's call for action on November 21.[76] As a result, scores of activists involved in the signature collection initiative joined the revolution and established the 14th self-defense unit "Free People."

An organizational infrastructure that emerged before, during, or after the 2004 Orange Revolution was activated to mobilize regime challengers.[77] Data from oral history projects reveal that many participants in the Revolution of Dignity were connected to organizations that were active during a previous episode of contention. For example, the Foundation of Regional Initiatives (FRI) founded on the eve of the Orange Revolution distributed guidelines on

---

[73] Den. 2013. "Aktyvisty zaklykauit studentiv zapysuvatys do Studentskoi sotni." December 11. https://day.kyiv.ua/news/271221-aktyvisty-zaklykayut-studentiv-zapysuvatys-do-studentskoyi-sotni.

[74] Emily Channell-Justice. 2022. *Without the State: Self-Organization and Political Activism in Ukraine*. Toronto: University of Toronto Press.

[75] UINP interview with Maiia Moskvych, February 23, 2015.

[76] UINP interview with Rada Kishka.

[77] On the role of an organizational infrastructure in autocracies, see Paul D. Almeida. 2003. "Opportunity Organizations and Threat-Induced Contention: Protest Waves in Authoritarian Settings." *American Journal of Sociology* 109 (2): 345–400.

safety measures at a protest event and set up a call center to provide assistance for participants in the Revolution of Dignity. As a member of the Kyiv-based branch of FRI, Olena Litvishko volunteered in the call center and monitored police actions in downtown Kyiv. Taking calls from victims of police violence, Litvishko felt that "it was necessary to do absolutely everything so that it [the political system] would change and such things would never happen again."[78]

Established by former participants in the Orange Revolution in 2010, the civic movement *Vidsich* sought to counteract the resurgence of authoritarianism in Ukraine in the aftermath of the 2010 presidential election. In January 2011, Vidsich, jointly with FRI and *Priama diia*, organized protests against a new law on education.[79] Furthermore, Vidsich activists played a prominent role in mass protests against the 2012 law on language policy proposed by the Party of Region deputies. Under a new law, Russian could be granted the status of a regional language in localities with at least 10 percent of the local population considering Russian as a mother tongue.[80] Such a language policy reinforced the domineering role of the Russian language in some parts of Ukraine and aided Russia's exercise of soft power aimed at undermining Ukraine's sovereignty. To denounce Russia's meddling in Ukrainian politics, Vidsich also organized a protest campaign calling for a boycott of Russian products.[81] Given its active role in civil society, Vidsich built a network of activists across the country. When the first protest rally began on November 21, Vidsich activists started calling everyone in their databases of volunteers to bring people into the street.[82]

Religious Institutions

A sizeable portion of the Ukrainian population regularly attends religious services, albeit there is considerable within-country variation in the level of religiosity. One-quarter of the total population reported in 2013 that they attended religious services at least once a month.[83] However, the percentage of regular

---

[78] NaUKMA interview with Olena Litvishko. Qtd. from *Maidan. Svidchennia. Kyiv, 2013–2014 roky*, p. 182.

[79] Olha Aivazovska. 2011. "Alma Pater." *The Ukrainian Week*, February 3. https://ukrainianweek.com/alma-pater.

[80] On language policies in Ukraine, see Dominique Arel. 2017. "Language, Status, and State Loyalty in Ukraine." *Harvard Ukrainian Studies* 35 (1/4): 233–63; Volodymyr Kulyk. 2013. "Language Policy in the Ukrainian Media: Authorities, Producers and Consumers." *Europe-Asia Studies* 65 (7): 1417–43.

[81] Ukrainskii Tyzhden. 2013. "U sotsmerezhakh ukraintsiv zaklykauit boikotuvaty rosiiski tovary." August 15. https://tyzhden.ua/u-sotsmerezhakh-ukraintsiv-zaklykaiut-bojkotuvaty-rosijski-tovary.

[82] UINP interview with Yaryna Chornohuz, August 10, 2014.

[83] Oleh Kozlovsky. 2013. "Dynamika rozvytku relihiinykh konfesii protiahom 10 rokiv (z 2003 po 2013 rr)." In *Ukrainske suspilstvo 1992–2013: Stan ta dynamika zmin. Sotsiolohichnyi monitorinh*, eds. Valerii Vorona and Mykola Shulha. Kyiv: Institute of Sociology, National Academy of Science of Ukraine, pp. 411–16, 414.

churchgoers was four times higher in the western part of Ukraine than in the eastern part (57.1 percent vs. 13.1 percent). In addition, there were gender differences in church attendance. In 2013, 34.6 percent of women and 13.8 percent of men attended places of worship at least once a month.[84] In light of these trends, religious institutions might have been more influential in mobilizing women in favor of social justice.

The Ukrainian Greek Catholic Church (UGCC) was especially vocal in conveying the importance of human dignity and supporting citizens' struggle for justice.[85] Opinion polls indicate that Greek Catholics represented 7.6 percent of the adult population in 2014, while 78.8 percent of Ukrainians self-identified with the Ukrainian Orthodox Church.[86] Yet, additional statistics reveal that Greek Catholics were quite active in professing their religious beliefs.[87] In 2014, UGCC had 3,763 registered parishes (*hromady*) and managed 1,291 Sunday schools.[88] For comparison, the Ukrainian Orthodox Church–Kyiv Patriarchate had 4,651 registered parishes and 1,461 Sunday schools that year. At the start of mass protests in November 2013, Major Archbishop Shevchuk expressed his solidarity with protesters and extolled the importance of commitment to nonviolence.[89] Following the killing of over a hundred movement participants in February 2014, Borys Gudziak, Bishop for Ukrainian Catholics in France, Belgium, the Netherlands, Luxemburg, and Switzerland, urged Ukrainians to reflect on the lives of the Heavenly Hundred and consider their martyrdom as "a source of understanding truth and a return to our dignity."[90]

The Prayer Tent (*Molytovnyi namet*) was a major meeting place for the faithful inside the Kyiv-based encampment. This interfaith initiative provided

---

[84] Kozlovsky. "Dynamika rozvytku relihiinykh konfesii protiahom 10 rokiv (z 2003 po 2013 rr)," p. 415.
[85] On the role of churches during Euromaidan, see Natalia Kochan. 2016. "Shaping Ukrainian Identity: The Churches in the Socio-Political Crisis." In *Churches in the Ukrainian Crisis*, eds. Andrii Krawchuk and Thomas Bremer. Cham: Palgrave Macmillan, pp. 105–21; Denys Shestopalets. 2020. "Churches, Politics, and Ideological Struggles in Ukraine: The Case of the Euromaidan Protests (2013–2014)." *Politics, Religion and Ideology* 21 (1): 46–67.
[86] Viktor Stepanenko. 2019. "Ukrainian Churches and Civil Society in the Euromaidan and the Russian-Ukrainian Conflict: A Sociological Analysis." In *Religion during the Russian-Ukrainian Conflict*, eds. Elizabeth Clark and Dmytro Vovk. London: Routledge, pp. 107–27, 116.
[87] Michał Wawrzonek. 2020. "Ukrainian Greek Catholic Church as an Agent of the Social Life in Ukraine." *Baltic Worlds* 13 (2–3): 113–24.
[88] Ministry of Culture of Ukraine. 2014. *Zvit pro merezhu tserkov i relihiinykh orhanizatsii v Ukraini stanom na 1 sichnia 2014 roku*. March 19. https://zakon.rada.gov.ua/rada/file/text/23/f421358n13.xls.
[89] Religious Information Service of Ukraine. 2013. "Head of UGCC in Solidarity with Participants of EuroMaidan and Warns Against Bloodshed." November 25. https://risu.ua/en/head-of-ugcc-in-solidarity-with-participants-of-euromaidan-and-warns-against-bloodshed_n65915.
[90] Religious Information Service of Ukraine. 2014. "UGCC Bishop Borys Gudziak on EuroMaidan's Heroes." February 21. https://risu.ua/en/ugcc-bishop-borys-gudziak-on-euromaidan-s-heroes_n67387.

an opportunity for believers to come together for a daily interfaith prayer or an informal conversation over a cup of tea.[91] Evangelicals organized a public discussion about the interpretation of the Biblical verses on the submission to state authorities. As a student at the Ukrainian Evangelical Theological Seminary, twenty-six-year-old Kateryna Zhytska joined this initiative through her church.

Once after the worship service in my church, our priest was going to Maidan to bring tea, coffee, sugar, and cookies, and he invited me to come along. That's how I got there. And it turned out that there was a prayer tent on Maidan in which I met a lot of my acquaintances. I was told that they had a shortage of volunteers because there were a lot of people, and it was necessary to fix tea, make sandwiches, and speak with people, pray with them. I stayed there because I became very interested in watching what was happening. I was simply awe-struck and surprised at the warm and family-like atmosphere there.[92]

In addition to Christian clergy, religious leaders from other faith traditions supported nonviolent resistance.[93] In December 2013, several influential figures in Ukrainian society, including Refat Chubarov, Chairman of the Mejlis of the Crimean Tatar People, and Josef Zissels, Chairman of the Association of Jewish Organizations and Communities of Ukraine (Vaad Ukraine), signed an open statement to the international democratic community, urging pro-democracy forces to condemn violence against peaceful demonstrators in Kyiv and "support the aspirations of the Ukrainian people toward freedom and democracy."[94] As a former member of the Ukrainian Helsinki Group and a political prisoner in the Soviet Union, Zissels urged Jewish communities to decide whether they stood "with the authoritarian power or with the democratic part of their society that aspires to join European space."[95]

---

[91] Tetiana Mukhomorova. 2013. "Vid uchora na Maidani die Molytovnyi mizhkonfesiinyi namet." *Religious Information Service of Ukraine*, December 6. https://risu.ua/vid-uchora-na-maydani-diye-molitovniy-mizhkonfesiyniy-namet_n66119.

[92] UINP interview with Kateryna Zhytska, October 12, 2014.

[93] See, for example, Mikics David. 2014. "The Head of the Jewish Community of Ukraine Speaks Out Against Putin." *The Tablet Magazine*, April 29. www.tabletmag.com/sections/news/articles/josef-zissels-yivo; Radio Free Europe/Radio Liberty. 2013. "Ukraine's Crimean Tatars Support Pro-EU Protesters." December 10. www.rferl.org/a/ukraine-crimean-tatars-euromaidan/25195844.html; Religious Information Service of Ukraine. 2014. "UAOC Bishop Thanks Jews and Crimean Tatars for Supporting EuroMaidan." February 2. https://risu.ua/en/uaoc-bishop-thanks-jews-and-crimean-tatars-for-supporting-euromaidan_n67015; Michael Yakubovich. 2014. "Ukrainian Muslims and Maidan." *Religious Information Service of Ukraine*, March 3. https://risu.ua/en/ukrainian-muslims-and-maidan_n67584.

[94] The full text of the Open Statement to the International Democratic Community of December 12, 2013, is available on the webpage of the Kharkiv Human Rights Protection Group. https://khpg.org/en/1386872906.

[95] Joseph Zissels. 2013. "Joseph Zissels Gave an Interview to JNS.org." *NaUKMA News*, December 17. www.ukma.edu.ua/eng/index.php/news/483-joseph-zissels-gave-an-interview-to-jns-org.

Region of Residence

Self-identification with a subnational political community was another motive for citizens' self-organization, given low levels of membership in a political party or a civic organization. Several self-defense units were formed by groups of individuals from a specific locality within Ukraine. As a native of Vinnytsia, a city located 124 miles southwest of Kyiv, Yelyzaveta Hrynenko joined the Vinnytsia Squad, also known as *Haidamatska Varta*[96]:

> Everybody has her own little Motherland that we would like to protect and above all protect our children from all of this, and then our brothers and our blood brothers, and those who are here ... It is our land, and we need to defend it. Our ancestors had been fighting for it, and we should safeguard it too.[97]

Some Kyiv residents who were born outside the capital city were drawn into the protest movement via their identification with compatriots from their place of birth (*zemliaky*). Anastasiia Maksymchuk, for example, was born in Chernivtsi oblast, but she moved to Kyiv to pursue an undergraduate degree and stayed in the capital city after graduation. When she ran into movement participants from her home region, it stirred a gamut of emotions in her. Maksymchuk started providing accommodation for out-of-town protesters.

> The office of a tourism company in which I worked happened to be located within a short distance from Maidan. Once I was walking to work through Independence Square and met people from Chernivtsi oblast, my compatriots (*zemliaky*). And it caught my attention. If even they came here, then I should do something. And that's how it all started for me.[98]

The data from oral history projects indicate that attachment to a subnational political community facilitated mass mobilization against the national government.

Political Parties

Trust in political parties is dismally low in contemporary Ukraine. Opinion polls show that only 6.6 percent of Ukrainians in 2013, compared to 8.5 percent in 2004, placed some trust in political parties.[99] Opposition politicians across the political spectrum failed to demonstrate their resolve to implement democratic reforms, uproot corruption, and mobilize the population against the entrenchment of authoritarianism. In part, citizens' distrust of political

---

[96] *Haidamaky* were paramilitary units that led several uprisings against the Polish nobility in the eighteenth century and demanded the abolition of serfdom and the free exercise of the Orthodox faith.
[97] UINP interview with Yelyzaveta Hrynenko, March 5, 2014.
[98] UNIP interview with Anastasiia Maksymchuk, November 12, 2014.
[99] Vorona and Shulha. *Ukrainske suspilstvo 1992–2013*, p. 483.

parties derived from widespread disenchantment with the inept performance of the political opposition during and after the Orange Revolution. Back in 2004, many people pinned their hopes on Yushchenko, but he did not live up to people's expectations in the wake of his electoral victory.[100] Public trust in President Yushchenko declined from 49.2 percent in 2005 to 23.2 percent in 2008.[101] Reflecting a wide chasm between voters and political parties, Mila Ivantsova described her attitude toward Ukrainian politicians of different stripes as follows:

> I did not believe them, those faces on the billboards irritated me. I realized even before the revolution that our people were on our own, and the ruling elite was left to its own devices. And people can self-organize. I had full confidence in our nation.[102]

Furthermore, leaders of three opposition political parties tried to persuade protesters to leave the encampment in the capital city. On February 21, 2014, Vitali Klitschko (UDAR), Oleh Tiahnybok (Svoboda), and Arsenii Yatseniuk (Batkivshchyna) cut a deal with the incumbent president and declared that protesters should go home in exchange for Yanukovych's alleged promise to hold presidential elections no later than December 2014.[103] The opposition politicians were booed by the crowd. In defiance of a deal negotiated by the political elite, a leader of a self-defense unit took to the mic and shamed politicians for shaking their hands with the authoritarian ruler responsible for the deaths of dozens of Ukrainians. Speaking on behalf of rank-and-file protesters, Parasiuk issued an ultimatum to the incumbent president. "We, ordinary citizens, tell politicians who stand behind my back, 'No way that Yanukovych is going to be the president for the whole year! Tomorrow by 10:00 a.m. he must go'."[104] Parasiuk warned the tyrant that people would storm his mansion in case of his refusal to step down the next day. In turn, Yanukovych took a helicopter to eastern Ukraine and subsequently settled down in the Russian Federation.

THE IMPACT OF BIOGRAPHICAL AVAILABILITY

A prominent argument in social movement literature is that biographical availability affects the likelihood of protest participation.[105] Specifically, parenthood might impose constraints on women's engagement in social movement

---

[100] On this point, see, for example, UINP interview with Iryna Panchenko, September 15, 2015.
[101] Vorona and Shulha. *Ukrainske suspilstvo 1992–2013*, p. 481.
[102] UINP interview with Mila Ivantsova, October 21, 2014.
[103] BBC. 2014. "Ukrainian President and Opposition Sign Early Poll Deal." February 21. www.bbc.com/news/world-europe-26289318.
[104] James Rupert. 2014. "Beyond the Crisis, Hope for Ukraine." *New Atlanticist* [blog], March 14. www.atlanticcouncil.org/blogs/new-atlanticist/beyond-the-crisis-hope-for-ukraine.
[105] Beyerlein and Bergstrand, "Biographical Availability." .

The Impact of Biographical Availability

activity.[106] Given women's responsibility as primary care givers in many Ukrainian households, women with little children are most likely to grapple with the challenge of combining motherhood with civic activism. Data from oral history projects reveal different ways in which women tackled this issue.[107]

In line with the biographical availability argument, some mothers of little children could not be physically present on Kyiv's Independence Square due to their childcare responsibilities. Vterkovska, for example, recalled how she had to stay at home to take care of her little daughter, while her spouse regularly visited the protest site.

Mainly, students were there [on the square] during the day. And I did not have such a possibility because I was staying at home with the sick child, my younger daughter got sick. But my spouse regularly went there. According to my estimates, there were 1,000 supporters per student standing there.[108]

A few middle-aged participants in the Revolution of Dignity mentioned that they were able to participate in the 2013–2014 protests more actively than in the 2004 postelection protests due to less intense childcare responsibilities. Thirty-three-year-old Iryna Kyselova, for example, noted that she was able to devote more time to volunteering during Euromaidan because her daughters were adolescents by that time.[109]

Many women with preschool children tried to carve out some free time for themselves by turning to their parents or friends as a source of tuition-free childcare. The likelihood of women's physical presence on Maidan increased if grandparents temporarily assumed responsibility for childcare. The Lviv native Khrystia Hrunyk, for example, left her six-year-old son in the care of her parents and went to Kyiv to participate in the revolution.[110] Twenty-nine-year-old Hrunyk took up a leadership position in a self-defense unit, patrolling the barricades. The Kyiv-based doctor Oksana Syvak sent her children abroad so that they could be in a safe environment, and she could devote more time to volunteering. "We moved our children away so we were free: we went to work during the day and volunteered at night," Syvak said. "Everyone at work knew

---

[106] Kay Lehman Schlozman, Nancy Burns, Sidney Verba, and Jesse Donahue. 1995. "Gender and Citizen Participation: Is There a Different Voice?" *American Journal of Political Science* 39 (2): 267–93.

[107] The interview guides did not include a question about the interviewee's family structure. However, several respondents mentioned parenthood as a constraint on their engagement in the protest movement.

[108] UINP interview with Nelia Vterkovska, September 21, 2015.

[109] UINP interview with Iryna Kyselova, March 17, 2017.

[110] Vasylyna Duman. 2014. "Na tretii barykadi. Yak tenditna divchyna kerue Nichnoiu vartoiu (spetsproekt Mekhanizm Maidanu)." *Texty*, January 13. https://texty.org.ua/articles/50989/Na_tretij_barykadi_Jak_tenditna_divchyna_keruje-50989.

what I was doing, and they showed me some understanding, I could leave a little bit early and come a little bit late."[111]

Another women's strategy was the scheduling of weekend visits to the encampment. Some out-of-town protesters arrived in Kyiv on Fridays and left on Sundays. A mother of little children, for example, traveled from Dnipro to Kyiv on weekends, bringing a wealth of medical supplies. "She managed to carry an unbelievable quantity of medical supplies and surgical instruments," stated the head of medical services in the first self-defense unit.[112]

Concurrently, many women tried to combine their childcare duties with involvement in the revolution by virtue of social media. As a self-described "Internet fighter," Ivanna Kobeleva noted that citizens could contribute to the common cause without standing on the barricades. "Not everyone could go and join a *sotnia* on Maidan, and spend nights there. Some people, for example, had little children. But they could do something useful via Facebook."[113]

Alternatively, some women brought their little children to protest rallies and street actions. The children's literature writer Olesia Mamchych, for example, took her children on some car rides to picket the mansions of high-profile government officials.

> I had two little children. And it really constrained me. I remember that the most active period of my going to Maidan [square] occurred during the Student Euromaidan. Then my parents got tired of constantly taking care of my kids, and my schedule changed. My spouse fully immersed himself in AutoMaidan. I did not see him either during the day or at night. Whenever possible, I joined the car caravans. When there were car rides that children could endure, when we did not drive too far.[114]

A close examination of qualitative data reveals gender differences in the impact of parenthood on participation in a contemporary revolution. Fathers of little children were able to get involved in street actions more frequently than mothers due to dominant social norms about parenting. Several women indicated that motherhood imposed constraints on the level of their involvement in civil resistance because they were expected to take care of little children. Moreover, women routinely delegated their childcare duties to other women, which decreased the overall level of women's physical presence inside the encampment.

CONCLUSION

In line with a hybrid model of women's participation in a revolution, this chapter shows a wide range of women's motivations for action, including

---

[111] NaUKMA interview with Oksana Syvak. Qtd. from *Maidan. Svidchennia. Kyiv, 2013–2014 roky*, p. 648.
[112] NaUKMA interview with Evheniia Yanchenko. Qtd. from *Maidan. Svidchennia. Kyiv, 2013–2014 roky*, p. 262.
[113] NaUKMA interview with Ivanna Kobeleva. Qtd. from *Maidan. Svidchennia. Kyiv, 2013–2014 roky*, p. 703.
[114] UINP interview with Olesia Mamchych, June 17, 2014.

Conclusion

public outrage over police violence, dissatisfaction with the quality of governance, motherhood, civic duty, professional service, and solidarity with protesters. Specifically, empirical evidence suggests that police violence can fuel citizens' dissatisfaction with the regime and bring together people from different backgrounds.

Despite women's assertion of agency under precarious conditions, most female interviewees did not mention feminism as a catalyst for their initial involvement in the Revolution of Dignity. There might be several reasons why the concept of feminism was not explicitly discussed in women's narratives about the revolution. Some women might have avoided the use of a concept infused with rather negative connotations in the postcommunist society.[115] Others might have subsumed their support for gender equality into a broader discussion about the importance of democracy and human dignity.

Furthermore, this chapter uncovers a wide range of social networks conducive to mass mobilization in a society with a rather underdeveloped party system and a low level of formal membership in civic organizations. Data from oral history projects indicate that many people learned about the first protest events via social media. Activists extensively used Facebook to implement crowdsourcing initiatives and coordinate diverse networks of volunteers. However, offline social networks, including friends, classmates, and colleagues, played a critical role in sustaining citizens' involvement in nonviolent resistance. In addition, some civic initiatives and social movements formed during or after the 2004 Orange Revolution facilitated the development of an organizational infrastructure in support of the protest movement. According to a Euromaidan participant, mass mobilization signified the process of "de-virtualization," offline meetings with people with whom one had previously been in contact on Facebook.[116]

---

[115] On the mass perceptions of feminism in Ukrainian society, see Tamara Martsenyuk. 2018. *Chomu ne varto boiatysia feminizmu*. Kyiv: Komora.

[116] NaUKMA interview with Ivan Hrihorev. Qtd. *from Maidan. Svidchennia. Kyiv, 2013–2014 roky*, p. 341.

4

Women's Roles During a Revolution

On November 30, following police violence against peaceful protesters and an escalation in state repression, the Kyiv-based Center for Civil Liberties (CCL) launched the civic initiative *Euromaidan SOS* to provide legal assistance for participants in the Revolution of Dignity.[1] The human rights defender Oleksandra Matviichuk became a coordinator of the Euromaidan SOS, placing victims of state repression in contact with lawyers and building a database of human rights violations during this period of mass mobilization. The civic initiative began with two Facebook posts. The first post ran like this, "We have three hotlines, please call if you are a witness, a relative, or a victim [of violence]. We will provide legal aid for you." The second post stated, "If you are a lawyer or an attorney and you want to provide pro bono legal services for people, call us, and we will put you in touch with them." "And it started working … by the end of the day we had 10,000 subscribers," Matviichuk said.[2] For several months, CCL staff and volunteers delivered pro bono legal aid for the wounded, arbitrarily jailed, and tortured protesters, documented human rights violations, and disseminated information to fight against the regime on the legal front. Meanwhile, other women raised funds for the social movement, offered urgent medical care for the injured, provided media coverage of protest events, picketed army barracks, or joined self-defense units to sustain mass mobilization.

This chapter highlights a diversity of women's roles during the Revolution of Dignity to demonstrate a hybrid model of women's participation in a contemporary revolution. The book challenges a binary construction of women's involvement in stereotypically feminine or stereotypically masculine

---

[1] For an overview, see the webpage of the Center for Civil Liberties, https://ccl.org.ua/tools/yevromajdan-sos.

[2] UINP interview with Oleksandra Matviichuk, July 5, 2014.

activities during a period of mass mobilization. The patriarchal model of women's participation in a revolution assumes a gender-based division of labor within a revolutionary movement, which reinforces preexisting patriarchal norms in society. The emancipatory model, on the contrary, views gender equality as a key principle of mass mobilization and assumes women's access to formal positions of leadership within the movement. Located between these two extremes, the hybrid model of women's participation in a revolution acknowledges the diversity and fluidity of women's roles. According to the hybrid model, women might adopt three different strategies: (1) acquiescence to a traditional gender-based division of labor, (2) appropriation of the masculine forms of resistance, and (3) adoption of gender-neutral roles or switching from stereotypically feminine to stereotypically masculine roles. The hybrid model enables us to better capture a full spectrum of women's roles during a revolution than a binary distinction between patriarchal and emancipatory revolutions.

Table 4.1 summarizes twelve main domains of women's activism during the Revolution of Dignity, including art production, crowdsourcing, food provision, legal aid, medical services, public order, and public relations. Food provision and urgent medical care are typically viewed as "caretaking" tasks performed by women. In contrast, the provision of public order is frequently seen as a men's domain. However, there exists a broad spectrum of critical tasks that fall somewhere between stereotypically masculine and stereotypically feminine roles. Moreover, the revolutionary situation opens up an opportunity for the contestation of dominant gender norms and the fluidity of women's

TABLE 4.1 *Main domains of women's participation in a revolution*

Domain	Example
Crowdsourcing	Raised funds via social media and managed the purchase of supplies critical to the maintenance of the encampment's infrastructure and the physical well-being of revolutionaries
Culture of resistance	Designed posters and wrote poems in support of the revolutionary cause; painted the protesters' gear
Education	Organized public lectures inside the encampment
Food	Coordinated the provision of food supplies
Housing	Facilitated the provision of temporary housing for out-of-town movement participants
Legal aid	Provided pro bono legal aid for movement participants
Library services	Maintained an encampment library
Medical services	Provided counseling and urgent medical care
Public order	Formed self-defense units and patrolled the barricades
Public relations	Posted news on social media and published newsletters
Street actions	Picketed government buildings and military barracks
Transportation	Coordinated the transportation of movement participants from provinces to the capital city

roles. The empirical analysis highlights diverse forms of women's activism during a twenty-first-century revolution. In addition, this chapter explores how the deployment of lethal force against protesters influenced modes of citizens' participation in the revolution. In particular, data from the oral history projects show that police killings of armless protesters had a profound impact on mass attitudes toward the use of violence to bring down the current regime.

FOOD PROVISION, HOUSING, AND TRANSPORTATION

For nearly three months, volunteers secured an adequate provision of food supplies and prepared meals for thousands of protesters who stayed inside the encampment and weathered harsh winter conditions. The length of civil resistance, as well as the size of the protest movement, makes it self-evident that the provision of food was not a trivial task. It required a great deal of coordination and the capacity to work on a tight schedule. Given the growth of the protest movement and the development of a food supply system, volunteers switched from making sandwiches to providing hot meals for movement participants in mid-December 2013.[3] According to some estimates, 1,600 people worked in three shifts around the clock in the dining hall of the Trade Unions Building on Khreshchatyk Street – the movement's headquarters – to feed revolutionaries.[4] Between 500 and 1,000 volunteers daily completed a shift in the Trade Unions Building in December 2013.[5] Olena Hrechaniuk, along with her mother and twin sister, joined another team of volunteers based in the building of the Kyiv City Council (*Kyivska miska derzhavna administratsiia*, KMDA) on Khreshchatyk Street. Hrechaniuk described her work schedule as follows:

Breakfast was served at 7:30 a.m. Our cook Ira got up at 5:00 a.m. to get it ready. We cooked food outdoors, in giant pots ... When everybody finished a meal, we closed the kitchen, but if someone was late, we gave them food, we could not leave a person without breakfast. Then we cooked lunch. It began around 2:00 p.m. We quickly peeled potatoes for borsch or soup. When we put it on the stove to get cooked, we could take a break and switch to making sandwiches. After a post-lunch clean-up, we tried to go to Maidan [square] to see what was happening there, it was sort of a break for us. We walked, spoke with people whom we had previously met during the food service, and then we went back to cook dinner. Dinner was served between 6 p.m. and 7 p.m.

---

[3] Televiziina sluzhba novyn. 2013. "Rozblokovanyi Evromaidan pereide na povnotsinne 3-razove kharchuvannia." *Channel 1+1*, December 13. https://kyiv.tsn.ua/kyiv/rozblokovaniy-yevromaydan-pereyde-na-povnocinne-3-razove-harchuvannya-325265.html.
[4] Lustration in Ukraine. n.d. "Headquarters of the Revolution and Nearby." www.lustration.in.ua/article.php.
[5] Liudmyla Osadchuk. 2013. "Na kukhni Evromaidanu robota kypyt tsilodobovo." *Molodyi Bukovynets*, December 14. https://molbuk.ua/photo_news/66706-na-kuhn-yevromaydana-u-robota-kipit-clodobovo.html.

Food Provision, Housing, and Transportation 105

After dinner, we cleaned up everything, did the dishes, and somewhere around 11:00 p. m. or midnight I headed home.[6]

Consistent with the results of on-site surveys, data from the oral history projects reveal that men and women from different parts of Ukraine joined civil resistance and volunteered on Maidan. Natalka Serdiuk, an artist from Zaporizhzhia, was impressed with the diversity of people whom she encountered during her volunteer work.

A young woman from Brovary [a city in Kyiv oblast] who volunteered next to me had two children, she took turns with her spouse [to volunteer in the kitchen]. There was a woman who might have been sixty or seventy years old. Mrs. Liubov came from Luhansk. Then there was a young man from western Ukraine. He was a professional chef, and he streamlined the logistics. Once I worked with him in the coffee department. He organized a small unit [specializing in making coffee]. There was a young woman named Mariia. There was a handsome man, of short stature, tanned. He said, "I am from Odesa, and I am the best chef in Odesa." There were volunteers from Kharkiv.[7]

There was a visible presence of men in field kitchens, cooking soup or making tea in huge cauldrons over a fire in the open air. Many of these field kitchens were self-organized by groups of volunteers from a region of Ukraine. For example, a group of five men from Donetsk oblast boiled tea and cooked soup every 2.5 hours in 80-liter cauldrons outdoors.[8] Plenty of men also cooked *kulish* (millet porridge), the traditional Ukrainian dish prepared by Zaporozhian Sich Cossacks during military campaigns.[9]

Yet, media reports provided a gendered coverage of civil resistance, suggesting that women were primarily involved in the preparation and distribution of food.[10] Furthermore, media reports indicated that there existed a gender-based division of labor in food services. Men were often charged with the task of carrying heavy boxes packed with food, lifting huge pots of borsch, or cracking walnuts, while women made tons of sandwiches and fixed tea with sliced lemon.[11]

In many cases, kitchens inside the encampment served as a safe space for women's discussion of Ukrainian politics and the development of feminist

---

[6] UINP interview with Olena Hrechaniuk, November 10, 2014.
[7] NaUKMA interview with Natalka Serdiuk. Qtd. from *Maidan. Svidchennia. Kyiv, 2013–2014 roky*, p. 307.
[8] Nazar Hrynyk. 2013. "Kukhnia z Donbasu na Evromaidani u Kuevi." *NazarGryn* [YouTube channel], December 10. https://youtu.be/bwDqrArj5Iw.
[9] Annabelle Chapman. 2013. "Revolution on Ice." *The Slate*, December 13. https://slate.com/news-and-politics/2013/12/ukrainian-protesters-endure-freezing-temperature-inside-kievs-euro maidan-tent-city.html.
[10] Radio Free Europe/Radio Liberty. 2023. "Inside the 'Euromaidan' Kitchen." December 13. www.rferl.org/a/ukraine-euromaidan-protests/25200088.html.
[11] Nataliia Sedletska. 2013. "Kukhnia Evromaidanu: Hory zapasiv, krasa po-ukrainski ta narodni pisni. Fotoreportazh." *Radio Svoboda*, December 13. www.radiosvoboda.org/a/25199839.html.

consciousness. Though many women cooked meals inside buildings adjacent to Independence Square, they routinely stepped outside to interact with movement participants and stay informed about current events. Moreover, for some female protesters, kitchens were an entry point into the movement, which led to their engagement in other movement activities.

The provision of housing and transportation for out-of-town revolutionaries was another key task that required considerable coordination among movement participants. Some women provided housing for out-of-town protesters on an ad hoc basis. Others tried to tackle this logistical challenge systematically. A group of volunteers compiled a database of Kyiv residents who were willing to provide temporary housing for out-of-town movement participants. In addition, activists established contacts with business owners to shelter protesters in offices located within walking distance from Independence Square. The Civic Sector of Euromaidan housed almost 10,000 people in the exhibition center KyivExpoPlaza during the first weeks of mass mobilization.[12]

MEDICAL SERVICES

The provision of urgent medical care was critical to the revolutionary movement, especially with an escalation in police violence. State authorities interfered with the work of emergency medical services and kidnapped injured protesters from public hospitals. In turn, hundreds of women with professional experience in the healthcare sector and medical school students volunteered to provide first aid for the injured in the encampment's medical stations and underground hospitals. According to Olha Bohomolets, a coordinator of Maidan's medical services, more than one thousand healthcare volunteers worked under precarious conditions in February 2014.[13] The obstetrician-gynecologist Natalia Leliukh, for example, joined the Medical Services of Maidan in December 2013, but she did not anticipate that she would need to brush up on her knowledge of battlefield medicine:

After the first [police] shots, I realized that it was time to read about field surgery, it was time to watch how a stun grenade has an impact [on civilians], it was time to recall certain things that I should never have thought about, given my peacetime occupation as an ob-gyn.[14]

---

[12] Liubov Velychko and Ivan Tertyi. 2013. "Hromadskyi sektor Maidanu. Vid poselennia aktyvistiv do vyhotovlennia ahitproduktsii." *Texty*, February 3. https://texty.org.ua/articles/51516/Gromadskyj_sektor_Majdanu_Vid_poselenna_aktyvistiv_do-51516.

[13] Vladislav Davidzon. 2014. "Maidan's Mother Teresa Talks Ukraine's Future." *Tablet Magazine*, May 23. www.tabletmag.com/sections/news/articles/maidans-mother-teresa-talks-ukraines-future.

[14] NaUKMA interview with Nataliia Leliukh. Qtd. from *Maidan. Svidchennia. Kyiv, 2013–2014 roky*, p. 268.

Medical Services

Consistent with the findings from on-site and nationally representative surveys, data from the oral history projects reveal diverse backgrounds of volunteers for the medical services of Maidan. A sizeable share of healthcare professionals came from the western part of Ukraine. The Kyiv-based homeopathic doctor Olena Finberg, for example, saw "many young doctors from western Ukraine, from Uzhhorod and Lviv" when she came to the Trade Unions Building to sign up for volunteering at a makeshift hospital.[15] Data from oral history projects also demonstrate that people from different ethnic and religious backgrounds volunteered inside the Kyiv-based encampment. Svitlana Abaeva, a rehabilitation doctor from Khmelnytskyi, described her volunteer experience as follows. "Our medical station was very unusual. Natan was a wonderful neurologist and an Orthodox Jew, Amina [Okueva] was a Chechen Muslim woman, and I was an evangelical Christian. And there was no enmity among us, we had very gentle relations."[16]

In addition to professional doctors, some women were willing to learn on the spot how to provide first aid for movement participants. Yuliia Pishta, for example, joined a medical team in response to the rising need for healthcare personnel.

On December 11, during an attempted police attack, I was on the barricades, on Instytutska Street, and I lost consciousness because of tear gas. So I decided that I should learn something about first aid; otherwise, somebody would lose consciousness and I would not know what to do. Then I became acquainted with Yaroslav Kravchenko ... I remember how he gathered us – six or seven women – and gave us a master class, showed how to provide first aid, put a bandage, do cardiopulmonary resuscitation, put salt on a cotton pad when a person is unwell.[17]

Many religious institutions supported the protest movement by providing space for temporary medical stations. Olena Hantsiak-Kaskiv, head of the Patriarchal Society in Kyiv (*Patriarshe Tovarystvo*) aimed at the unification of all Ukrainian churches, assumed a leadership role in converting local churches into underground infirmaries for protesters.[18] St. Michael's Golden-Domed Monastery, belonging to the Ukrainian Orthodox Church of the Kyiv Patriarchate, provided a safe space for regime opponents during Euromaidan. On November 30, scores of students chased by the riot police found refuge inside the monastery. In February 2014, the monastery opened its doors again to protesters in need of urgent medical care.[19] In collaboration with the Red Cross, a group of Ukrainian medics, informally

---

[15] NaUKMA interview with Olena Finberg. Qtd. from *Maidan. Svidchennia. Kyiv, 2013–2014 roky*, p. 597.
[16] NaUKMA interview with Svitlana Abaeva. Qtd. from *Maidan. Svidchennia. Kyiv, 2013–2014 roky*, p. 637.
[17] UINP interview with Yuliia Pishta, September 18, 2015.
[18] UINP interview with Olena Hantsiak-Kaskiv, December 25, 2014.
[19] Matt Robinson. 2014. "Kiev Monastery: A Sanctuary for the Bloodied and Bruised." *Reuters*, February 19. www.reuters.com/article/us-ukraine-church/kiev-monastery-a-sanctuary-for-the-bloodied-and-bruised-idUSBREA1I11520140219.

dubbed Michael's Medics (*Mykhailivski medyky*), set up a medical station and a storage space for medical supplies inside a monk's cell.[20] The German Evangelical Lutheran Church of St. Catherine, located close to the epicenter of civil resistance on Luteranska Street, was another important site of support for participants in the Revolution of Dignity.[21] The congregation welcomed everyone to rest and pray. With an escalation in police violence, the Lutheran Church was increasingly used as a temporary medical station for protesters.[22] The medical personnel provided urgent medical care on the first floor, while professional psychologists offered counseling on the second floor.

Crisis counseling was an important dimension of medical treatment, given the immense amount of psychological stress among revolutionaries. The Psychological Services of Maidan (*Psyholohichna sluzhba Maidanu*) was set up by licensed psychologists and psychotherapists on December 2, 2013. As noted by Halyna Tsyhanenko, psychologists started self-organizing and made a schedule of shifts so that professionals could deliver counseling services around the clock.[23] As the first step, psychologists tried to change mass attitudes toward their profession and emphasize the importance of mental health. Viktoriia Kochubei, for example, tirelessly worked to build rapport with protesters to overcome the social stigma associated with mental health.

I realized that I would be more helpful if I directed my efforts in a professional channel … We had green aprons, with the word "Psychologist" written in white. When we started walking in green aprons, some people shied away from us, especially men were saying to us, "Psychologist? No! We don't need your services." But three weeks, a month passed by. And they began to say, "Oh, psychologist! Come! Come!" Trust was formed. There emerged some understanding of what we could offer.[24]

CROWDSOURCING AND PUBLIC RELATIONS

A steady flow of resources was vital to the maintenance of the encampment's infrastructure and the physical well-being of revolutionaries. For this purpose, the protest movement heavily relied upon crowdsourcing as a tool for soliciting ideas and services in support of the revolution.[25] By the same token, women played an active role in crowdfunding, raising funds by soliciting small

---

[20] UINP interview with Kateryna Korniiko, September 24, 2015.
[21] Religious Information Service of Ukraine. 2014. "A Drop in the Sea: Stories of Ministering on Maidan from the Lutheran Church." February 4. https://risu.ua/en/a-drop-in-the-sea-stories-of-ministering-on-maidan-from-the-lutheran-church_n67044.
[22] The Lutheran World Federation. 2014. "Ukrainian Bishop Calls for an End to the Violence." February 20. www.lutheranworld.org/news/ukrainian-bishop-calls-end-violence.
[23] UINP interview with Halyna Tsyhanenko, October 30, 2015.
[24] UINP interview with Viktoriia Kochubei, February 16, 2015.
[25] On this point, see Tetyana Bohdanova. 2014. "Unexpected Revolution: The Role of Social Media in Ukraine's Euromaidan Uprising." *European View* 13 (June): 133–42, 137–38.

contributions from a large number of people, especially the online community. Vita Bazan, a project coordinator at Spilnokosht, Ukraine's first and largest crowdsourcing platform launched in September 2012, became involved in civic initiatives aimed at raising funds for Euromaidan.[26] In December 2013, Spilnokosht supported the project "Warm Up and Feed Maidan" (*Zihrii ta nahodui Maidan*) initiated by the civic organization "Kyivites – for Reforms" (*Kyiany – za reformy*) to buy tents, warm clothes, and food for the protest movement. Within three days, the project reached its goal of raising Hr 100,000,[27] and the campaign ended with a total of Hr 261,890 (approximately $30,000) from 1,060 people.[28] In addition, people from all over the country provided in-kind support and donated clothes, food, generators, and tents for the Kyiv-based encampment.[29]

Much effort has been directed to the provision of medical supplies for medical stations inside the encampment. Healthcare professionals realized that they could put their medical training to use by managing the movement's stock of medical supplies. Sholoiko, for example, volunteered to gather, sort out, and distribute medical supplies.

Someone stopped by a pharmacy, purchased everything, and gave it in a bundle, with a receipt. And a grandma looked through her first aid kit at home and brought some bandages, brilliant green dye (*zelionka*), medical cotton, an open pack of pills, but everything was labeled. It was a touching moment. Everyone helped in a different way.[30]

Another crowdsourcing initiative launched by the Institute of Mass Information, in collaboration with the international human rights organization Reporters without Borders, focused on the provision of personal protective equipment for journalists. Initially, the Institute distributed orange vests and construction hats; later, they began purchasing snowboard helmets to protect journalists against rubber bullets. As the level of police violence escalated, the Institute made arrangements for the distribution of bullet-proof vests for local reporters. "It was a totally horizontal movement, there was no superior who would issue orders," recalled Oksana Romaniuk, director of the Institute of Mass Information and a representative of the Reporters without Borders in Ukraine.[31]

---

[26] Ahata Shapran. 2014. "Kak sobrat s miru po nitke." *NeFormat* [Mariupol-based magazine] 13: 4–7.
[27] Den. 2013. "Initsiatyva 'Zihrii ta Nahodui Maidan' nabrala bilshe 100 tysiach hryven." December 3. https://day.kyiv.ua/news/271221-initsiatyva-zihriy-ta-nahoduy-maydan-nabrala-bilshe-100-tys-hrn.
[28] The Big Idea. 2013. "Zihrii ta nahodui Maidan." https://biggggidea.com/project/385/#
[29] Maria Shamota. 2013. "Donations Pour in to Feed and Clothe EuroMaidan." *Kyiv Post*, December 13. www.kyivpost.com/post/10315.
[30] UINP interview with Nataliia Sholoiko, December 4, 2014.
[31] UINP interview with Oksana Romaniuk, June 11, 2015.

The collection and distribution of warm clothes was another domain of women's activism. In January 2014, the average temperature in Kyiv hovered around 23°F (-5°C), but it dropped below zero Fahrenheit at night.[32] Given the weather conditions and the use of firewood for heat, revolutionaries needed to have a large supply of warm and sturdy clothes. "We took in tons of warm clothes, sorted it out, and then distributed," Yuliia Votcher said.[33] Having volunteered at an on-site medical station, Votcher felt emotionally drained from her daily work with victims of police brutality. To remain engaged in civil resistance, she switched her sphere of activities and spent the whole month inside a building on Khreshchatyk Street to sort out and distribute clothes.

Women's engagement in crowdsourcing initiatives often resulted in their physical absence from the encampment on Independence Square. For example, Oleksandra Dubicheva, a founding member of the civic initiative People's Hospital (*Narodnyi hospital*), worked mostly from home. Dubicheva assumed responsibility for the provision of medical instruments and equipment for on-site medical stations.

I saw somewhere on the Internet a list of necessary medical supplies. It was a breaking moment for me. Some surgical materials and instruments were on the list. I found them via the Internet and brought to the medical station, the one to which [Serhii] Nihonian was brought after being wounded ... I was a "person on the phone," in front of my laptop, on the Internet. Once journalists came to interview me and asked, "Please describe your typical day." I replied, "I don't remember." And I asked a friend who had spent the previous day with me, "Listen, describe my previous day." He said, "You spent eighteen hours in front of the computer. Then you took my sandwich, ate half of it, and fell asleep on the chair."[34]

In addition, women played a vital role in spreading the news about protest events both among protesters and a wider audience. As noted by the journalist Bohdana Babych, there was a need to break down the oligarchs' control over the mass media and create an alternative platform for an intellectual discussion of political, socioeconomic, and cultural developments in the country.[35] Formed in the spring of 2013, the TV channel *Spilno* provided around-the-clock live streaming from Independence Square to keep the media spotlight on the main encampment in the capital city. Similarly, *Hromadske Radio* launched by another team of journalists in the summer of 2013 produced a series of podcasts *Holosy Maidanu* (Voices of Maidan).[36] Furthermore, in December 2013, *Hromadske Radio* journalists Iryna Slavinska and Nataliia Sokolenko

---

[32] For details, visit the webpage Time and Date AS, www.timeanddate.com/weather/ukraine/kyiv/historic?month=1&year=2014.
[33] UINP interview with Yuliia Votcher, September 21, 2015.
[34] UINP interview with Oleksandra Dubicheva, September 4, 2015.
[35] UINP interview with Bohdana Babych, December 9, 2014.
[36] For details, visit the webpage of Hromadske Radio, https://hromadske.radio/podcasts/golosy-maydanu.

joined the Euromaidan-centered marathon on the airwaves of the radio station *Europe Plus*.[37]

There was also a dramatic growth in citizen journalism. Tetiana Movchan, for example, played a pivotal role in publishing the daily *Teritoriia voli* (Territory of Freedom). "This newspaper was coming from the people to the people," Movchan said. "[It was named] *Territory* because Maidan was conceived as Zaporozhian Sich [a military and political center of Ukrainian Cossacks in the 16th–18th centuries], wherein there was an organizational structure, a code of rules, certain relations between people."[38] The first issue of January 16, 2014, featured an interview with a farmer who was killed by the riot police four days later. Under these circumstances, the women-produced publications swiftly became not only a news source but also a medium for archiving eyewitness accounts of Euromaidan and commemorating the fallen heroes of the revolution. Another prominent newsletter, titled *Khronika tekushchikh sobytii* (The Chronicle of Current Events), was published by a team of activists affiliated with the Civic Sector of Euromaidan to spread the movement's key messages among Russophones. A Russian-language underground magazine with the same title used to be published during the Brezhnev period to document state repression against dissidents and expose political processes in the Soviet Union. Likewise, the Chronicle of Current Events tried to deliver uncensored news to the Russian-speaking audience in post-Soviet Ukraine. The newsletter's circulation grew from 1,177 copies on February 1 to 150,000 copies on February 19.[39]

Complementing the emergence of ad hoc print publications, some websites of existing civic organizations were aptly transformed into news outlets for revolutionaries. These organizational changes facilitated a rapid response to the protesters' needs. Tetiana Motsak, for example, contributed stories to the news portal *Sil'* (Salt):

> Our website had up to 500 unique visitors before Maidan. We had over 10,000 visitors during Maidan. We made an effort to write our own texts, not copy and paste. We reacted immediately because we were on Maidan [square], we had an opportunity to do interviews, speak with people, provide an expert opinion ... Our approach to the delivery of Maidan news was a reflection of our own thinking, our opportunity to discuss real problems with people and help them meet some urgent needs.[40]

---

[37] Detector Media. 2013. "*Hromadske Radio* tretii den pospil vede onlain-marafon pro Evromaidan." December 3. https://stv.detector.media/radio/read/417/2013-12-03-gromadske-radio-tretiy-den-pospil-vede-onlayn-marafon-pro-ievromaydan.

[38] UINP interview with Tetiana Movchan, August 20, 2014.

[39] For details, see the Facebook page of the Chronicle of Current Events, www.facebook.com/uachronicle.

[40] UINP interview with Tetiana Motsak, March 24, 2015.

LEGAL AID

Since the collapse of communism, the Ukrainian government deployed an unprecedented amount of violence against regime opponents, including the use of rubber bullets, stun grenades, tear gas, and water cannons against civilians, as well as the kidnapping and torture of civic activists.[41] Among targets of state violence were, for example, members of the grassroots initiative AutoMaidan. State-sponsored thugs (*titushki*) organized physical attacks on activists and set their cars on fire. Journalists and doctors who assisted protesters also became targets of state repression.[42] An escalation in police violence occurred at dawn on November 30, 2013; the riot police ruthlessly dispersed several hundred peaceful protesters inside the encampment by hitting people with batons and inflicting serious injuries, including broken legs and concussions.[43] Another spike in violence, involving a series of sniper shootings, resulted in the deaths of nearly 100 people on February 18–20, 2014.[44]

Given a staggering level of state repression, scores of lawyers volunteered to offer pro bono legal aid for revolutionaries.[45] By the end of the revolution, the hotline Euromaidan SOS alone had a list of 400 lawyers.[46] "This legal community was quite heterogeneous, ranging from owners of big law firms to individuals with limited legal experience. But they called [the hotline] and they were ready to help people," pointed out Matviichuk. The Euromaidan SOS identified several priorities for their work, focusing on legal aid for the detained protesters and the search for missing persons. Mariia Ivanyk, an active member of the Foundation of Regional Initiatives, was a hotline coordinator:

It is fair to say that we lived there [in the office of CCL]. My colleague and I were tied to our phones that never went silent because people were calling all the time. We were just collecting information about their [legal] needs.[47]

---

[41] Human Rights Watch. 2015. "World Report 2015: Ukraine." www.hrw.org/world-report/2015/country-chapters/ukraine; Kharkiv Human Rights Protection Group. 2014. *Human Rights Violations Associated with Euromaidan.* http://khpg.org/en/index.php?r=2.5.43.
[42] Human Rights Watch. 2014. "Ukraine: Police Attacked Dozens of Journalists, Medics." January 30. www.hrw.org/news/2014/01/30/ukraine-police-attacked-dozens-journalists-medics.
[43] Human Rights Watch. 2013. "Ukraine: Excessive Forces against Protesters." December 3. www.hrw.org/news/2013/12/03/ukraine-excessive-force-against-protesters; Kyiv Post. 2013. "Police Violently Break Up Independence Square Protests at 4 A.M. Today; Many Injuries Reported." November 30. www.kyivpost.com/article/content/euromaidan/reports-police-forcefully-break-up-protest-site-on-maidan-nezalezhnosti-this-morning-332674.html.
[44] The Office of the United Nations High Commissioner for Human Rights. 2014. "Report on the Human Rights Situation in Ukraine." April 15. www.ohchr.org/EN/Countries/ENACARegion/Pages/UAReports.aspx.
[45] For an in-depth treatment of the topic, see Sophia Wilson. 2017. "Cause Lawyering in Revolutionary Ukraine." *Journal of Law and Courts* 5 (Fall): 267–88.
[46] UINP interview with Oleksandra Matviichuk, July 5, 2014.
[47] UINP interview with Mariia Ivanyk, August 12, 2014.

Culture and Art of Resistance 113

Similarly, Iryna Mukhina stayed in the office of CCL and spent the bulk of her time on the phone, which made her work less visible to many people inside the encampment:

Since I coordinated the work of the hotline, I did not have a chance to be on Maidan at all. And I missed all the beautiful things that were happening on Maidan. I was upset about it, I wanted to go [there] to make sandwiches or bandage a wound. I wanted to do some very practical things, with a clearly visible outcome. When you volunteer for a hotline, it is very difficult to observe an outcome [of your work]. Not everyone would call back and report what had happened in the long run ... But we, all the Euromaidan SOS volunteers, were aware of the importance of this line of work, and we did it.[48]

CULTURE AND ART OF RESISTANCE

Women played a vital role in producing the art of resistance to sustain the spirit of revolutionaries and document this critical moment in Ukrainian history through visual art, music, and poetry.[49] To that end, a group of artists, writers, and musicians set up the Art Squad (*Mystetska sotnia*). One of the projects launched by the Art Squad focused on shield painting (*shchytopys*). Based upon their encounters with protesters, artists elegantly painted protesters' hard hats and wooden shields.[50] An artist named Natalka, for example, received a lot of requests from members of self-defense units to paint St. Michael the Archangel [patron saint of Kyiv] or St. Gabriel the Archangel on their gear to protect them against police violence.[51] Having received professional training at the Kharkiv Art School, Kateryna Tkachenko was drawn to this civic initiative.

I was looking for ways in which some artistic achievements could come in handy on Maidan so that I could serve people through art. I went to the Ukrainian House, which had been occupied by protesters by then, to figure out whether poems might be recited or art exhibits might be held on Maidan [square]. I was referred to a young woman, Maryna Matilda, and she told me, "Oh, we are organizing the Art Squad right now. Artists, painters, musicians got united: we should do something for Ukraine, for Maidan [movement]." That's how I found myself in the Art Squad, and the Art Squad entered my life.[52]

Women generated a broad spectrum of creative work to convey their visions of the revolution. Having joined the creative department in the Civic Sector of

---

[48] UINP interview with Iryna Mukhina, August 27, 2014.
[49] For details, see Tetiana Kovtunovych and Tetiana Pyvalko, eds. 2016. *Maidan vid pershoi osoby: Mystetsvo na barykadakh* [Maidan from the First Person: Art on the Barricades]. Kyiv: Ukrainian Institute of National Memory.
[50] UAInfo. 2014. "Khudozhnyky rozpysaly boiovi shchyty voiakam Samooborony Maidanu. Foto." February 10. https://uainfo.org/blognews/273759-hudozhniki-rozpisali-boyov-schiti-voyakam-samooboroni-maydanu-foto.html.
[51] NaUKMA interview with Natalka. Qtd. from *Maidan. Svidchennia. Kyiv, 2013–2014 roky*, p. 720.
[52] Kovtunovych and Pyvalko. *Maidan vid pershoi osoby*, pp. 161–62.

Euromaidan, Oleksandra Navrotska and Nata Obvintseva designed a series of special posters, capturing the essence of Euromaidan.[53] In addition to visual art, Euromaidan engendered the growth of literary works, fostering a sense of collective identity and articulating a wide gamut of emotions that prevailed among movement participants during these tumultuous events. The Ukrainian poet and librarian Olha Strashenko, for example, wrote a poem dedicated to the memory of Yurii Verbytskii, a Euromaidan activist who was tortured and killed in January 2014. In addition to the commemoration of fallen heroes of the liberation struggle, some literary work sought to draw a stark contrast between Ukrainian and Russian culture. Having observed the condescending attitude of Russians toward Ukrainians and the systematic misrepresentation of Euromaidan on Russian TV channels, the budding poet Anastasiia Dmytruk penned a Russian-language poem *Nikogda my ne budem brat'iami* (We will never be brothers).[54] Well-known cultural figures also gave a powerful voice to the movement by making media appearances and delivering guest lectures aimed at educating the foreign audiences about Ukraine's national struggle for independence. Representing a generation of Ukrainian women writers, Oksana Zabuzhko, an award-winning poet and a key figure in the Ukrainian feminist movement, delivered countless talks, gave media interviews, and wrote essays on the significance of cultural resistance to Russia's foreign policy.[55]

The Open University of Maidan – a series of outdoor lectures on Independence Square – was a civic initiative aimed at educating revolutionaries and stimulating a public debate on the pressing issues in Ukrainian society. Between December 2013 and January 2014, the Open University hosted nearly 300 lectures by outstanding scholars, businessmen, and artists. Yuliia Tychkivska, an alumna of the National University of Kyiv-Mohyla Academy, was a cofounder and coordinator of this initiative. In late December, Svitlana Taranenko assumed a key role in developing the University's programming. According to Tychkivska, three priorities underpinned the Open University's programming:

First, it was about a new Ukraine, we tried to convey the idea of reforms. [Talk] about things that might be changed, about the country that we would like to have. Second, [speakers were] people who were successful and inspiring. Third, content that stimulated personal growth. We told people about the development of their leadership potential. We also had a series of art lectures. There was a wide range of topics.[56]

This educational initiative reached a diverse body of Euromaidan participants. Initially, civic activists considered young people as the primary audience

---

[53] UINP interview with Oleksandra Navrotska, April 15, 2016.
[54] The full text of the poem is available at https://dmytruk.com.ua/nykohda-myi-ne-budem-bratyamy.
[55] For an overview, see Oleksandra Wallo. 2020. "New National Chronicles." In *Ukrainian Women Writers and the National Imaginary: From the Collapse of the USSR to the Euromaidan*. Toronto: University of Toronto Press, pp. 131–48.
[56] UINP interview with Yuliia Tychkivska, April 28, 2015.

for the lecture series. However, it quickly became obvious to organizers that many middle-aged protesters from provinces were hungry for knowledge about Ukrainian culture. "It was as if there was arid land that wasn't watered for a long time, and then water came down. The floodgates have opened," recalled Taranenko.[57] She scheduled four lectures about Ukrainian literature and Taras Shevchenko due to high demand for such content.

The creation of an on-site library filled with inspirational literature was another civic initiative aimed at sustaining the spirit of Maidan. This initiative was spearheaded by Inna and Viktor Bisovetski in January 2014 and supported by scores of volunteers. Located inside the Ukrainian House, an exhibition hall on Khreshchatyk Street, the Maidan Library drew a large number of visitors. "Kyivites would bring books and revolutionaries would read them," recalled Anastasiia Makarenko.[58] Ukrainian-language prose about prior liberation struggles was especially popular with Euromaidan participants. For example, Vasyl Shkliar's novel *The Black Raven* (*Chornyi voron*) and Yurii Horlis-Horsky's novel *The Cold Ravine (Kholodnyi Yar)*, portraying the Ukrainian resistance movement against the Russian Bolsheviks in the early 1920s, were in high demand. Euromaidan participants drew inspiration from heroic sagas of Ukrainians who fought for national independence in the twentieth century.

NONVIOLENT ACTION

Women's repertoire of contention encompassed a variety of nonviolent methods, ranging from the performance of folk songs in front of police cordons and the picketing of army barracks to the organization of car caravans to the homes of government officials and the night guard at hospitals. A network of activists comprising the Civic Sector of Euromaidan championed the idea of nonviolent resistance by organizing innovative street actions. In waging nonviolent resistance, movement participants targeted such state actors as the riot police, the internal troops under the jurisdiction of the Ministry of Internal Affairs, the national parliament, the judiciary, and public universities. Moreover, civic activists conceived a wide array of nonviolent methods to foster the movement's growth.

At the start of mass mobilization, some activists tried to challenge the power of regime-friendly university rectors and propel the student population into action. Activists blocked entry to university buildings, disrupted lectures, and visited dormitories to mobilize students against the regime. In particular, Vidsich activists tried to develop contacts with students at Kyiv-based institutions of higher education, wherein the university administration closely monitored student attendance of classes and pressured students into political

---

[57] NaUKMA interview with Svitlana Taranenko. Qtd. from *Maidan. Svidchennia. Kyiv, 2013–2014 roky*, p. 172.
[58] UINP interview with Anastasiia Makarenko, June 10, 2014.

conformity. Maryna Hohulia, for example, campaigned among students at the Kyiv Linguistic University:

We would enter the student dormitory with drums and whistles that soccer fans would use. And we would run from one floor to another, distribute leaflets, and urge them to join a student strike and have an impact.[59]

Similarly, the Civic Sector of Euromaidan sought to mobilize the population against the regime. To mark a month since the violent dispersal of protesters, activists organized a public campaign, titled "Don't be afraid – a million will turn out" (*Ne biisia – vyide million*). People were prompted to make posters with the abovementioned slogan and stand in small groups in public spaces for an hour on December 30, 2013.[60] On the same day, activists organized a street action directed at the police. For half an hour, women held large mirrors in front of the police cordon on Hrushevska Street so that police officers could look themselves in the eye and reflect upon their role in the movement's confrontation with the incumbent government.[61]

The civic activist and a former member of the youth movement Pora Olha Salo believed that "women are the force that can stop aggression. It is just necessary to stand between the two sides – and then there will be no aggression on either side."[62] When there emerged some tensions between the police and male protesters on December 1, a few female activists rushed to the site in an attempt to de-escalate the situation:

Back then, it was not difficult to come up to the police cordon. We realized right away what we should do: we moved between the [police] shields and the guys who tried to get into a brawl with the police, spoke with some, tried to persuade others [not to use violence].[63]

In general, a wide range of women-led street actions targeted the riot police and the internal troops to reduce the incidence of violence against participants in the protest movement. Women gathered near the military bases located in Kyiv to plead with soldiers to disobey an imminent order to shoot at protesters. Likewise, groups of women approached cordons of the riot police with a plea for humane treatment of protesters. Young women painted hearts on the police shields and tied blue-and-yellow ribbons. Meanwhile, middle-aged women drew on their maternal identity to appeal against the use of lethal force.[64]

---

[59] UINP interview with Maryna Hohulia, August 9, 2014.
[60] Daily Lviv. 2013. "U ponedilok – zahalnoukrainska aktsiia Evromaidanu." December 28. https://dailylviv.com/news/polityka/u-ponedilok-zahalnoukrayinska-aktsiya-ievromaidanu-3264.
[61] Ihor Lutsenko. 2013. "Anons. Tsarstvo moroku – v otochenni!" *Ukrainska Pravda* [blog entry], December 29. https://blogs.pravda.com.ua/authors/lutsenko/52c02addb19d4/page_2.
[62] UINP interview with Olha Salo, January 30, 2015.   [63] Ibid.
[64] NaUKMA interview with Zoriana Sokhatska. Qtd. from *Maidan. Svidchennia. Kyiv, 2013–2014 roky*, p. 496.

Wearing the sign "Mother" on their winter coats, women stood between a police cordon and movement participants.

Women activists tried to exploit the dominant patriarchal norms, casting policemen as protectors of women. A group of 20–30 female musicians led by the musical band *Dakh Daughters* developed a repertoire of folk songs and performed them in front of the police cordons near the parliamentary building in early December 2013.[65] While singing folk songs, women held self-made posters aimed at deterring police violence against female participants in the revolution. Invoking the traditional gender norms, Hanna, for example, made a poster with the slogan, "Protect me, I cook well."[66] Another woman's poster stated, "Don't beat me up, I have a hungry cat at home." Similarly, a group of young women, carrying flowers, paper cut hearts, and posters with the slogan "Don't Beat! Love and Protect" (*Ne byi! Kokhai ta zakhyshchai*), approached the police cordon on December 8 to emphasize the nonviolent character of the protest movement.[67] Inha Vyshnevska, one of the organizers of the women-led street action and the head of the press service for Ukrainian Fashion Week, cherished the hope that such peaceful actions could break the wall of misunderstanding between protesters and the police.[68]

Yet, women's efforts to engage in a dialog with the riot police produced mixed results. "We asked them not to beat us. We told them [the police] that we wanted a better life. We were talking, but we did not hear anything in response," recalled Iryna Zemliana, a participant in a street action near the presidential administration.[69] Likewise, following police violence against protesters in mid-December, some female artists became disillusioned with the effectiveness of such outreach and focused on the use of art as a means of lifting the spirit of regime opponents. With an escalation in police violence against protesters, it became increasingly difficult to converse with the internal troops and especially the riot police unit Berkut.

The making of a ceremonial towel (*obrichnyi rushnyk*) was another method of nonviolent resistance pursued by women activists.[70] A group of five women,

---

[65] Butkevych Bohdan. 2014. "Muzychni anarkhistky." *Ukrainskyi Tyzhden*, March 22. https://tyzhden.ua/muzychni-anarkhistky.

[66] NaUKMA interview with Hanna. Qtd. from *Maidan. Svidchennia. Kyiv, 2013–2014 roky*, p. 153.

[67] UNIAN. 2013. "Divchata pid Kabminom provely aktsiui 'Ne byi, kokhai ta zakhyshchai'." December 8. www.unian.ua/politics/860711-divchata-pid-kabminom-proveli-aktsiyu-ne-biy-kohay-ta-zahischay.html.

[68] NV.ua. 2015. "Maidan ochyma Inhy Vyshnevskoi." December 2. https://nv.ua/ukr/project/story-of-maidan-by-vishnevskay-40003190.html.

[69] UINP interview with Iryna Zemliana, February 12, 2015.

[70] On the ritual use of rushnyky, see Frank Sciacca. 2014. "Ukrainian Rushnyky: Binding Amulets and Magical Talismans in the Modern Period." *FOLKLORICA – Journal of the Slavic, East European, and Eurasian Folklore Association*17 (January). https://doi.org/10.17161/folklorica.v17i0.4677.

including the historian of dress and ethnographer Liudmyla Sivtseva-Klymuk, decided to perform a ritual of making a special embroidered towel as an amulet to protect the encampment against evil spirits.[71] Following the Ukrainian tradition, they worked in silence from the sunset to the sunrise. In the morning, women brought the embroidered towel, along with freshly baked bread and a cross, to the encampment so that they could complete the ritual by walking through the area in need of heavenly protection.

In response to the increasing number of victims of police violence, Anna Sarapion and Inna Sovsun launched the civic initiative titled the Hospital Guard (*Varta v likarni*) in January 2014.[72] The injured protesters faced the threat of being taken to police stations and denied access to medical services so the Hospital Guard held vigils at hospitals. Given the dearth of public information about in-patients, activists tried to keep a record of the injured protesters in the care of local hospitals and facilitate a search for missing persons. In addition, activists coordinated the provision of homemade meals for the injured.[73] More than 200 people filled out an online form via Facebook, volunteering to keep vigil at a Kyiv hospital on short notice.[74] According to Sarapion, proponents of nonviolent resistance joined this initiative:

> Most of us are women. Maybe, they are not going to Hrushevska Street [where there are clashes between the police and protesters], but they do not want to sit at home either. We take shifts in hospitals where activists are treated. We find out what they need as to medicine, clothes, food.[75]

Another civic initiative titled the Night Guard (*Nichna varta*) was spearheaded by the 2004 Eurovision winner Ruslana to sustain the spirit of movement participants during the most precarious moments. According to Anhelina Husar,[76] a member of the Night Guard, guest speakers had been brought in to provide spiritual nourishment for those who braved the cold weather and faced the threat of police violence at night. Every hour of the Night Guard service from midnight until dawn was punctuated with the Ukrainian national anthem and an interfaith prayer.

The civic initiative AutoMaidan provided one of the most precarious venues for women's activism because AutoMaidan activists were prime targets of police violence. Car owners staged protests in front of the opulent homes of

---

[71] UINP interview with Liudmyla Sivtseva-Klymuk, February 29, 2016.
[72] Anastasiia Moskvychova. 2014. "Pobytoho avtomaidanivtsia ia vpiznala po shnurkah – koordnynatorka Varty v likarni." *Radio Svoboda*, November 27. www.radiosvoboda.org/a/26712856.html.
[73] UINP interview with Oleksandra Dvoretska, April 5, 2016.
[74] Ukrainska Pravda. 2014. "'Varta u likarni': Iak riatuvaly poranenykh vid militsii." January 27. https://life.pravda.com.ua/society/2014/01/27/150107/.
[75] Iryna Virtosu. 2014. "Ne buterbrodom edynym, abo Navishcho Maidanu Zhinocha sotnia." *Ukrainska Pravda*, February 5. https://life.pravda.com.ua/society/2014/02/5/151445/.
[76] UINP interview with Anhelina Husar, October 15, 2014.

Nonviolent Action

high-level government officials who obstructed Ukraine's European integration. "Our main task was to bring Maidan to the homes of the powerholders," said Kateryna Kuvita. "When Maidan was happening on Independence Square, it did not bother them so much. But when we drove to their homes, made public their home addresses, it made them very angry."[77] On December 29, 2013, for example, a caravan of cars and bikes drove to Mezhyhiria, the main presidential residence, and dropped off an empty coffin near the president's palace, implying an end to Yanukovych's political career.[78] Another caravan of over 200 cars picketed the mansion of Viktor Medvedchuk, former head of the presidential administration and the Kremlin's ally, in January 2014.[79] In response, the police placed AutoMaidan activists on a watch list. If captured, activists were subject to severe police beatings and put on trial. On top, thugs set fire to activists' vehicles, which imposed constraints on the initiative's daily operations.

Kateryna Butko joined AutoMaidan in early December, and after spending two days in the passenger seat, she quickly realized that she could have a bigger impact by organizing original actions (*aktsii*). Butko recalled how activists tried to outwit the traffic police through deception:

We announced that we would drive to one person, but in reality, we drove to someone else. When we organized one of our last car caravans prior to the February events and drove to [Viktor] Pshonka, we announced that we would drive to [Vitalii] Zakharchenko. We did send 3–4 cars to Zakharchenko, and all the local police met them there. Meanwhile, we drove to Pshonka whose house was located in another part of the city. And for a long time, the police cars that followed us could not figure out where we were heading.[80]

Concurrently, some pedestrians participated in a lying-down protest. In December 2013, tens of men and women laid down on the sidewalk near the entrance to the Prosecutor's Office to demand the release of protesters detained that month. Some activists affiliated with the Democratic Alliance held a poster with the following message, "If you trampled on the law, trample down on citizens of Ukraine."[81] Indeed, most judges ignored protesters, stepping over people to enter the building. In turn, protesters chanted *Han'ba!* (Shame!), shaming judges for lack of judicial independence.

Many women were quite vocal in condemning the deployment of violence. For example, Tetiana Mazur, director of Amnesty International in Ukraine,

---

[77] UINP interview with Kateryna Kuvita, September 23, 2015.
[78] Ukrainska Pravda. 2013. "Do Yanukovycha u Mezhyhiria ide truna." December 29. www.pravda.com.ua/news/2013/12/29/7008813/.
[79] Radio Svoboda. 2014. "Avtomaidan 'naikhav' na Yanukovycha i Medvedchuka." January 12. www.radiosvoboda.org/a/25227774.html.
[80] UINP interview with Kateryna Butko, October 3, 2014.
[81] Ukrainska Pravda. 2013. "Pid viknamy Pshonky lezhachyi protest, pidtiahuiut Berkut." December 6. www.pravda.com.ua/news/2013/12/6/7005077.

believed that the movement's strength lay in its adherence to nonviolence.[82] In the winter of 2013, there erupted an intense public debate about the demolition of statues of leaders of the Communist Party of the Soviet Union. On December 8, a group of men toppled the statue of Vladimir Lenin in downtown Kyiv and smashed it into pieces, triggering the so-called Leninopad – removal of monuments to Lenin – across the country.[83] Ruslana Lyzhychko openly criticized this type of action:

> We do not want to be far from the European standards and principles of humanism. At a time when our peaceful initiative requires the cohesion and unity of everyone around Maidan and peaceful protests for the resignation of the criminal government, the demolition of monuments and calls for aggression are nothing but a movement in the opposite direction from European integration and humane society.[84]

In addition, data from oral history projects reveal that many male protesters opposed the deployment of violence against their opponents. Specifically, the Civic Sector of Euromaidan championed the idea that it was impossible to win with the use of force. "First, it immediately places the protest outside the bounds of the law, and second, it is absolutely unfeasible in terms of resources to fight with the use of force against the army and the police," said Andrii Meakovskyi, an activist affiliated with the Civic Sector of Euromaidan. "That's why we made every effort, took any action to prevent such a turn of events."[85] However, proponents of nonviolent action could not check the emergence of a radical flank. A violent clash between protesters and the police that erupted in January 2014 marked a new phase in mass mobilization. Some men, especially those without prior military service, grappled with the new reality:

> There was some perplexity and lack of understanding: you have been going to a peaceful protest for two months, and it is unclear how to participate in this [type of action]. But on the other hand, it is clear that it is irreversible. I got used to tear gas, [the fact that] one needs to cover up, look for a respirator ... With every new visit [to Maidan], you get used to it, and it seems to you that it is a normal course of events. Under these circumstances, it is necessary to look for ways in which you can be helpful.[86]

Police violence against peaceful protesters, along with the parliament's adoption of repressive laws on January 16, 2014, caused the rise of a radical

---

[82] NaUKMA interview with Tetiana Mazur. Qtd. from *Maidan. Svidchennia. Kyiv, 2013–2014 roky*, p. 129.
[83] Serhii Plokhii. 2014. *Goodbye Lenin: A Memory Shift in Revolutionary Ukraine*. Cambridge: Ukrainian Research Institute, Harvard University, https://gis.huri.harvard.edu/leninfall.
[84] Ruslana Lyzhychko. 2013. "My ne khochemo, shchob Tvorcha Revoluitsiia peretvorylasia u pohromu." *Ukrainska Pravda* [blog entry], December 8. https://blogs.pravda.com.ua/authors/ruslana/52a4c2e3b8b13.
[85] NaUKMA interview with Andrii Meakovskyi. Qtd. from *Maidan. Svidchennia. Kyiv, 2013–2014 roky*, p. 147.
[86] NaUKMA interview with Andrii Ostrikov. Qtd. from *Maidan. Svidchennia. Kyiv, 2013–2014 roky*, p. 349.

Nonviolent Action

flank and entailed a shift in mass perceptions about the effectiveness of nonviolent methods. According to Pavlo Kucher, an eyewitness to a protesters' clash with the police on January 19, 2014, "the first Molotov cocktails were tossed somewhat gingerly."[87] But both sides appeared to have reached a point of no return. There was a growing understanding among activists that the ruling elite would not stop at anything to decimate the protest movement. Even self-proclaimed pacifists realized that the likelihood of a peaceful turnover of power was rapidly evaporating. For example, Kateryna Overchenko, a member of the Civic Sector of Euromaidan, changed her perspective on the use of radical tactics after she witnessed the violent police beating of young women on November 30.

> Actually, I am a pacifist. I was always against violence, against war. But I cannot be a pacifist now when a rifle, a baton, a grenade, or something else is directed at you. I think that I was not the only one who underwent this transformation. I distributed peaceful leaflets, but I understood that such [nonviolent] methods would not work.[88]

Data from oral history projects indicate that the attitudes of many male protesters also changed from the total rejection of violence to the acceptance of radical tactics as the most viable method for attaining the movement's goals and removing the incumbent from office. Petro Didula, for example, recalled how the violent events of January 18–19 had a profound impact on his mode of participation in the revolution.

> I have changed dramatically on Maidan. At the early phase [of events] on Hrushevskoho, I was a pacifist, [Vitali] Klitschko's call for the non-use of force was very close and lucid to me. I believed that it was possible to endure, to achieve something by virtue of such a method as the steadfast, daily standing on Maidan ... And what do I do [on January 18]? I put down my camera, which cost 6,000 dollars, simply put it down on the pavement ... and I start digging up cobblestones, and some tranquility, peace of mind descends upon me ... I could not throw stones. But I could tear up cobblestones ... There was a synthesis [within the protest movement], wherein everyone could realize oneself.[89]

Similarly, Yuliian, a philosophy alumnus at NaUKMA, observed the transformative impact of state repression on modes of citizens' resistance to the regime. There emerged a near consensus that the use of violent tactics was necessary to counteract police killings of protesters.

> At the beginning, there was a confrontation between proponents of radical tactics and people who came to Maidan as if it were a festival, singing Christmas songs (*koliadky*)

---

[87] NaUKMA interview with Pavlo Kucheriv. Qtd. from *Maidan. Svidchennia. Kyiv, 2013–2014 roky*, p. 317.

[88] NaUKMA interview with Kateryna Overchenko. Qtd. from *Maidan. Svidchennia. Kyiv, 2013–2014 roky*, p. 222.

[89] NaUKMA interview with Petro Didula. Qtd. from *Maidan. Svidchennia. Kyiv, 2013–2014 roky*, p. 381–82.

and lighting up flashlights. After the first deaths [of protesters], these arguments were over. There was simply the will to go until the end.[90]

The findings presented in the chapter reveal the limitations of nonviolent action in bringing down the authoritarian incumbent who is willing to use live ammunition against peaceful protesters. Under such conditions, regime opponents are faced with a choice of surrendering to the coercive apparatus or modifying their tactics to defeat the regime. Data from the oral history projects show that most Ukrainian activists were determined to fight until the incumbent's removal from power.

SELF-DEFENSE OF MAIDAN

The Self-Defense of Maidan (*Samooborona Maidanu*) was an integral part of civil resistance. Following the ruthless police beating of peaceful protesters on November 30, people started forming self-defense units (*sotni*), comprised of approximately 100 people.[91] Modeled on the military organization in the Zaporozhian Sich, each *sotnia* was divided into a group of ten (*rii*), and a platoon (*chota*) consisted of 30–40 people within a self-defense unit. By late December, seventeen sotni were responsible for guarding the Kyiv-based encampment.[92] In February 2014, Andrii Parubii, the commandant of the encampment on Independence Square and head of Samooborona, announced that Samooborona enlisted 12,000 people in thirty-nine sotni.[93] Bracing for an escalation in police violence, Parubii urged citizens to form self-defense units throughout Ukraine so that they could not only defend the main encampment in the capital city but also transform the whole country into Maidan. According to Andrii Levus, Parubii's deputy, each member of the Self-Defense was a "revolutionary political soldier."[94] Among the members of self-defense units were veterans of the Soviet war in Afghanistan. "We have become a live shield between the authorities, riot police, and the people so that blood, the blood of our children, is not spilled," said the war veteran Vasyl Hryhorenko.[95]

---

[90] NaUKMA interview with Yuliian. Qtd. from *Maidan. Svidchennia. Kyiv, 2013–2014 roky*, p. 578.
[91] The Ukrainian-language word *sotnia* literally means a hundred. *Centuria* is a Latin term for a legion in the Roman army, consisting of approximately 100 soldiers. In US military, a squad consists of 10 soldiers, a platoon consists of a few dozen soldiers, and a company has between several dozen and 200 soldiers. For details, see US Department of Defense. "Military Units: Army." www.defense.gov/Multimedia/Experience/Military-Units/Army.
[92] Levko Stek. 2013. "Samooborona Evromaidanu: Zavdannia, Struktura, Metody Roboty." *Radio Svoboda*, December 21. www.radiosvoboda.org/a/25207800.html.
[93] UNIAN. 2014. "U strukturi Samooborony Maidanu vzhe diiut 39 soten – Parubii." February 2. www.unian.ua/politics/881819-u-strukturi-samooboroni-maydanu-vje-diyut-39-soten-parubiy.html.
[94] Ibid.
[95] Maria Danilova. 2013. "Bonfires, Borscht, Humor in Kiev Protest Camp." *AP News*, December 7. https://apnews.com/article/2086086704694c8b918c28a93844c9be.

Self-Defense of Maidan

Women, albeit outnumbered by men, actively participated in the self-defense of Maidan. Some women joined men-led *sotni*. For example, there existed a women's *chota* (platoon) within the 16th sotnia formed by the civic movement Vidsich. Liubov Halan, an undergraduate student at NaUKMA and a Vidsich activist, along with other members of the women's platoon, agitated among the security forces to convince the internal troops of Ukraine to withdraw their involvement in a crackdown on protesters.[96] Khrystia Hrunyk, coordinator of the Lviv-based branch of Vidsich, came to Kyiv and became the head of the night guard at one of the barricades. Hrunyk managed a group of mostly male guards:

It is my responsibility to keep an eye on the guards so that they are always at their checkpoint, behave properly, and do not drink [alcohol]. I deal with all the unforeseen situations – when a car might enter, bring something, or take something away. Of course, I also make sure that guys do not get fatigued – eat, sleep, and feel well.[97]

A few women drew on their experiences within a man-led self-defense unit to establish their own. For example, Anna Kovalenko first joined the 11th sotnia and later established the 39th women's squad (*zhinocha sotnia*).[98] Members of the women's squad participated in violent clashes with the police on February 19–21, 2014, and provided first aid for the wounded.[99] Kovalenko was convinced that women should use whatever means necessary to bring down the current regime:

After [police] violence, all of us understood [that] something was wrong and we should decide: Can we live with this police reality, when the police can just beat up [people] whenever it wants? Or should we fight the system? And fighting the system meant going to the end. So we decided to go until the end.[100]

---

[96] Hromadske. 2014. "Kerivnyk komendatury samooborony Maidanu Andrii Levus ta uchasnytsia zhinochoi choty 16 sotni Liubov Halan v studii *Hromadske.TV*." January 6. https://youtu.be/1YW5fb4Bogw?t=62.

[97] Vasylyna Duman. 2014. "Na tretii barykadi. Yak tenditna divchyna kerye Nichnoiu vartoiu (spetsproekt Mekhanizm Maidanu)." *Texty*, January 13. https://texty.org.ua/articles/50989/Na_tretij_barykadi_Jak_tenditna_divchyna_keruje-50989.

[98] The English-language use of the phrase "women's squad" is somewhat misleading in describing the size of such a unit during the Revolution of Dignity. In line with US military terminology, the phrase "women's company" is more accurate to denote a women's self-defense unit.

[99] Hromadske. 2014. "Zhinky, iaki proishly cherez Maidan, prodovzhuiut borotbu u hariachykh tochkakh Ukrainy, – sotnyk Anna Kovalenko." June 12. https://hromadske.radio/podcasts/intervyu/zhinki-yaki-proyshli-cherez-maydan-prodovzhuyut-borotbu-u-garyachih-tochkah-ukrayini-sotnik-anna-kovalenko.

[100] Qtd. from Olga Oliker and Jeffrey Mankoff. 2017. "Of Revolutions, Old and New." In *Russian Roulette* [Podcast Program]. Episode No. 25, March 10. Washington, DC: The Center for Strategic and International Studies. https://soundcloud.com/csis-57169780/of-revolutions-old-and-new.

The women's squad named after Olha Kobylianska was formed in February 2014 to unite women based upon the principles of solidarity, sisterhood, and self-respect. In a public manifesto, the women's squad declared its belief that "women do not help make a revolution, they are making a revolution."[101] The women's squad sought to counteract any manifestation of sexism within the protest movement and support women's initiatives during Euromaidan. In addition, feminists stressed their commitment to nonviolent methods of resistance:

> The women's squad uses in its work education methods, methods of nonviolent resistance, and, in the most extreme cases, self-defense with a minimum impact.[102]

Upon the initiative of Olena Shevchenko, master of sports in sambo and freestyle wrestling, the women's squad named after Olha Kobylianska organized self-defense workshops to build women's physical and emotional strength.[103] As a prominent LGBTQ+ activist and head of the civic organization Insight, Shevchenko was previously involved in the organization of street actions in support of LGBTQ+ rights in Ukraine.[104] According to the civic activist and sociologist Nina Potarska, the women's squad brought together women of different backgrounds: "women athletes, lawyers, human rights activists, simply women who came to Maidan [square] and did not find their place there because of [facing] an alternative of either being in the kitchen or putting on a helmet and going to the barricades."[105] Despite the military connotations associated with the term *sotnia* and the organization of self-defense workshops, the women's squad was intent on using nonviolent methods of resistance in their struggle for social change.

THE IMPACT OF GENDER NORMS ON MODES OF WOMEN'S ACTIVISM

It is reasonable to assume that dominant gender norms influence how women and men participate in a revolution. Specifically, a traditional gender-based division of labor relegates women to the kitchen and the hospital ward, while men are expected to form the frontline on the barricades. Indeed, media reports indicate that some male revolutionaries attempted to reproduce a gender-based

---

[101] Zhinocha sotnia imeni Olhy Kobylianskoi. 2014. *Live Journal*, February 17. https://feminism-ua.livejournal.com/958347.html.
[102] Ibid.
[103] Anastasiia Melnychenko. 2014. "Navishcho Ukraini Zhinocha sotnia?" Heinrich-Böll Stiftung, March 25. https://ua.boell.org/uk/2014/03/25/navishcho-ukrayini-zhinocha-sotnya.
[104] See, for example, Council of LGBT Organizations of Ukraine. 2013. *LGBT-Vektor Ukrainy: Stanovyshche LGBT v Ukraini (lystopad 2011 – 2012)*. Kyiv: Center Nash Svit. www.gay.org.ua/publications/lgbt_ukraine_2012-u.pdf.
[105] Anastasiia Moskvychova. 2014. "Zhinky na Maidani: Abo kukhnia, abo barykady?" *Radio Svoboda*, February 4. www.radiosvoboda.org/a/25252319.html.

The Impact of Gender Norms on Modes of Women's Activism 125

division of labor within the protest movement. The display of such signs as "Woman, please clean up if you see the mess, it will please the male revolutionary" or "Entry to the Ukrainian House is allowed only for men with a special permit and for women with a smile" signified the presence of patriarchal views among movement participants.[106] In line with this perspective, a high level of women's involvement in food preparation and medical services might be interpreted as a reproduction of traditional gender norms inside the encampment. However, it should be kept in mind that many women pushed back against such a rigid division within the protest movement. Furthermore, data from in-depth interviews reveal a variety of reasons for women's involvement in certain types of activities.

A close inspection of women's motivations for their involvement in such a stereotypically feminine activity as the provision of food vividly illustrates the multiplicity of factors associated with a woman's mode of engagement in the revolution. Some women accepted dominant social norms and wholeheartedly devoted themselves to preparing hot meals in the encampment's field kitchens. Others considered cooking as an instrument for circumventing state repression. For example, several Kyiv-based students who faced the threat of expulsion for skipping classes in broad daylight opted to volunteer in the kitchen at night.[107] Additionally, some women viewed cooking as a viable method for combining their participation in the revolution with full-time employment or education. For example, cooking was an optimum choice for balancing employment and civic engagement for Olena Sychenko and her colleagues:

When we realized that it was not a rally for a day or two, that it would stay for a long time, we as business people sat down and began to discuss how we could help Maidan [movement] so that it would last as long as possible. Since we were all young, we did not have a whole lot of financial resources. But we could donate our time. We had daytime jobs and we tried to quickly finish our work and then cook food. From the second half of the day onwards, we cooked food and brought it to Maidan [square].[108]

Another major factor that influenced women's mode of participation was access to certain resources. For example, the work schedule, along with car ownership, was a key factor for Kateryna Kuvita's decision to join AutoMaidan.

The schedule of my being on Maidan was as follows: I went home after work in the evening, quickly changed clothes, and then rushed to Maidan until 2 a.m. or 3 a.m. And this very schedule (a chance to have a quick rest in the evening) soon brought me to AutoMaidan. I could not just come to Maidan, bring my body there and do nothing constructive, it was not interesting for me. I had a car, and in two weeks, once AutoMaidan was formed, I joined it.[109]

---

[106] Virtosu. "Ne buterbrodom edynym, abo navishcho Maidanu Zhinocha sotnia".
[107] UINP interview with Viktoriia Kochubei, February 16, 2015.
[108] UINP interview with Olena Sychenko, August 13, 2015.
[109] UINP interview with Kateryna Kuvita, September 23, 2015.

Women's prior professional experience served as a catalyst for their involvement in the protest movement and influenced the mode of their participation in the revolution. In particular, healthcare professionals put their medical training to use by joining on-site medical stations and offering urgent medical care for the injured. Likewise, many female lawyers offered pro bono legal aid for protesters. In addition, female journalists and NGO activists put their professional skills to use by developing crowdsourcing initiatives and counteracting Russia's propaganda machine. Under these circumstances, occupational segregation – the prevalence of women in certain professions – affected modes of women's engagement in the protest movement.

An invocation of traditional gender norms – the men's imperative to protect women – was most frequently articulated during periods of an escalation in police violence. In early December 2013, Parubii estimated that the self-defense units could withstand a police attack for at least 5–15 minutes, which would be sufficient for the evacuation of women and the arrival of additional forces in support of the movement.[110] On December 9, Parubii urged men to advance to the edge of the encampment bordering Mykhailivska Street and guard the barricades, while women and children were asked to move to a safer location.[111]

In turn, women's contestation of dominant gender norms gave rise to women's squads. "The women's squad was formed to create the optimum conditions for women's activism on Maidan," stated Nadia Parfan, a film director and civic activist. "It was important for us to find a way for each woman to get involved in the Maidan movement as she wants and as she can."[112] Many women refused to act within the parameters of the "caretaking" roles and pursued alternative modes of activism. Furthermore, an escalation in police violence and the radicalization of the protest movement brought some women into self-defense units. Yet, the emergence of women's squads stirred a debate about the extent to which such action challenged the prevailing gender norms or reinforced the militarization of the protest movement.[113]

---

[110] Oleksandr Mikhelson. 2013. "Plan oborony Maidanu: 'afhantsi' i 7 tysiach u rezervi." *Ukrainskyi tyzhden*, December 5. https://tyzhden.ua/plan-oborony-majdanu-afhantsi-j-7-tysiach-u-rezervi.

[111] Interfax-Ukraine. 2013. "Parubiy Urges Men to Guard Barricades, Asks Women and Children to Move to Tent Camp on Maidan." December 9. https://en.interfax.com.ua/news/general/180304.html.

[112] Melnychenko. "Navishcho Ukraini Zhinocha sotnia".

[113] On this debate, see Maria Mayerchyk. 2014. "Do 8 bereznia: Pro pereplavku smysliv." *Krytyka*, March. https://krytyka.com/ua/articles/do-8-bereznya-pro-pereplavku-smysliv; Tamara Martsenyuk. "Do 8 bereznia: Zhinocha sotnia abo pravo na smysly (Vidpovid na stattiu Marii Mayerchyk)." *Krytyka*, March. https://krytyka.com/ua/articles/do-8-bereznya-zhinocha-sotnya-abo-pravo-na-smysly-vidpovid-na-stattyu-mariyi.

CONCLUSION

In sum, women performed a variety of critical functions during the Revolution of Dignity, which is consistent with a hybrid model of women's participation in a revolution. Women's repertoire of contentious collective action did not boil down to a binary choice between standing on the barricades and making sandwiches for male revolutionaries. Moreover, female activists not only implemented critical tasks but also shaped the development of movement tactics. Women assumed leadership roles in various civic initiatives, including the Art Squad, AutoMaidan, the Euromaidan SOS, the Night Guard, the Hospital Guard, and the People's Hospital. As noted by Olena Podobed-Frankivska, "Maidan [movement] turned out to be a living organism with a cluster of services that worked really well."[114] Every deed no matter how small or big sustained the movement's survival.[115] The lawyer Olena Nozhovnik, for example, observed how everyone tried to contribute to the liberation struggle in their own way. "There were people with different backgrounds, and everyone did whatever they could," Nozhovnik said. "But the most important thing is that they came out, they expressed it [their demand for freedom]."[116]

Data from oral history projects uncover a broad spectrum of factors associated with women's involvement in certain types of activities. A match between women's professional skills and the movement's needs frequently affected women's decisions to concentrate on volunteer work in a specific domain. In response to the movement's urgent needs, some women switched from one activity to another. In addition to working as a journalist and organizing a literary marathon, Olena Maksymenko, for example, volunteered to pick up garbage, distribute tea, bring tires, and tore up cobblestones at various points during the revolution. "I would just come to Maidan and try to understand what the most urgent issue was."[117] Moreover, in many cases, the performance of the so-called caretaking tasks was driven by the desire to combine activism with full-time employment.

One of the findings that emerges from oral history data is that most women and men favored the idea of nonviolent action. However, the disproportionate use of force against peaceful protesters backfired. Rather than crushing the protest movement, police violence caused public outrage and raised the stakes of citizens' opposition to the current regime. In particular, the police shooting of armless protesters triggered a shift in methods of resistance and a reconsideration of the utility of radical tactics. A call for action was succinctly summarized in a popular slogan, "No – to the discotheque, yes – to the revolution"

---

[114] UINP interview with Olena Podobed-Frankivska, August 21, 2014.
[115] On this point, see, for example, UINP interview with Valentyna Davydenko, December 1, 2014.
[116] UINP interview with Olena Nozhovnik, September 22, 2015.
[117] NaUKMA interview with Olena Maksymenko. Qtd. from *Maidan. Svidchennia. Kyiv, 2013–2014 roky*, p. 468.

(*Dyskotetsi – ni, revoliutsii – tak*). "We saw that people gathered [on Maidan]. But we understood that one would not change anything by just standing and singing," said Solomiia Farion, an activist of the Youth Nationalist Congress.[118]

Nonetheless, given the heavy physical presence of male protesters during the most violent phases of public confrontation with the ruling elite, women's participation in the revolution might have been less visible than men's in the mass media. The takeaway message is that scholars should look beyond the barricades to uncover different modes of citizens' engagement in a contemporary revolution. Scores of Ukrainian women fought for political change by working on a laptop in their homes or taking phone calls in a volunteer hub. In the aftermath of protest events, many women continued to press for democratic development and gender equality through their engagement in various civic initiatives and their participation in the Russia–Ukraine war.

---

[118] UINP interview with Solomiia Farion, May 12, 2015.

5

Gender Outcomes of the Revolution and the Russia–Ukraine War

Participation in the Revolution of Dignity has become a pathway to women's engagement in domestic politics, civil society, and the Armed Forces of Ukraine. In response to Russia's military aggression against Ukraine in 2014, many activists became involved in crowdsourcing efforts to provide supplies for the cash-strapped army. Others joined volunteer battalions and fought on the frontlines. The medical battalion *Hospitallers*, for example, was formed by eighteen-year-old Yana Zinkevych who participated in Euromaidan and subsequently joined a volunteer battalion in eastern Ukraine. She conceived the idea of organizing a group of volunteer paramedics during her service on the frontline, and the battalion's name was inspired by a chaplain's story about a religious military order founded in Jerusalem in the eleventh century and known for its humanitarian work.[1] In July 2019, Zinkevych was elected to the national parliament on the list of the political party European Solidarity and became the head of the interim parliamentary committee on veteran affairs.[2]

This chapter seeks to trace the impact of women's participation in Euromaidan and the ensuing Russia–Ukraine war on gender equality in contemporary Ukraine.[3] Drawing upon social movement literature,[4] the analysis distinguishes several types of outcomes: (1) political outcomes, measured by legal changes and women's representation in different branches of government;

---

[1] Dmytro Lykhovyi and Lesia Shovkun. 2019. "Yana Zinkevych: 'Ztsipliuiu zuby i idu dali'. Velyke interv'iu z komandyrom 'Hospital'eriv'." *Novynarnia*, July 18. https://novynarnia.com/2019/07/18/yana-zinkevych.

[2] Dzerkalo tyzhnia. 2019. "Zinkevych ocholyt komisiiu z pytan veteraniv." August 26. https://zn.ua/ukr/POLITICS/zinkevich-ocholit-komisiyu-z-pitan-veteraniv-321678_.html.

[3] The empirical analysis presented in this chapter focuses on the period from 2014 to 2021.

[4] For an overview, see Lorenzo Bosi, Marco Giugni, and Katrin Uba, eds. 2019. *The Consequences of Social Movements*. New York: Cambridge University Press.

(2) economic outcomes, measured by unemployment rate, the gender wage gap, and occupational segregation; and (3) cultural outcomes, measured by mass attitudes toward gender equality and women's empowerment. Using statistical data, this chapter compares the level of gender equality before and after the Revolution of Dignity. Consistent with a hybrid model of women's participation in a revolution, this chapter registers various degrees of progress in different spheres. In addition, based on data from oral history projects and media interviews with female activists, this chapter illustrates the biographical consequences of women's participation in Euromaidan.

An empirical analysis of gender outcomes is methodologically challenging for several reasons. First, it is necessary to distinguish between aftermaths – immediate effects – and legacies – long-term patterns associated with a revolution.[5] It might take several decades to detect vestiges of profound transformations in society. Second, empirical analysis is compounded by the temporal proximity of the Revolution of Dignity (November 2013–February 2014) and the Russia–Ukraine war (February 2014–present). Regardless of the passage of time, wars tend to have more pronounced effects on society. At least, this chapter catalogs cross-time patterns in gender equality, which can provide an empirical basis for a more robust estimation of the relationship between revolutionary events and women's empowerment in contemporary Ukraine.

LEGAL FRAMEWORK

Article 24 of the Constitution of Ukraine adopted in 1996 posits that "citizens have equal rights and freedoms and are equal before law."[6] The Constitution further states that gender equality is guaranteed by granting women and men equal opportunities in various domains. In line with constitutional provisions, the national parliament passed the Law on the provision of equal rights and opportunities for women and men in the wake of the Orange Revolution in September 2005.[7] To implement these legal provisions, the Cabinet of Ministers adopted a four-year state program on the advancement of gender equality in Ukrainian society under Yushchenko's presidency in 2006.[8] The Cabinet of Ministers under Yanukovych's presidency adopted a revised version of the state program in 2013, removing the phrase "gender equality" from the

---

[5] On this distinction, see Mark Beissinger. 2022. *The Revolutionary City*Princeton: Princeton University Press, p. 363.
[6] Constitution of Ukraine. June 28, 1996. https://zakon.rada.gov.ua/laws/show/254k/96-вр#Text.
[7] Law on the provision of equal rights and opportunities for women and men (*Zakon Ukrainy Pro zabespechennia rivnykh prav ta mozhlyvostei zhinok i cholovikiv*). No. 2866-IV. September 8, 2005. https://zakon.rada.gov.ua/laws/show/2866-15#Text.
[8] State program on the advancement of gender equality in Ukrainian society for the period until 2010 (*Postanova Pro zatverdzhennia Derzhavnoi programy z utverdzhennia hendernoi rivnosti v ukrainskomu suspilstvi na period do 2010 roku*). No. 1834. December 27, 2006. https://zakon.rada.gov.ua/laws/show/1834-2006-n#Text.

Legal Framework

title of the law and instead emphasizing the government's efforts to combat sex-based discrimination.[9] The next state program on gender equality adopted under Poroshenko's presidency in April 2018 declared the government's commitment to "European standards of equality."[10]

The Orange Revolution set into motion the adoption of laws aimed at combating gender discrimination in the economic sphere. In compliance with the 2005 Law on the provision of equal rights and opportunities for women and men, Verkhovna Rada introduced amendments to the Labor Code in 2008.[11] The 2012 Law on measures to prevent and combat discrimination in Ukraine laid out key principles of nondiscrimination.[12] Amendments to the law adopted in May 2014 broadened the definitions of discrimination and indirect discrimination.[13] According to Article 184 of the Labor Code, for example, it is prohibited to deny employment or lower wages to women on the sole basis of their pregnancy or having a child under the age of three. Yet, pregnant women and women with little children continue to face discrimination in the labor market.

To remedy the problem, the notion of gender equality was gradually incorporated in collective agreements signed by representatives of employers and trade unions. The 2010 general agreement (*Heneralna uhoda*) recommended that collective agreements between an employer and a labor union should guarantee gender equality for employees.[14] Following protracted negotiations

---

[9] State program on the provision of equal rights and opportunities for women and men for the period until 2016 (*Postanova Pro zatverdzhennia Derzhavnoi programy zabespechennia rivnykh prav ta mozhlyvostei zhinok ta chilovikiv na period do 2016 roku*). No. 717. September 26, 2013. https://zakon.rada.gov.ua/laws/show/717-2013-n#Text

[10] State social program on the provision of equal rights and opportunities for women and men for the period until 2021 (*Postanova Pro zatverdzhennia Derzhavnoi sotsialnoi programy zabespechennia rivnykh prav ta mozhlyvostei zhinok ta chilovikiv na period do 2021 roku*). No. 273. April 11, 2018. https://zakon.rada.gov.ua/laws/show/273-2018-n#Text

[11] Law on amendments to some legislative acts of Ukraine in regard to the adoption of the Law of Ukraine on the provision of equal rights and opportunities for women and men (*Pro vnesennia zmin do deiakykh zakonodavchikh aktiv Ukrainy u zviazku z pryiniattiam Zakonu Ukrainy pro zabespechennia rivnykh prav ta mozhlyvostei zhinok i cholovikiv*). No. 274-VI. April 15, 2008. https://zakon.rada.gov.ua/laws/show/274-17#Text.

[12] Law on measures to prevent and combat discrimination in Ukraine (*Pro zasady zapobihannia ta protydii dyskryminatsii v Ukraini*) No. 5207-VI. September 6, 2012. https://zakon.rada.gov.ua/laws/show/5207-17.

[13] On amendments to some legislative acts of Ukraine pertaining to the prevention and combat against discrimination (*Pro vnesennia zmin do deiakykh zakonodavchykh aktiv Ukrainy shchodo zapobihannia ta protydii dyskryminatsii*). No. 1263-VII. May 13, 2014. https://zakon.rada.gov.ua/laws/show/1263-18#n11.

[14] General agreement on the regulation of key principles and norms regarding the implementation of socioeconomic policy and labor relations in Ukraine for 2010–2012 (*Heneralna uhoda pro rehuliuvannia osnovnykh pryntsypiv i norm realizatsii sotsialno-ekonomichnoi polityky i trudovykh vidnosyn v Ukraini na 2010–2012 roky*). November 9, 2010. https://zakon.rada.gov.ua/laws/show/n0006120-10#Text.

over minimum wages,[15] the general agreement signed in September 2016 dropped a reference to gender equality.[16] More recently, however, the 2019 general agreement recommended that employers should conduct gender audits and develop plans for gender equality.[17]

Another piece of legislature pertaining to women's participation in the labor market was spearheaded by Iryna Suslova, leader of the civic initiative "Woman Can Do Everything," and supported by the acting Minister of Health Ulana Suprun in October 2017.[18] The Ministry of Health of Ukraine abolished the Decree No. 256 that banned women's employment in 450 occupations deemed hazardous to women's reproductive health.[19] Effective 2017, women could take up a wider range of jobs in such industries as chemical, copper, metallurgical, shipbuilding, and transportation. Yet, the Decree No. 241, banning women to lift weight larger than 7 kgs (15.4 pounds) and thus prohibiting employment in certain occupations, remained intact.[20]

Meanwhile, women engaged in the Russia–Ukraine war demanded women's access to combat positions in the Armed Forces of Ukraine. The government's adoption of the national action plan for the implementation of the United Nations Security Council's Resolution (UNSCR) 1325 on women, peace, and security in February 2016 served as a catalyst for greater provision of women's rights in the Ukrainian military.[21] The Cabinet of Ministers of Ukraine adopted

---

[15] Federation of Trade Unions of Ukraine. 2016. "Pozytsiia profspilok. Heneralna uhoda mae buty ne kamenem spotykannia, a novoiu iakistiu trudovykh vidnosyn." March 17. https://fpsu.org.ua/nasha-borotba/9785-pozitsiya-profspilok-generalna-ugoda-mae-buti-ne-kamenem-spotikannya.

[16] General agreement on the regulation of key principles and norms regarding the implementation of socioeconomic policy and labor relations in Ukraine (*Heneralna uhoda pro rehuliuvannia osnovnykh pryntsypiv i norm realizatsii sotsialno-ekonomichnoi polityky i trudovykh vidnosyn v Ukraini roky*). August 23, 2016. https://zakon.rada.gov.ua/laws/show/n0001120-16#Text.

[17] General agreement on the regulation of key principles and norms regarding the implementation of socioeconomic policy and labor relations in Ukraine for 2019–2021 (*Heneralna uhoda pro rehuliuvannia osnovnykh pryntsypiv i norm realizatsii sotsialno-ekonomichnoi polityky i trudovyh vidnosyn v Ukraini na 2019–2021 roky*). April 14, 2019. https://zakon.rada.gov.ua/laws/show/n0001120-19#Text.

[18] UNIAN. 2017. "Suslova: MOZ hotovyi skasuvaty nakaz pro 450 zaboronenykh dlia zhinok profesii." June 13. www.unian.ua/society/1972651-moz-gotoviy-skasuvati-nakaz-pro-450-zaboronenih-dlya-jinok-profesiy.html.

[19] Ministry of Health of Ukraine. "Decree on abolishing the decree of the Ministry of Health of Ukraine of 29 December 1993 No. 256" (*Nakaz pro vyznannia takym, shcho vtratyv chynnist nakazu Ministerstva okhorony zdorovia Ukrainy vid 29 hrudnia 1993 roku No. 256*). No. 1254. October 13, 2017. https://zakon.rada.gov.ua/laws/show/z1508-17#Text.

[20] Ministry of Health of Ukraine. "Decree on the approval of norms on lifting and moving heavy objects by women" (*Nakaz pro zatverdzhennia Hranychnykh norm pidiimannia i peremishchennia vazhkykh rechei zhinkamy*). No. 241. December 12, 1993. https://zakon.rada.gov.ua/laws/show/z0194-93#Text.

[21] Cabinet of Ministers of Ukraine. "Decree on the adoption of a national action plan for the implementation of the UN Security Council Resolution 1325 'Women, Peace, Security' until 2020" (*Rozporiadzennia pro zatverdzhennia Natsionalnoho planu dii z vykonannia rezoliutsii*

Legal Framework

an updated version of the national action plan in October 2020.[22] Under Soviet-era laws, women could be officially employed as seamstresses, cooks, or nurses in the military. In reality, however, many women who joined volunteer battalions performed a far wider range of tasks on the frontlines in eastern Ukraine. Decree No. 292 of June 2016 allowed women to take up a number of combat positions and officially serve as scouts, snipers, or drivers of infantry fighting vehicles, to name a few.[23] Another decree of 2018 reaffirmed the idea of equal rights and opportunities for men and women serving in the military.[24] Furthermore, the Decree No. 26 of February 2020 allowed women to assume officer ranks in different branches of the military.[25] To advance through the military ranks, women also pressed for greater access to military education. In 2019, for example, female adolescents were allowed for the first time to apply for admission to the military lyceum.[26] In line with NATO's policy on the implementation of UNSCR 1325, the Armed Forces of Ukraine created a network of 400 gender advisors to provide guidance on how to integrate a gender perspective into the training, procedures, and operations of

---

Rady Bezpeky OON 1325 'Zhinky, myr, bezpeka' na period do 2020 roku). No. 113. February 24, 2016. www.kmu.gov.ua/npas/248861725.

[22] Cabinet of Ministers of Ukraine. "Decree on the adoption of a national action plan for the implementation of the UN Security Council Resolution 1325 'Women, Peace, Security' until 2025" (*Rozporiadzennia pro zatverdzhennia Natsionalnoho planu dii z vykonannia rezoliutsii Rady Bezpeky OON 1325 'Zhinky, myr, bezpeka' na period do 2025 roku*). No. 1544. October 28, 2020. https://zakon.rada.gov.ua/laws/show/1544-2020-%D1%80#Text.

[23] Ministry of Defense of Ukraine. "Decree on amendments to the temporary list of military occupations and full-time positions of private, sergeant and senior staff and servicewomen and tariff lists of the positions of the above-mentioned military personnel" (*Nakaz Pro zatverdzhennia zmin do tymchasovykh perelikiv viiskovo-oblikovykh spetsialnostei i shtatnykh posad riadovoho, serzhantskoho i starshynskoho sklady ta viiskovosluzhbovtsiv-zhinok i taryfnykh perelikiv posad vyshchezaznachenykh viiskovosluzhbovtsiv*). No. 292. June 3, 2016. https://zakon.rada.gov.ua/laws/show/z0880-16#n10.

[24] Verkhovna Rada. "Law on amendments to some laws of Ukraine as to the provision of equal rights and opportunities for women and men during their service in the Armed Forces of Ukraine and other military formations" (*Zakon Pro vnesennia zmin do deiiakykh zakoniv Ukrainy shchodo zabespechennia rivnykh prav i mozhlyvostei zhinok i cholovikiv pid chas prokhodzhennia viiskovoi sluzhby u Zbroinykh Sylakh Ukrainy ta inshykh viiskovykh formuvan*). No. 2523. September 6, 2018. https://zakon.rada.gov.ua/laws/show/2523-19#Text.

[25] Ministry of Defense of Ukraine. "Decree on amendments to the list of officer ranks that can be held by servicewomen" (*Nakaz Pro zatverdzhennia zmin do Pereliku viiskovykh posad osib ofitserskoho skladu, iaki mozhut buty zamishcheni viiskovosluzhbovtsiamy-zhinkamy*). No. 26. February 5, 2020. https://zakon.rada.gov.ua/laws/show/z0188-20#Text.

[26] Cabinet of Ministers of Ukraine. "Decree on amendments to the decree of the Cabinet of Ministers of Ukraine of 17 July 2003 No. 1087" (*Postanova Pro vnesennia zmin do postanovy Kabinetu Ministriv Ukrainy vid 17 lypnia 2003 roku No. 1087*). No. 486. May 15, 2019. https://zakon.rada.gov.ua/laws/show/486-2019-%D0%BF#n10.

the Ukrainian military.[27] These legal changes made the military more accessible for women.

Since 2014, legal changes were also underway in the realm of electoral politics. Article 4 of the 2015 Law on Local Elections stated that representation of either sex on the candidate list under the proportional system must be no less than 30 percent.[28] However, the passage of this law only three months from Election Day (in violation of the recommendation of the Venice Commission), as well as the lack of any sanctions for noncompliance with the gender quota, weakened its impact on the electoral process. In September 2015, the Central Election Commission of Ukraine acknowledged that the party's failure to meet the gender quota would not constitute a sufficient ground for a non-registration of candidates.[29] The 2020 Electoral Code raised the gender quota to 40 percent in localities with over 10,000 voting-age population and extended its application to both local and national elections.[30] According to the Electoral Code, no less than two of five candidates on a party list should be of a different sex (*stat'*).

Taken as a whole, a brief overview of legal changes in the post-2014 period indicates that there was modest progress in laying the legal groundwork for gender equality. Yet, incompetent implementation, ineffective monitoring, and arbitrary enforcement of existing laws might pose a threat to the advancement of women's rights in a polity with fragile democratic institutions. The remainder of the chapter explores actual changes in women's participation in politics and economics in the aftermath of Euromaidan and the Russia–Ukraine war.

WOMEN IN GOVERNMENT

Women's representation in the national parliament is a common indicator of female participation in political life. Using this benchmark, Ukraine made some headway. As seen in Figure 5.1, women made up less than 10 percent of parliamentarians during the first two decades of Ukraine's independence. Meanwhile, the percentage of women in Verkhovna Rada gradually increased

---

[27] Oleksandr Kozubenko. 2021. "Iak u Zbroinykh Sylakh realizovuiut natovskyi plan dii shchodo zhinok, myru, bezpeky." *ArmyInform*, November 23. https://armyinform.com.ua/2021/11/23/yak-u-zbrojnyh-sylah-realizovuyut-natovskyj-plan-dij-shhodo-zhinok-myru-bezpeky.

[28] Law on local elections (*Zakon Pro mistsevi vybory*). No. 595. July 14, 2015. https://zakon.rada.gov.ua/laws/show/595-19#Text.

[29] Central Election Commission of Ukraine. "Decree on the clarification of some provisions of the Law on local elections over the course of the registration of candidates" (*Postanova Pro roz'iasnennia shchodo zastosuvannia deiakykh polozhen Zakonu Ukrainy Pro mistsevi vybory pid chas reestratsii kandydativ u deputaty...*). No. 362. September 23, 2015. https://zakon.rada.gov.ua/laws/show/v0362359-15#Text.

[30] Electoral Code of Ukraine (*Vyborchyi kodeks Ukrainy*). June 17, 2020. https://zakon.rada.gov.ua/laws/show/396-20#n4129.

Women in Government

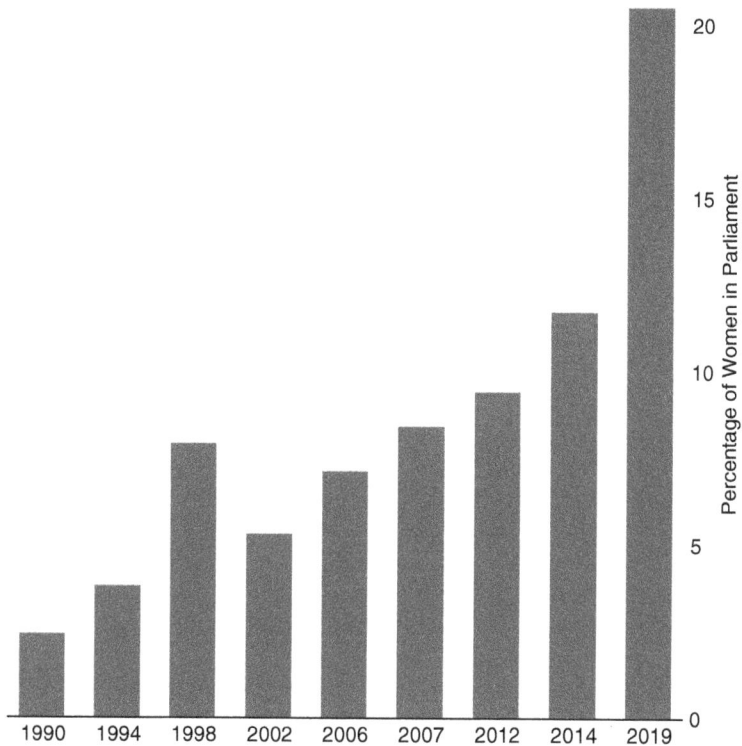

FIGURE 5.1 Women's representation in the national parliament.
Source: Inter-Parliamentary Union (IPU) Parline. 2020. *Historical Data on Women in National Parliaments*, https://data.ipu.org/historical-women.

from 3.8 in 1994 to 9.4 percent in 2012.[31] The first post-Euromaidan parliamentary elections held in October 2014 brought 11.7 percent of women in the national parliament. As a result of the 2019 snap elections, held three months after Volodymyr Zelensky's resounding win in the 2019 presidential election, women's representation in the national parliament reached 21 percent.

A palpable increase in the number of women in the ninth convocation of Verkhovna Rada might be attributed, in part, to the abovementioned changes in electoral laws and the emergence of such new political parties as Voice (*Holos*) and Servant of the People (*Sluha narodu*). The pro-European political party Voice was founded by Sviatoslav Vakarchuk, frontman of the popular rock band *Okean Elzy*, in 2019 and received twenty seats (5.8 percent) in the

---

[31] Inter-Parliamentary Union (IPU) Parline. 2020. *Historical Data on Women in National Parliaments*.https://data.ipu.org/historical-women.

parliament that year.³² In contrast, the near-virtual political party Servant of the People, which had neither active members nor regional offices two months prior to the 2019 parliamentary election, grabbed 43.1 percent of the vote due to Zelensky's savvy election campaign.³³ Women made up 45 percent of Voice deputies and 23 percent of Servant of the People deputies in 2019, compared to only 15 percent in Fatherland (*Batkivshchyna*) and 11 percent in the Opposition Platform "For Life."³⁴ Yet, political parties that claimed to focus on women's rights – the Solidarity of Women of Ukraine, Women for the Future, and Women of Ukraine – did not fare well at the ballot box. According to a nationally representative survey conducted in February 2020, 64 percent of the voting-age population concurred that Ukraine lacked a political party that adequately represented women's interests.³⁵

Women tend to gain larger representation in lower levels of legislative bodies. As a result of changes in electoral laws, women's representation in oblast legislatures increased from 12 percent in 2010 to 14.9 in 2015 and 27.8 percent in 2020. As seen in Figure 5.2, the proportion of women slightly improved in city councils (28 percent in 2010 vs. 32 percent in 2020), while it declined in village councils. These statistics offer a rather crude measure of women's participation in local politics. Some reports indicate that female deputies were pressured to step down shortly upon the conclusion of elections to vacate seats for male politicians.

Since its inception in 2011, the interparty caucus (*mizhfraktsiine ob'ednannia*, MFO) Equal Opportunities, bringing together women and men from different political parties, has established itself as a driving force behind the adoption of public policies in favor of gender equality. In 2012, the caucus cochaired by Iryna Herashchenko (*Udar*) and Olena Kondratiuk (*Batkivshchyna*) was comprised of twenty-six deputies; 38.5 percent of them (ten deputies) were men.³⁶ As a result of the 2014 parliamentary election, a total of 46 deputies, including 36 women and 10 men, joined the caucus in 2015.³⁷ In the wake of the 2019 parliamentary election, the caucus membership

---

[32] On foreign policy priorities of all the political parties competing in the 2019 parliamentary election, see Portal zovnishnoi polityky. 2019. "Parlamentska dyplomatiia Ukrainy." http://fpp.com.ua/elections_vr_2019.

[33] Sonia Koshkina and Diana Butsko. 2019. "Ruslan Stefanchuk: 'Use vyrishue Zelensky'." *LB.ua*, May 22. https://lb.ua/news/2019/05/22/427531_ruslan_stefanchuk_use_virishuie.html.

[34] Nataliia Patrikeeva. 2020. "Parlamentski partii: Khto i iak rozvyvae zhinoche liderstvo." *Chesno*, September 29. www.chesno.org/post/4915.

[35] Rating Group Ukraine. 2020. "Rol zhinok v ukrainskomu suspilstvi." March 4. https://ratinggroup.ua/research/ukraine/rol_zhenschin_v_ukrainskom_obschestve.html.

[36] Iryna Herashchenko. 2012. "Siohodni u VR my stvoryly Mizhfraktsiine deputatske obednannia Rivni mozhlyvosti." *Facebook*, December 25. www.facebook.com/iryna.gerashchenko/posts/383336731754146.

[37] Opora. 2016. "Sklad mizhfraktsiinykh deputatskikh ob'ednan. Hruden 2015." January 12. https://rada.oporaua.org/16-chitati/8584-sklad-mizhfraktsiinykh-deputatskykh-obiedan-hruden-2015.

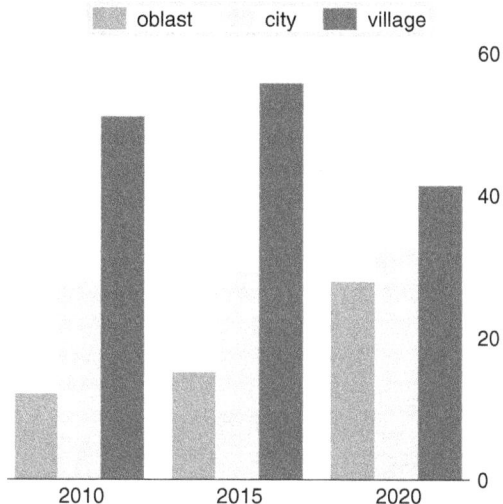

FIGURE 5.2 Women's representation in local legislative bodies.
Source: Committee of Voters of Ukraine.

rose to eighty-six in March 2020. Nearly half of the caucus members (forty people) were men, signifying joint efforts to bring about policy change. MFO members launched a variety of legislative initiatives to tackle the issue of gender equality. In 2017, for example, a group of parliamentarians coauthored a bill on the provision of equal rights and opportunities for women and men during their service in the Armed Forces of Ukraine and other military formations, which became a law the next year. Moreover, since 2017, the caucus annually held the Ukrainian Women's Congress that brought together scores of the most active and successful women and men from government, business, mass media, and the NGO sector to set an agenda on gender policy in contemporary Ukraine.[38]

Women's leadership within a political party can be viewed as another marker of women's standing in the political arena. According to reports submitted to the Central Election Commission of Ukraine in the run-up to local elections, the share of women-led political parties has recently increased.[39] Of 142 political parties that declared their intent to run in the 2015 local

---

[38] For details, visit the website of the Ukrainian Women's Congress, https://womenua.today/en/all-events-of-ukrainian-women-s-congress.

[39] Each political party is required to submit to the Central Election Commission names of party leaders whose signatures testify to the party's collective decision to participate in local elections. In many cases, more than one person is listed as a party leader who confirms the conduct of a party convention and voting on the matter.

election, 28 parties (19.7 percent) were (co-)chaired by women.[40] More recently, 52 of 194 political parties (26.8 percent) that decided to participate in the 2020 local election were (co-)chaired by women.[41] Many local political parties, as well as a handful of major political parties with a national reach, listed women as their leaders. These listings, however, provide incomplete information regarding the real distribution of power within a political party. For example, Svitlana Kharchuk designated as a leader of the Opposition Bloc was a token figure, without any real power in the opposition camp. In contrast, having been a minister of energy, a prime minister, and the founding member of the party Fatherland, Tymoshenko wielded considerable power in Ukrainian politics.[42] A closer look at the legislative work of female party leaders further illustrates a variation in the level of women's activism. Iryna Herashchenko, leader of the bloc European Solidarity in the ninth convocation of Verkhovna Rada (2019–2024), was named one of the most active party leaders in 2020, since she attended 86 percent of parliamentary sessions and took the floor 106 times.[43] For comparison, Tymoshenko attended only 54 percent of sessions and delivered speeches 63 times during the calendar year.

The representation of women in the Cabinet of Ministers is another indicator of women's empowerment. Between one and three women were represented in the Cabinet of Ministers during Mykola Azarov's two terms (2010–2012; 2012–2014). Women's appointment to ministerial positions increased under Prime Minister Volodymyr Groysman (2016–2019). Ivanna Klympush-Tsintsadze assumed the post of the Deputy Prime Minister for European and Euro-Atlantic Integration of Ukraine. Despite a high proportion of female employees in the education sector, Liliia Hrynevych was the first woman to be appointed as the Minister of Education and Science in 2016. In addition, Iryna Friz was placed in charge of the newly created Ministry of Veterans Affairs to provide more effective support for war veterans. The same number of women was appointed to ministerial positions under Oleksii Honcharuk (2019–2020). Hanna Novosad, for example, became the Minister of Education and Science, while Zoriana Skaletska was appointed the Minister of Health.

---

[40] Central Election Commission of Ukraine. 2015. *List of Political Parties That Made a Decision to Participate in the Elections of 25 October 2015.* https://cvk.gov.ua/vibory_category/mistsevi-vibori/vibori-deputativ-verhovnoi-radi-avtonomnoi-respubliki-krim-mistsevih-rad-ta-silskih-selishhnih-miskih-goliv-25-zhovtnya-2015-roku.html.

[41] Central Election Commission of Ukraine. 2020. *List of Political Parties That Made a Decision to Participate in the Elections of 25 October 2020.* www.cvk.gov.ua/wp-content/uploads/2020/10/perelik_patiy_20201009.doc.

[42] See, for example, Focus Ukraine. 2021. "Top 100 Most Influential Women of Ukraine, According to the Magazine Focus Ukraine." https://focus.ua/ratings/486307-100-samyh-vliyatelnyh-zhenshchin-ukrainy-po-versii-zhurnala-fokus-2021.

[43] Committee of Voters of Ukraine. 2021. "Herashchenko i Zhelezniak – naiefektyvnishi lidery fraktsii u 2020 rotsi." January 15. www.cvu.org.ua/nodes/view/type:news/slug:herashchenko-i-zhelezniak-naiaktyvnishi-lidery-fraktsii-u-2020-rotsi.

Furthermore, the appointment of women – Natalie Jaresko and Oksana Markarova – as the Minister of Finance challenged the conventional distribution of ministerial portfolios.

As shown in Table 5.1, the largest number of women held ministerial positions under Denys Shmyhal's prime ministership (2020–2024). In several cases, however, men were initially given ministerial positions and subsequently replaced by women. Furthermore, given frequent reshuffles, more than half of female appointees did not serve a full term in the twenty-first Cabinet of Ministers. Yuliia Laputina, for example, was appointed the Minister of Veterans Affairs in the wake of Serhii Bessarab's resignation in December 2020, and she resigned in February 2024.[44] Likewise, in November 2021, Yuliia Svyrydenko became the fourth Minister of Economics since the start of Shmyhal's prime ministership, replacing Oleksii Liubchenko six months after his initial appointment. That year, Iryna Vereshchuk replaced Oleksii Reznikov as the Minister for Reintegration of Temporarily Occupied Territories. A few women were appointed as acting ministers for a short period, for example, three months – the acting Minister of Environment Svitlana Fomenko and the acting Minister of Education and Science Liubomyra Mandzii, seven months – the acting Minister of Energy Olha Buslavets. Frequent cabinet reshuffles limited women's capacity to implement robust reforms. In her capacity as the Deputy Prime Minister for European and Euro-Atlantic Integration of Ukraine since June 2020, Olha Stefanishyna is currently the longest-serving female minister during Zelensky's presidency.

A hallmark of Groysman's prime ministership was the creation of a new government position, the Government Commissioner for Gender Policy. Nominated by the Vice-President for European and Euro-Atlantic Integration, the Commissioner is charged with the task of coordinating the implementation of gender policies by different government agencies and monitoring the incorporation of gender norms into Ukraine's legislature.[45] Since December 2017, Ukrainian human rights activist Kateryna Levchenko holds the post.

Notably, new cohorts of female politicians educated in the West are gradually entering the high echelons of power. Klympush-Tsintsadze (b. 1972) attended the summer school at Harvard University's Ukrainian Research Institute in 1992 and studied political science at Montana State University in 1993–1994. Oksana Markarova (b. 1976) received a master's degree in public

---

[44] NV.ua. 2024. "Rada pidtrymala vidstavku Laputinoi z posady ochylnytsi Minveteraniv." February 7. https://nv.ua/ukr/ukraine/politics/rada-pidtrimala-vidstavku-laputinoji-z-posadi-ochilnici-minveteraniv-50390685.html; Ukraina Moloda. 2020. "Verkhovna Rada vidpravyla u vidstavku Ministra u spravakh veteraniv Serhiia Bessaraba." December 16. https://umoloda.kyiv.ua/number/0/2006/152848.

[45] Cabinet of Ministers of Ukraine. "Decree on the Government Commissioner for Gender Policy" (*Pro Uriadovoho upovnovazhenoho z pytan hendernoi polityky*). No. 390. June 7, 2017. https://zakon.rada.gov.ua/laws/show/ru/390-2017-%D0%BF#n10.

TABLE 5.1 *Women in the Cabinet of Ministers of Ukraine*

Position	Name	Number of women in the cabinet
15th Cabinet of Ministers of Ukraine (March 2010–December 2012) President Viktor Yanukovych, Prime Minister Mykola Azarov		1
Vice Prime Minister, Minister of Health	Raisa Bohatyriova	
16th Cabinet of Ministers of Ukraine (December 2012–February 2014) President Viktor Yanukovych, Prime Minister Mykola Azarov		3
Minister of Health	Raisa Bohatyriova	
Minister of Social Policy	Nataliia Korolivska	
Minister of the Cabinet of Ministers	Olena Lukash (December 2012–July 2012)	
Minister of Justice	Olena Lukash (July 2012–February 2014)	
17th Cabinet of Ministers of Ukraine (February 2014–November 2014) Acting President Oleksandr Turchynov, Prime Minister Arsenii Yatseniuk		1
Minister of Labor and Social Policy	Liudmyla Denisova	
18th Cabinet of Ministers of Ukraine (December 2014–April 2016) President Petro Poroshenko, Prime Minister Arsenii Yatseniuk		3
Minister of Finance	Natalie Jaresko	
Minister of the Cabinet of Ministers	Hanna Onyshchenko	
Acting Minister of Environment	Hanna Vronska (February 2016–April 2016)	
19th Cabinet of Ministers of Ukraine (April 2016–August 2019) President Petro Poroshenko, Prime Minister Volodymyr Groysman		6
Minister of Veterans Affairs	Iryna Friz (November 2018–August 2019)	
Minister of Education and Science	Liliia Hrynevych	
Deputy Prime Minister for European and Euro-Atlantic Integration of Ukraine	Ivanna Klympush-Tsintsadze	
Acting Minister of Finance	Oksana Markarova (June 2018–November 2018)	
Minister of Finance	Oksana Markarova (November 2018–August 2019)	
Acting Minister of Health	Ulana Suprun (August 2016–August 2019)	
Acting Minister of Agriculture	Olha Trofimtseva (February 2019–August 2019)	
20th Cabinet of Ministers of Ukraine (August 2019–March 2020) President Volodymyr Zelensky, Prime Minister Oleksii Honcharuk		6
Minister of Regional Development	Aliona Babak (August 2019–February 2020)	
Minister of Veterans Affairs, Temporarily Occupied Territories and Internally Displaced Persons of Ukraine	Oksana Koliada	

Position	Name	Number of women in the cabinet
Minister of Education and Science	Hanna Novosad	
Minister of Finance	Oksana Markarova	
Minister of Health	Zoriana Skaletska	
Minister of Social Policy	Yuliia Sokolovska	
21th Cabinet of Ministers of Ukraine (March 2020–April 2024)[46]		9
President Volodymyr Zelensky, Prime Minister Denys Shmyhal		
Acting Minister of Energy	Olha Buslavets (April 2020–November 2020)	
Acting Minister of Culture and Information Policy	Svitlana Fomenko (March 2020–June 2020)	
Minister of Veterans Affairs	Yulia Laputina (December 2020–February 2024)	
Minister of Social Policy	Maryna Lazebna (March 2020–July 2022)	
Acting Minister of Education and Science	Liubomyra Mandzii (March 2020–June 2020)	
Deputy Prime Minister for European and Euro-Atlantic Integration of Ukraine	Olha Stefanishyna (June 2020–2024)	
First Prime Minister, Minister of Economic Development and Trade	Yuliia Svyrydenko (November 2021–2024)	
Vice Prime Minister, Minister for Reintegration of Temporarily Occupied Territories	Iryna Vereshchuk (November 2021–2024)	
Minister of Social Policy	Oksana Zholnovych (July 2022–2024)	

Note: The dates of a minister's appointment are listed in parentheses if the minister did not serve the full term in the Cabinet of Ministers. For the 21st Cabinet of Ministers, the analysis covers the period from March 2020 to April 2024.
Source: Government of Ukraine, www.kmu.gov.ua/uryad-ta-organi-vladi/team.

finance and trade from Indiana University in 2001. More recently, Hanna Novosad (b. 1990) graduated from Maastricht University in the Netherlands with a master's in European Studies in 2013. These socialization experiences are likely to have shaped their political outlook and strengthened their commitment to Ukraine's alliance with the EU.

---

[46] The list of ministerial positions under Prime Minister Denys Shmyhal reflects the distribution of portfolios in April 2024. In November 2023, all the political parties represented in Verkhovna Rada signed a memorandum, agreeing to postpone the conduct of presidential and parliamentary elections until the end of the Russia–Ukraine war and the end of the martial law in Ukraine. At the time of this writing, Shmyhal continues to hold the post of the prime minister.

Moreover, two Americans of Ukrainian descent served as agents of change in the Ukrainian government. Born into a Ukrainian family in 1965, Jaresko grew up in Illinois, studied accounting at DePaul University, and graduated with a master's degree from the Harvard Kennedy School. Jaresko seized an opportunity to move to Ukraine in 1992 and focused on the development of small and medium enterprises through her work at the US Embassy and the Western NIS Enterprise Fund. In 2014, Jaresko accepted the invitation to serve as the Minister of Finance, with a monthly wage of $300. "I'm doing this out of a sense of patriotism," Jaresko explained. "I have no other reason to do this, other than to make a difference. Ukraine must succeed. There is no room for any of us to fail."[47] Similarly, in her capacity as the acting Minister of Health, Ulana Suprun was on a crusade to bring about a sea change in the healthcare sector. Among other things, she focused her efforts on "busting myths of Soviet medicine."[48] Born in Detroit in 1963, Suprun earned a bachelor's degree in biology from Wayne State University and received her medical degree from Michigan State University. With over twenty years of medical work in Michigan and New York, Suprun moved to Ukraine in 2013 and volunteered as a doctor during Euromaidan. She subsequently founded the nongovernmental organization "Patriot Defense" to provide tactical medicine training and distribute NATO-standard improved first aid kits to the Ukrainian military.

An increasing representation of women in government might have far-reaching consequences for policymaking. Public opinion research suggests that women and men tend to take distinctive positions on various policy issues.[49] Specifically, women are more prone to support welfare spending. Yet, women ministers do not necessarily implement policies that improve women's welfare. For example, the Ministry of Social Policy under Liudmyla Denisova's leadership abolished state payments for mothers of children under the age of three in 2014.[50] In 2021, Tetiana Ostashchenko, the first female commander of the Medical Services of the Armed Forces of Ukraine, abolished the position of an advisor for gender policy in the military unit.[51]

---

[47] Brett Forrest. 2015. "The American Woman Who Stands Between Putin and Ukraine." *Bloomberg*, March 5. www.bloomberg.com/news/features/2015-03-05/putin-s-american-foe-in-ukraine-finance-minister-natalie-jaresko.

[48] Kennan Institute. 2019. "A Conversation with Former Ukrainian Minister of Health Ulana Suprun." September 30. www.wilsoncenter.org/event/conversation-former-ukrainian-minister-health-ulana-suprun.

[49] Mary-Kate Lizotte. 2020. *Gender Differences in Public Opinion: Values and Political Consequences*. Philadelphia: Temple University Press.

[50] The Ukrainian Helsinki Human Rights Union. 2014. "Dopomoha po dohliadu za dytynoiu do 3 rokiv skasovana ofitsiino." June 26. https://helsinki.org.ua/articles/dopomoha-po-dohlyadu-za-dytynoyu-do-3-rokiv-skasovana-ofitsijno.

[51] Novynarnia. 2021. "U Komanduvanni Medsyl ZSU skasuvaly posadu radnyka z hendernykh pytan." November 29. https://novynarnia.com/2021/11/29/u-komanduvanni-medsyl-zsu.

Moreover, women's presence in high-level cabinet positions does not necessarily signify less corruption in high echelons of power.[52] The Minister of Health Iryna Bohatyriova (2012–2014) was allegedly involved in opaque schemes for the procurement of medical supplies and received kickbacks from pharmaceutical companies.[53] Following Euromaidan, the Ukrainian government issued an arrest warrant for Bohatyriova, and the US Treasury Department's Office of Foreign Assets Control placed her on the sanctions list for misappropriation of state assets and actions that undermine democratic processes in Ukraine.[54] Likewise, the Minister of Justice Olena Lukash, Yanukovych's legal counsel during the Supreme Court hearings on electoral malpractices during the 2004 election, reportedly interfered with tender procedures and publicly endorsed police violence against participants in the Euromaidan protests.[55] Investigative journalists also reported that Minister Denisova allegedly tampered with tender procedures, which enabled food vendors notorious for the violation of food safety regulations to win the bid for the provision of food services for school canteens.[56] Some female politicians also lobbied for certain business interests in the national parliament. For example, the Institute of Legislative Ideas placed 24 women on the list of the top 100 parliamentarians who proposed bills with corruption risks between September 2019 and June 2021.[57] Given the ubiquity of corruption, only 23 percent of Ukrainians in 2020 believed that women were on the whole less corrupt than men.[58]

---

[52] There is a debate in comparative politics literature regarding women's role as "cleaners of corruption" in government. On this point, see, for example, David Dollar, Raymond Fisman, and Roberta Gatti. 2001. "Are Women Really the 'Fairer' Sex? Corruption and Women in Government." *Journal of Economic Behavior and Organization* 46 (4): 423–29; Anne Marie Goetz. 2007. "Political Cleaners: Women as the New Anti-Corruption Force?" *Development and Change* 38 (1): 87–105.

[53] Igor Kossov. 2020. "Patient Groups Warn of Deadly Drug Shortages." *Kyiv Post*, May 18. www.kyivpost.com/ukraine-politics/patient-groups-warn-of-deadly-drug-shortages.html.

[54] National Archives. 2015. "Sanctions Actions Pursuant to Executive Orders 13660 and 13685." *Federal Register: The Daily Journal of the United States Government* 80 (51), March 17. www.federalregister.gov/documents/2015/03/17/2015-06056/sanctions-actions-pursuant-to-executive-orders-13660-and-13685.

[55] Ukrinform. 2015. "U chomu vynna Olena Lukash?" November 6. www.ukrinform.ua/rubric-polytics/1910112-u-chomu-vinna-olena-lukash.html.

[56] Nashi Hroshi. 2014. "Denysova dala 110 milioniv na kharchi dlia shkoliariv 'rehionalu', iakyi torik hoduvav ditei koshtovnym nepotribom." May 19. https://nashigroshi.org/2014/05/19/denysova-roztenderyla-170-miljoniv-mizh-rehionalamy-udarivkoyu-i-hloptsem-korolevskoji/.

[57] Institute of Legislative Ideas. 2021. "Reiting narodnykh deputativ Ukrainy za kilkistiu podanykh zakonoproektiv, iaki mistiat' koruptsiohenni faktory." https://rge9.izi.institute/wp-content/uploads/2021/06/Rating__2021.html.

[58] Kateryna Potapenko, ed. 2020. *Ukraine in World Values Survey 2020: Resume of the Analytical Report*. Kyiv: Ukrainian Center for European Policy, p. 32.

The dearth of transparency in the recruitment of individuals for high-level government positions dampens women's ambitions to pursue a career in public service. Several scandals broke out in the mass media when women in their mid-20s, with rather dubious credentials, were appointed to high-level positions in government. In 2016, for example, the Minister of Interior Affairs Arsen Avakov came under criticism for appointing twenty-four-year-old Anastasiia Deeva as his deputy minister.[59] Despite legal requirements positing that a deputy minister should have at least ten years of work experience, the recent alumna of the Kyiv National University, with a master's degree in political science, landed one of the country's top jobs in law enforcement. Likewise, the appointment of twenty-five-year-old Hanna Serheeva as the Deputy Minister of Social Policy, with a monthly salary 2.5 times higher than President Zelensky's official salary, stirred a storm in July 2022.[60] Rather than setting a positive example for young women with political ambitions, such controversial appointments raise questions about the logic of recruitment and the degree of transparency in government agencies. Video recordings released in the spring of 2020 suggest that the brother of Andrii Yermak, head of the presidential administration, allegedly sought payments in exchange for lucrative jobs in the public sector.[61] In appointing individuals for high-level government positions, the incumbent appears to prioritize their loyalty and personal connections, rather than their professional qualifications.[62]

WOMEN'S BID FOR PRESIDENCY

A growing number of women around the globe run for executive office.[63] To date, only six women in postcommunist Ukraine registered as presidential candidates: Nataliia Vitrenko (1999 and 2004), Inna Bohoslovska (2010 and

---

[59] BBC. 2016. "Storm as Woman, 24, Gets Key Ukraine Job." November 23. www.bbc.com/news/world-europe-38076261; Anastasiia Ringis. 2016. "Anastasiia Deeva: tskuvannia mene mae svoho rezhysera. I adekvatna liudyna tse zrozumie." *Ukrainska Pravda*, November 15. www.pravda.com.ua/articles/2016/11/15/7126893.

[60] Liia Ilchenko. 2022. "Bloherku bez dosvidu roboty pryznacheno zastupnykom ministra sotspolityky iz zarplatoiu bilshe, nizh v Prezydenta." *Dzerkalo tyzhnia*, July 10. https://zn.ua/ukr/ECONOMICS/bloherku-bez-dosvidu-roboti-priznacheno-zastupnikom-ministra-sotspolitiki-iz-zarplatoju-bilshe-nizh-v-prezidenta.html.

[61] Bohdan Nahaylo. 2020. "Yermakgate Scandal Rocks Zelenskyy Administration." *The Ukrainian Weekly*, April 17. www.ukrweekly.com/uwwp/yermakgate-scandal-rocks-zelenskyy-administration.

[62] On this point, see, for example, Oleksandr Lemenov. 2022. "Khto takyi i chy bude nezalezhnym novyi henprokuror Andrii Kostin." *Dzerkalo tyzhnia*, July 27. https://zn.ua/ukr/internal/khto-takij-i-chi-bude-nezaleznim-novij-henprokuror-andrij-kostin.html; NV. 2022. "'Stavliat viddanykh, a ne profesionaliv'. Heneral Kryvonos rozpoviv pro vplyv Ofisu prezydenta na Zaluzhnoho ta kadrovi rishennia v ZSU." August 5. https://nv.ua/ukr/ukraine/politics/ofis-prezidenta-vplivaye-na-zaluzhnogo-ta-priznachennya-v-zsu-krivonos-novini-ukrajini-50261164.html.

[63] Rainbow Murray, ed. 2010. *Cracking the Highest Glass Ceiling: A Global Comparison of Women's Campaigns for Executive Office*. Santa Barbara: Praeger; Torild Skard. 2014.

TABLE 5.2 *Female presidential candidates*

Election year	Total number of candidates	Number of female candidates	Names of female candidates	Percent of vote
1994	7	0		
1999	13	1	Nataliia Vitrenko	10.97
2004	24	1	Nataliia Vitrenko	1.53
2010	18	3	Inna Bohoslovska	0.41
			Liudmyla Suprun	0.19
			Yuliia Tymoshenko	25.05
2014	21	2	Olha Bohomolets	1.91
			Yuliia Tymoshenko	12.81
2019	39	4	Olha Bohomolets	0.17
			Inna Bohoslovska	0.09
			Yuliia Lytvynenko	0.10
			Yuliia Tymoshenko	13.40

Note: The percentage of votes that a presidential candidate received in the first round of elections is reported in the table.
Source: Central Election Commission of Ukraine, www.cvk.gov.ua/vibory_category/vibori-prezidenta-ukraini-2.html.

2019), Liudmyla Suprun (2010), Olha Bohomolets (2014 and 2019), Yuliia Lytvynenko (2019), and Yuliia Tymoshenko (2010, 2014, and 2019). The full list of female presidential candidates, arranged chronologically by the year of election, is displayed in Table 5.2. Between 1994 and 2004, at most one female presidential candidate was placed on the ballot. In the first election since the Orange Revolution, 3 of 18 presidential contenders were women. In the wake of Euromaidan, female candidates comprised approximately 10 percent of candidates for executive office: two of twenty one in 2014 and four of thirty nine in 2019. As seen in Table 5.2, the number of women who run for the presidency is on the rise. To date, none of the female candidates succeeded in winning the plurality of votes, albeit Tymoshenko once broke through into the second round of the presidential elections.[64]

Women of Power: Half a Century of Female Presidents and Prime Ministers Worldwide. Bristol: Policy Press.

[64] According to electoral rules in Ukraine, the second round of elections is held if none of the candidates receives a majority of votes in the first round. Two candidates with the largest share of vote compete for presidency in the second round. Over the past three decades, only Poroshenko in 2014 and Zelensky in 2019 scored more than half of votes in the first round of the presidential election.

Born in 1951, Vitrenko launched her political career in the early 1990s and joined the newly formed Socialist Party of Ukraine. In light of her disagreements with the party's position on private property and double citizenship, she established and chaired the Progressive Socialist Party of Ukraine. Her political platform combined "fierce populism, nostalgia for the Soviet era, and strong anti-Western sentiments."[65] As a stern critic of the West, Vitrenko lashed out against the International Monetary Fund, opposed Ukraine's alliance with the EU and NATO, and lobbied for a strategic partnership with Russia. Given her first electoral victory in the city of Konotop and her virulent rhetoric, Vitrenko was dubbed the witch of Konotop (*Konotopska vid'ma*) in the mass media.[66] However, mass support for her candidacy dropped from 10.9 percent of the vote in 1999 to 1.5 percent in 2004.[67] In the wake of Euromaidan, Vitrenko moved to Moscow and endorsed Russia's aggression against Ukraine.[68]

Bohoslovska (b. 1960) was another female politician known for her vitriol on talk shows and her controversial policy stance.[69] Bohoslovska, for example, voted in favor of the Russian naval base in Crimea and an upgraded status of the Russian language in the early 2010s. The civic organization *Chesno* (Honestly) uncovered that the native of Kharkiv had paid in Russian rubles for her campaign ads on Facebook in 2019.[70] Over the span of her political career, Bohoslovska switched parties several times, and she was closely associated with the bloc Team of the Winter Generation (*Komanda ozymoho pokolinnia*), the political party Council (*Viche*), and the Party of Regions. Having lived through the hard times of the 1990s (the winter), Bohoslovska claimed that her team would bring about socioeconomic renewal in the 2000s.[71] Yet, the Team of the Winter Generation failed to get into the parliament, and Bohoslovska eventually joined the Party of Regions. In 2010, Bohoslovska

---

[65] Jan Maksymiuk. 1999. "Genie Out of the Bottle?" *RFE/RL Poland, Belarus, and Ukraine Report*1 (19), October 5. www.rferl.org/a/1142006.html.

[66] The witch of Konotop was the main character of a well-known nineteenth-century book by Ukrainian writer Hryhorii Kvitka-Osnovianenko.

[67] Central Election Commission of Ukraine. 2000. *Vybory Prezydenta Ukrainy 1999: Informatsiino-analitychne vydannia*. Kyiv: CVK, p. 294.

[68] Vholos. 2019. "'Zachystyty ukraintsiv': maty odnoho iz kerivnykiv Naftohazu u Moskvi rozpovila, iak nenavydyt Ukrainu." November 11. https://vgolos.ua/news/zachystyty-ukrayintsiv-maty-odnogo-iz-kerivnykiv-naftogazu-u-moskvi-rozpovila-yak-nenavydyt-ukrayinu-video_1101858.html.

[69] Znaj. 2019. "Inna Bohoslovska: Dos'e, biohrafiia i kompromat na ukrainskoho polityka." https://znaj.ua/dossier/34-inna-bogoslovska-dosye-biografiya-i-kompromat-na-ukrajinskogo-politika#kompromat-i-chutki.

[70] Chesno. 2019. "Aby povydomyty cholovikiv, shcho ide v Prezydenty, Bohoslovska platyla sotsmerezhi Facebook rubliamy." March 22. www.chesno.org/post/1101.

[71] Pavlo Solodko. 2012. "2002: Peredvyborchui rolyk 'Komandy ozymoho pokolinnia'." *Ukrainska Pravda*, June 15. www.istpravda.com.ua/videos/2012/06/15/88717/.

temporarily suspended her party membership to run for the presidency against a slate of candidates, including Yanukovych and Tymoshenko. As a presidential contender, Bohoslovska concentrated on attacking Tymoshenko and received 0.4 percent of the vote in 2010.[72] Only 0.09 percent of voters cast their ballot for Bohoslovska during the 2019 presidential election.[73]

Another female presidential candidate in the 2010 election was forty-five-year-old Liudmyla Suprun. In 2002, she was elected to the parliament on the ticket of the regime-friendly political alliance For United Ukraine (*Za edynu Ukrainu*). She subsequently disapproved of the Orange Revolution and promoted the idea of the confederation of Russia, Belarus, and Ukraine.[74] Moreover, her spouse Mykola Suprun was an advisor to Yanukovych, and he allegedly aided corruption in the government.[75] Concurrently, Suprun assumed a leadership role in the Civic Parliament of Women of Ukraine (*Hromadianskyi parlament zhinok Ukrainy*) that sought to collaborate with the national parliament to strengthen gender equality in Ukrainian society. In 2003, for example, Suprun championed the idea of gender quotas, positing that women should comprise at least 20 percent of Verkhovna Rada deputies.[76] Suprun failed to enter the parliament in 2006 and 2007, and she received 0.19 percent of the votes in the 2010 presidential election.

Having been the personal physician for President Yushchenko, Bohomolets (b. 1966) herself ran for the presidency in 2014 and 2019. Coming from a well-known dynasty of doctors, Bohomolets played a prominent role in coordinating the provision of urgent care for participants in Euromaidan and subsequently facilitated the rehabilitation of injured protesters abroad.[77] Having served in the Kyiv city council during Yushchenko's presidency, she was no stranger to politics either. Following the Revolution of Dignity, Bohomolets decided to run for executive office, with a mission to "transform a government of bandits into a government that serves the people through the creation of

---

[72] Central Election Commission of Ukraine. 2010. "Protokol Tsentralnoi vyborchoi komisii pro rezultaty holosuvannia u den vyboriv Prezydenta Ukrainy 17 sichnia 2010 roku." January 25. www.cvk.gov.ua/vibory_category/vibori-prezidenta-ukraini/vibori-prezidenta-ukraini-17-sichnya-2010-roku.html.

[73] Central Election Commission of Ukraine. 2019. "Protokol Tsentralnoi vyborchoi komisii pro rezultaty holosuvannia u den vyboriv Prezydenta Ukrainy 31 bereznia 2019 roku." April 7. www.cvk.gov.ua/vibory_category/vibori-prezidenta-ukraini/vibori-prezidenta-ukraini-2019.html.

[74] The Epoch Times. 2011. "Pavel Borodin za 'Narodnoe bolshinstvo Rossii, Ukrainy, Belorussii'." December 17. www.epochtimes.ru/content/view/56084/9.

[75] Ukraina Moloda. 2017. "Eks-radnyk Yanukovycha Mykola Suprun aktyvno spilkuetsia z ukrainskymy suddiamy." February 10. https://umoloda.kyiv.ua/number/0/180/108620.

[76] Iryna Kukhar. 2003. "'Henderni nosylky' i kvoty na 'rivnist'." *Den*, April 10. https://m.day.kyiv.ua/uk/article/den-ukrayini/genderni-nosilki-i-kvoti-na-rivnist.

[77] Espreso. 2014. "Bohomolets: Na Maidani utvorylasia paralelna systema okhorony zdrov'ia." January 30. https://espreso.tv/news/2014/01/30/bohomolec_na_maydani_utvorylasya_paralelna_systema_okhorony_zdorovya.

mechanisms of economic transparency."[78] Yet, notwithstanding her socialist agenda, emphasizing the need for free education and universal health care, Bohomolets received only 1.9 percent in the 2014 presidential election.[79] Known as an ardent critic of reforms spearheaded by the acting Minister of Health Suprun,[80] Bohomolets finished the 2019 presidential race with 0.17 percent of the vote.

The female presidential contender with the least political experience was forty-two-year-old Yuliia Lytvynenko. Originally from Kryvyi Rih, an industrial town in Dnipropetrovsk oblast, Lytvynenko moved to Kyiv to pursue a career in journalism. The TV host was viewed as a "technical candidate," an individual who was registered as a candidate with the sole purpose of drawing votes from other presidential contenders to benefit a certain politician. An analysis of Lytvynenko's campaign ads indicates that she primarily targeted Zelensky and, to a lesser extent, Tymoshenko and Anatolii Hrytsenko, which was beneficial for Poroshenko's bid for reelection.[81] Lytvynenko received 0.10 percent of the vote in the 2019 election and subsequently disappeared from the political landscape.

In contrast, Tymoshenko (b. 1960) is the most well-known female politician in contemporary Ukraine. Once nicknamed the "gas princess," she made a fortune in the energy sector and set up the political party Fatherland. Despite electoral losses, corruption scandals, and imprisonment, she weathered all the storms and became a fixture in Ukrainian politics.[82] In 2010 and 2014, she came second in the presidential race. The seasoned politician received 13.4 percent of the vote in the 2019 presidential election. According to the 2021 ranking of Top 100 Most Successful Women in Ukraine by the Kyiv-based magazine *NV* (New Voice), Tymoshenko remained one of the most

---

[78] Vladislav Davidzon. 2014. "Maidan's Mother Teresa Talks Ukraine's Future." *The Tablet*, May 23. www.tabletmag.com/sections/news/articles/maidans-mother-teresa-talks-ukraines-future.

[79] Central Election Commission of Ukraine. 2014. "Protokol Tsentralnoi vyborchoi komisii pro rezultaty holosuvannia u den vyboriv Prezydenta Ukrainy 25 travnia 2014 roku." June 2. www.cvk.gov.ua/vibory_category/vibori-prezidenta-ukraini/pozachergovi-vibori-prezidenta-ukraini-25-travnya-2014-roku.html.

[80] A team of policy analysts concluded that most of Bohomolets's critical statements were based upon the manipulation of facts. For details, see Yaroslav Kudlatskyi, Olena Shkarpova, and Yuliia Zhaha. 2018. "Ten Accusations from Olga Bogomolets towards the Ministry of Health and Ulana Suprun." *VoxCheck*, May 15. https://voxukraine.org/en/ten-accusations-from-olga-bogomolets-towards-the-ministry-of-health-and-ulana-suprun-voxcheck.

[81] Oleskii Pivtorak. 2019. "Finzvit Lytvynenko: ofitsiino bez vytrat na Facebook, YouTube ta telereklamu." *Chesno*, March 25. www.chesno.org/post/951.

[82] Ray Furlong. 2019. "Prisoner to President? Ukraine's 'Gas Princess' Aims For the Pinnacle of Power." *Radio Free Europe/Radio Liberty*, March 29. www.rferl.org/a/ukraine-tymoshenko-profile/29849755.html.

influential women in Ukraine.[83] Yet, the politician peddled a populist agenda devoid of a well-defined gender policy.[84]

To date, a female candidate failed to win the presidential elections in Ukraine. Clearly, women who registered as presidential candidates between 1999 and 2019 did not represent the full spectrum of political forces in the country and predominantly advanced a populist or leftist agenda. Strikingly, female politicians appeared to be more visible in the political camp associated with a pro-Russian foreign policy and authoritarian tendencies in government. Though women's representation in the national parliament increased in the post-2014 period, Ukrainian society has yet to see the ascendance of female presidential aspirants with a clean public record and a vigorous commitment to enact policy reforms in favor of the country's democratic development and European integration.

ECONOMIC OUTCOMES

Research on the economic consequences of social unrest shows that political instability adversely affects economic growth.[85] Consistent with this finding, Ukraine experienced an economic slowdown in the wake of political revolutions in 2004 and 2013–2014. As shown in Figure 5.3, gross domestic product (GDP) per capita growth was negative in the 1990s. Meanwhile, a streak of positive economic growth transpired for a few years preceding the Orange Revolution. GDP per capita growth dropped from 12.6 percent in 2004 to 3.8 percent in 2005, but it rose to 8.3 percent in 2006. The Great Recession caused a dramatic decline in economic activity, with -14.7 percent GDP per capita growth in 2009. The economy bounced back in 2010, with 4.5 GDP per capita economic growth. Yet, the size of the national economy again contracted in the wake of Euromaidan and the war. Nonetheless, between 2016 and 2019, Ukraine saw positive economic growth. The COVID-19 pandemic caused economic hardship, but Ukraine's economy showed signs of recovery in 2021 until it plummeted the next year.

---

[83] NV. 2021. "Zhurnal *NV* nazyvae 100 naiuspishnishykh zhinok Ukrainy." March 6. https://nv.ua/ukr/ukraine/events/top-100-nayuspishnishih-zhinok-ukrajini-za-versiyeyu-zhurnalu-nv-novini-ukrajini-50145627.html.

[84] Olena Sorotynska. 2019. "Women as Presidential Candidates: Who Are They, and Why Are They Silent about Women's Rights?" *Ukraine World*, March 19. https://ukraineworld.org/articles/russian-aggression/women-presidential-candidates-who-are-they-and-why-are-they-silent-about-womens-rights.

[85] Ari Aisen and Francisco José Veiga. 2013. "How Does Political Instability Affect Economic Growth?" *European Journal of Political Economy* 29 (March): 151–67; Alberto Alesina, Sule Özler, Nouriel Roubini, and Phillip Swagel. 1996. "Political Instability and Economic Growth." *Journal of Economic Growth* 1 (2): 189–211; Richard Jong-A-Pin. 2009. "On the Measurement of Political Instability and Its Impact on Economic Growth." *European Journal of Political Economy* 25 (1): 15–29.

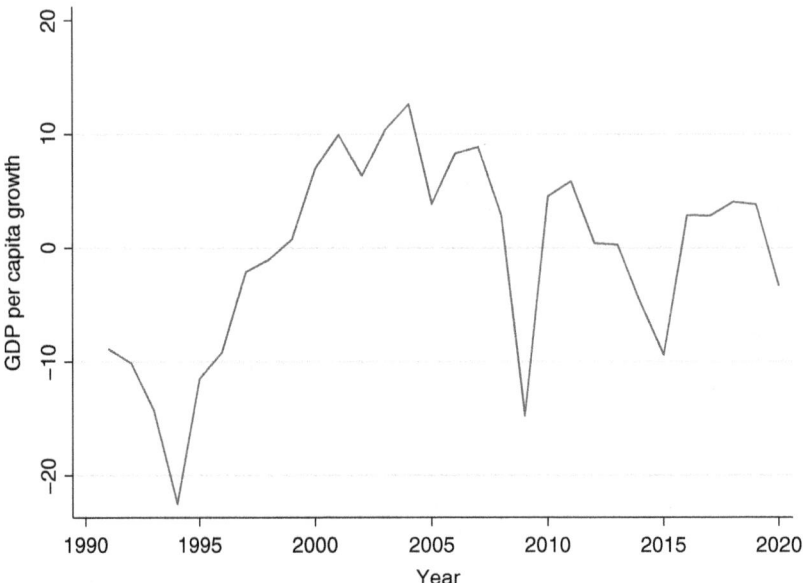

FIGURE 5.3 Gross domestic product (GDP) per capita growth.
Note: The annual percentage growth rate of GDP per capita based on constant local currency is displayed in the figure.

Source: World Bank. 2022. World Development Indicators [database], https://databank.worldbank.org/source/world-development-indicators.

Corruption is a major impediment to economic development in Ukraine.[86] Despite citizens' demands for the eradication of corruption during the Orange Revolution and the Revolution of Dignity, Ukrainian politicians displayed a lack of political will to uphold the rule of law.[87] For example, the Ukrainian government sabotaged the appointment of the head of the Specialized Anti-Corruption Prosecutor's Office for two years under Zelensky's presidency (2020–2022), which blocked the investigation of grand corruption and damaged Ukraine's relations with its Western partners.[88] The case of Oleh Tatarov,

---

[86] Erik Herron. 2020. *Normalizing Corruption: Failures of Accountability in Ukraine*. Ann Arbor: University of Michigan Press.

[87] See, for example, Felix Blatt and Caroline Schlaufer. 2021. "The Influence of Civil Society on Ukrainian Anti-Corruption Policy After the Maidan." *Central European Journal of Public Policy* 15 (1): 15–30; Bohdan Harasymiw. 2019. "Civil Society as an Anti-Corruption Actor in Post-Euromaidan Ukraine." *Canadian Slavonic Papers* 61 (3): 288–320.

[88] Radio Free Europe/Radio Liberty. 2022. "Ukraine Appoints New Anti-Corruption Prosecutor after Long Delay." July 28. www.rferl.org/a/ukraine-appoints-new-anti-corruption-prosecutor/31963876.html; Oleg Sukhov. 2021. "Panel Head Blocks Appointment of Anti-graft Prosecutor, Wants SBU to Check Winner." *The Kyiv Independent*, December 24. https://kyivindependent.com/national/panel-head-blocks-appointment-of-anti-graft-prosecutor-wants-sbu-to-check-winner.

deputy chief of the presidential administration, suggests that President Zelensky and Andrii Yermak, head of the presidential administration, interfere with corruption investigations and disregard evidence of corruption within their inner circle.[89] Reflecting these trends, Ukraine's score on the Corruption Perceptions Index barely improved from 26 in 2012 to 32 in 2021 on a scale from 0 (highly corrupt) to 100 (very clean).[90] For comparison, Estonia's score rose from 64 in 2012 to 74 in 2021. The two former Soviet republics – Georgia and Lithuania – scored, respectively, 55 points and 61 points in 2021. Despite the government's rhetoric, Ukraine lagged behind countries that implemented more robust reforms during their transition from communism. Against this backdrop, women navigated the labor market in Ukraine.

Over the past three decades, women comprised half of the labor force.[91] In the short term, the Revolution of Dignity and the first phase of the war (February 2014–January 2022) had a modest impact on women's participation in the labor market. The percentage of women in the total labor force slightly dropped from 49.5 percent in 2013 to 47.7 percent in 2020. According to the estimates of the International Labor Organization, approximately 60 percent of working-age women were "economically active" in Ukraine in the 2010s. Yet, official statistics might inaccurately register the level of women's participation in the labor market. Based on a survey of businessmen, the Kyiv International Institute of Sociology estimated that the shadow economy was worth 38 percent of the country's GDP in 2018.[92] In light of the size of the informal economy, the level of women's participation in the labor market is likely to be higher. Women, for example, tend to perform paid domestic work without signing an employment contract.[93]

Gender gap in unemployment is another indicator of gender inequality in the labor market. According to the official statistics, the unemployment rate in Ukraine was slightly lower for working-age women than working-age men throughout the 2010s. The average unemployment rate for the 2007–2013

---

[89] Transparency International Ukraine. 2021. "A Year After: What Problems Does Tatarov's Case Reveal?" December 1. https://ti-ukraine.org/en/blogs/a-year-after-what-problems-does-tatarovs-case-reveal.

[90] For details, see Transparency International. *The 2021 Corruption Perceptions Index.* www.transparency.org/en/cpi/2021.

[91] Data on women's participation in the labor market are retrieved from the World Bank's World Development Indicators, https://databank.worldbank.org/source/world-development-indicators.

[92] Kyiv International Institute of Sociology. 2019. "Shadow Economy in Ukraine: Results of the 2019 Survey." [press release], October 11. https://kiis.com.ua/?lang=eng&cat=reports&id=897&page=1&t=9.

[93] Alissa Tolstokorova. 2014. "Mary Poppins Comes Back: The Revival of Paid Domestic Work in the Informal Labour Market in Ukraine." *Südosteuropa. Zeitschrift für Politik und Gesellschaft* 62 (4): 479–99.

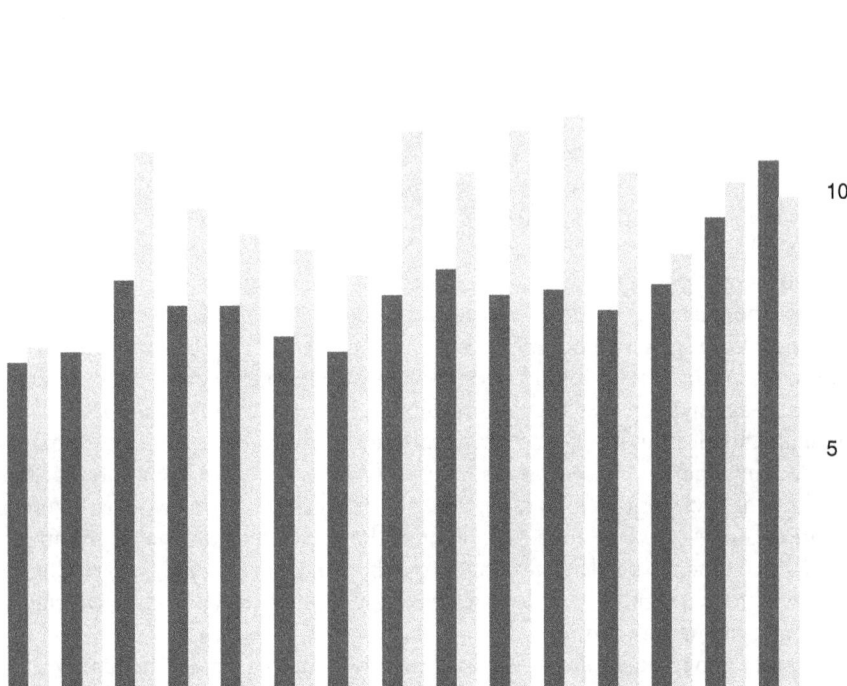

FIGURE 5.4 Unemployment rate among working-age women and men.
Source: State Statistics Service of Ukraine, http://ukrstat.gov.ua.

period was 7.3 percent for women and 8.7 percent for men. In the wake of Euromaidan, the average unemployment rate for the 2015–2021 period increased to 8.6 percent for women and 10.3 percent for men. As seen in Figure 5.4, the unemployment rate was, for example, 7.7 percent for women and 10.4 percent for men in 2018.

Next, the analysis considers the gender wage gap as an indicator of gender inequality in the economic sphere. State Statistics Service of Ukraine measures this gap as the difference in average monthly earnings between men and women who are employed by an entity with at least ten employees. As shown in Figure 5.5, the gender wage gap was slowly narrowing down in the past two decades. In 2002, women earned 69 *kopiika* to every *hryvnia* earned by

Economic Outcomes 153

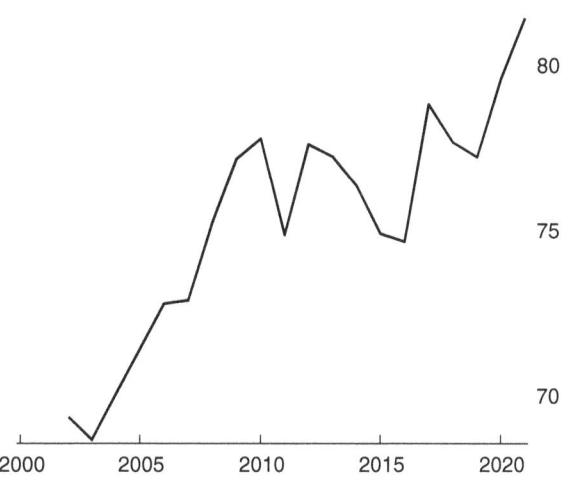

FIGURE 5.5 Gender wage gap, 2002–2021
Note: The gender wage gap refers to the difference in average monthly wages of men and women. It is reported in percentages.
Source: State Statistics Service of Ukraine, www.ukrstat.gov.ua/operativ/operativ2017/gdn/smzp_zs/smzp_zs_ek/smzp_zs_ek_u.htm.

men.[94] By 2012, women earned 77 *kopiika* for every *hryvnia* a man earned. The wage disparities further shrank in 2020. In 2021, women earned, on average, 81 *kopiika* to every *hryvnia* earned by men. However, the magnitude of the gender wage gap varied across different sectors of the economy. On the one hand, the gender wage gap in the financial sector ranged from 53.4 percent in 2002 to 68.1 percent in 2021. On the other hand, the gender wage gap in the education sector decreased from 78.9 percent in 2002 to 95.9 percent in 2021. Women appeared to fare better in the education sector. Yet, one should keep in mind the pay scale in different industries. The average monthly wages in 2021 were UAH 30,610 for men and UAH 20,841 for women in the financial and insurance sector, and UAH 12,209 for men UAH 11,708 for women in the education sector. The gender wage gap within an industry stems in part from unequal chances of promotion.

Occupational segregation – gender-based distribution of workers across and within occupations – is another marker of inequalities in the labor market. Traditionally, women represent a lion's share of employees in the education

[94] *Kopiika* is a monetary subunit of *hryvnia*, Ukraine's national currency. One kopiika is the lowest denomination coin; it is equivalent to 0.01 of hryvnia.

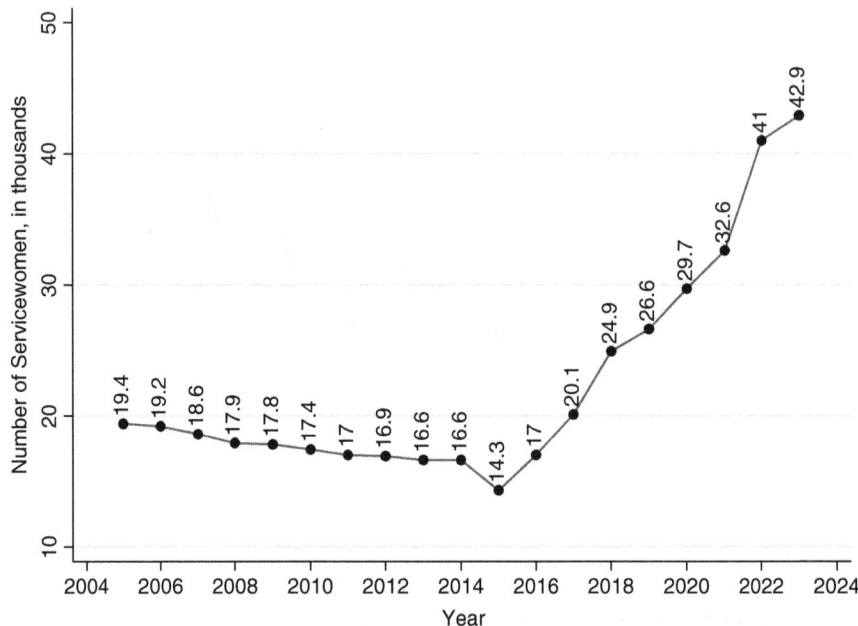

FIGURE 5.6 Servicewomen in the Armed Forces of Ukraine.
Source: *ArmiaInform*. 2021. "Skilky zhinok-viiskovosluzhbovtsiv sluzhat u zbroinykh sylakh Ukrainy – novi dani Kadrovoho tsentru." December 4. https://armyinform.com.ua/2021/12/04/skilky-zhinok-vijskovosluzhbovcziv-sluzhat-u-zbrojnyh-sylah-ukrayiny-novi-dani-kadrovogo-czentru.

and health sectors. For example, 81.9 percent of employees in the health sector in 2002, as well as 81.6 percent in 2013, were women. Likewise, women made up more than two-thirds of employees in the education sector: 75.4 percent in 2002 and 76.6 percent in 2013. Meanwhile, the share of women in public administration was on the rise. The percentage of female employees in public administration (*derzhavne uprvalinnia*) increased from 52.9 percent in 2002 to 65.1 percent in 2013.[95]

The Russia–Ukraine war had a profound impact on women's service in the Armed Forces of Ukraine. As shown in Figure 5.6, the number of servicewomen was gradually decreasing from 19,366 in 2005 to 16,962 in 2012. With the mobilization of Ukrainian society against the aggressor state, this trend was reversed. The number of women who served in the military doubled from 16,557 in 2013 to 32,569 in 2021.[96] For comparison, the average

---

[95] O. O. Karmazina, ed. 2014. *Dity, zhinky ta sim'ia v Ukraini*. Kyiv: State Statistics Service of Ukraine, p. 146.

[96] These statistics reflect only the number of servicewomen. In addition, thousands of women are employed as civilian personnel in the military. In 2021, for example, women held 54 percent of civilian jobs in the Armed Forces of Ukraine. For details, see Olha Mosondz. 2021. "U nashomu

representation of military women across NATO member states increased from 10.5 percent in 2013 to 12 percent in 2019.[97] According to Klympush-Tsintsadze, the Deputy Prime Minister for European and Euro-Atlantic Integration of Ukraine (2016–2019), the percentage of women in the Armed Forces of Ukraine was similar to the average percentage of women in the armed forces of NATO member states in 2019.[98] "Over the course of Maidan, we saw that men and women were on equal footing," Klympush-Tsintsadze said. "Subsequently, women took an active part in building the Armed Forces from scratch, or even from a negative baseline, and also stood up for the defense of Ukraine with weapons in their hands."[99] Given the growing number of women in the military, women activists expanded the scope of their activities to combat gender discrimination and change mass attitudes toward women in male-dominated occupations.

PUBLIC OPINION ON GENDER EQUALITY

Public opinion literature distinguishes between values and attitudes. Values denote "concepts or beliefs about desirable end states or behaviors that transcend specific situations, guide selection or evaluation of behavior and events, and are ordered by relative importance."[100] Values are usually seen as a product of preadult socialization and endure over the life span. In contrast, attitudes are more volatile and might change in response to new evaluative information.[101] An attitude is "an individual's disposition to respond favorably or unfavorably to an object, person, institution, or event, or to any other discriminable aspect of the individual's world."[102] This section focuses on mass attitudes toward women's leadership role in political life as a dimension of gender equality. The underlying assumption is that attitudes influence behavior and thus affect the status of women in society.

---

viisku sluzhyt ponad 31 tysiacha zhinok." *ArmiiaInform*, March 4. https://armyinform.com.ua/2021/03/04/v-nashomu-vijsku-sluzhyt-ponad-31-tysyacha-zhinok.

[97] NATO. 2019. *Summary of the National Reports of NATO Member and Partner Nations to the NATO Committee on Gender Perspectives*. Brussels: NATO. www.nato.int/cps/en/natohq/topics_132342.htm.

[98] UkrInform. 2019. "V ZSU sluzhyt takyi samyi vidsotok zhinok iak v armiiakh NATO – Klympush-Tsintsadze." January 23. www.ukrinform.ua/rubric-society/2624767-u-zsu-sluzit-takij-samij-vidsotok-zinok-ak-v-armiah-nato-klimpuscincadze.html.

[99] Ibid.

[100] Shalom H. Schwartz. and Wolfgang Bilsky. 1987. "Toward a Universal Psychological Structure of Human Values." *Journal of Personality and Social Psychology* 53 (3): 550–52, p. 551.

[101] Gerd Bohner and Nina Dickel. 2011. "Attitudes and Attitude Change." *Annual Review of Psychology* 62 (1): 391–417.

[102] Icek Ajzen. 2014. "Attitude Structure and Behavior." In *Attitude Structure and Function*, eds. Anthony R. Pratkanis, Steven J. Breckler, and Anthony G. Greenwald. New York: Psychology Press, pp. 241–74, p. 241.

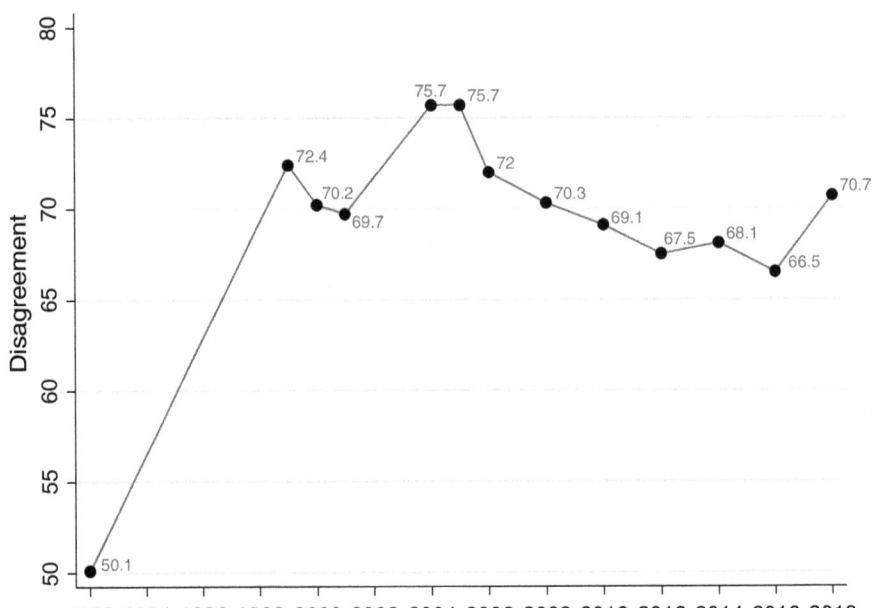

FIGURE 5.7 Disagreement with the statement, "Women Should Not Hold Leadership Positions."
Note: The percentage of survey respondents who disagree with the statement "Women should not hold leadership positions" is displayed in the figure.
Source: Institute of Sociology, National Academy of Sciences of Ukraine. *Ukrainian Society-2014: Social Monitoring*.

Opinion polls annually conducted by the Institute of Sociology, the National Academy of Sciences of Ukraine, reveal that approximately one-third of the adult population disapproved of having women in leadership positions.[103] As seen in Figure 5.7, only half of the survey respondents in 1992 disagreed with the statement, "Women should not hold leadership positions (*kerivni posady*)." Mass attitudes toward women's leadership roles improved in the late 1990s and underwent minor fluctuations throughout the past two decades. Approval of women in leadership positions peaked at 75.7 percent in 2004, dropped to 67.5 percent in 2012, and then reached 70.7 percent in 2018.

Survey data from the World Values Survey allow us to distinguish mass attitudes toward women's leadership in business and politics.[104] Empirical

[103] Survey results are retrieved from Valerii M. Vorona and Mykola O. Shulha, eds. 2018. *Ukrainske suspilstvo: monitorinh sotsialnykh zmin*. Kyiv: Institute of Sociology, National Academy of Sciences of Ukraine, p. 439.

[104] The latest three waves of the World Values Survey were conducted in Ukraine on November 15–November 25, 2006 (wave 6), December 1–December 12, 2011 (wave 7), and July 7–August 17, 2020 (wave 8). For details, see Ronald Inglehart, et al., eds. 2020. *World Values*

analysis finds that 44.1 percent of survey respondents in 2006, as well as 53.8 percent in 2011 and 51.3 percent in 2020, disagreed or strongly disagreed with the statement "On the whole, men make better business executives than women." In other words, nearly half of the adult population assumed that men would deliver better performance in executive positions. Attitudes toward female political leaders were even less favorable than attitudes toward female business executives. In November 2006, 40.8 percent of WVS respondents disagreed or strongly disagreed with the statement, "On the whole, men make better political leaders than women do." By the summer of 2020, 49 percent of the survey respondents expressed support for women's political leadership through their disagreement with the abovementioned statement. The survey results suggest that mass attitudes toward gender equality undergo a gradual change. Yet, women with political ambitions need to overcome a variety of challenges, including gender stereotypes in politics.

Public support for a female presidential candidate is widely regarded as a telling example of dominant gender norms. Since 1937, opinion polls conducted by the US leading polling company Gallup regularly included the following survey question, "If your party nominated a generally well-qualified person for president who happened to be a woman, would you vote for that person?" Using a similar survey item, the Kyiv International Institute of Sociology gauged mass attitudes toward a female presidential candidate in Ukraine in the 2010s.[105] The first nationally representative survey, including the abovementioned survey item, was conducted in March 2011, more than two years prior to Euromaidan (N = 1,020). The second survey was administered in October–November 2018, four years after the Revolution of Dignity (N = 2,044). The survey results register the stability of public opinion on this matter: 70 percent of Ukrainians in 2011 and 72 percent in 2018 would vote for a woman if she was nominated by a political party.[106] Similarly, 73 percent of Americans in 1975 were inclined to vote for a female aspirant for the executive office.[107] It is plausible to assume that the emergence of third-wave feminism in the 1990s influenced public opinion on women's status in American politics.[108] By 2011, 9 out of 10 Gallup respondents in the US reported their willingness to vote for a female presidential candidate. Meanwhile, one-quarter of voting-age

---

Survey: All Rounds – Country-Pooled Datafile. Madrid, Spain and Vienna, Austria: JD Systems Institute and WVSA Secretariat. www.worldvaluessurvey.org/WVSDocumentationWVL.jsp.

[105] Volodymyr Paniotto. 2011. "Komu vazhko staty prezydentom Ukrainy?" *KMIS Review* 9 (2): 13–14. www.kiis.com.ua/materials/KMIS-Review/02(10-2011)/ds.php?file=02_KR.pdf.

[106] Volodymyr Paniotto and Tetiana Pashkovska. 2018. "Komu vazhko staty prezydentom Ukrainy?" [press release]. November 30. Kyiv International Institute of Sociology, Kyiv. www.kiis.com.ua/index.php?lang=ukr&cat=reports&id=805&t=1&page=15.

[107] On cross-time attitudinal patterns in the US, see Gallup. 2022. "Topics A to Z: Presidency." https://news.gallup.com/poll/4729/Presidency.aspx.

[108] For an overview, see Jennifer Drake. 1997. *Third Wave Agenda: Being Feminist, Doing Feminism*. Minneapolis: University of Minnesota Press.

adults in contemporary Ukraine appear to assume that women are not well fit for the presidency.

Popular assumptions regarding the division of labor within a household impose constraints on women's pursuit of political ambitions. In addition to full-time employment, women are expected to perform a lion's share of household chores and childcare in Ukraine. The Kyiv International Institute of Sociology, for example, reported that only 22 percent of men in 2015 were willing to share equally domestic work with their spouses.[109] Likewise, according to the 2018 National Survey on Equality between Men and Women, the majority of Ukrainians assumed that women should be primarily responsible for cleaning the house and cooking for the family.[110] In line with traditional gender norms, 83.5 percent of Ukrainians in 2020 agreed with the statement, "The most important women's task is to take care of home and family."[111] In addition, 75 percent of survey respondents agreed that men's primary responsibility was to earn money.

Meanwhile, there is a growing acceptance of gender equality as an attribute of the democratic political system. WVS respondents were prompted to report the degree to which the provision of equal rights for women and men is essential for democracy on a scale from 1 ("not at all an essential characteristic of democracy") to 10 ("an essential characteristic of democracy"). The proportion of Ukrainians who regarded gender equality as an essential attribute of democracy and chose the maximum score of 10 increased from 43.7 percent in 2006 to 61.8 percent in 2020.[112] Yet, the level of public confidence in women's organizations remained quite low. Only one-third of respondents in 2006 (37 percent) and 2020 (34 percent) had "a great deal" or "quite a lot" of confidence in women's organizations. Low levels of trust in nongovernmental organizations entailed a low membership in NGOs. According to the results of the seventh wave of WVS, only 1 percent of the adult population were active members of women's organizations in 2020.[113] Nonetheless, data from oral history projects and media reports indicate that women's participation in the

---

[109] Kyiv International Institute of Sociology. 2015. "Chy zhodni ukraintsi zminyty stereotypy, rozdilyvshy porivnu domashni obov'iazky ta dohliad za ditmy? Rezyltaty doslidzhennia KMIS" [press release], October 30. www.kiis.com.ua/?lang=ukr&cat=reports&id=563&page=1&t=8.

[110] Office of Vice Prime Minister Ivanna Klympush-Tsintsadze. 2018. *The 2018 National Survey on Equality between Men and Women.* N = 2,558. This research was designed and executed by the National Democratic Institute and funded by Sweden and UK Aid. www.ndi.org/sites/default/files/Ukraine%20National%20Survey%20on%20Equality%20Between%20Men%20and%20Women%20July%202018.pdf.

[111] Rating Group Ukraine. "Rol zhinok v ukrainskomu suspilstvi."

[112] The mean for the ten-point scale increased from 8.4 in 2006 to 8.8 in 2020.

[113] An additional 4.5 percent of survey respondents reported that they were "inactive" members of women's organizations in 2020.

Revolution of Dignity had a profound impact on their identity and civic engagement.

BIOGRAPHICAL CONSEQUENCES OF ACTIVISM

A growing body of research demonstrates that participation in social movement activity can have far-reaching biographical consequences.[114] Participants in anti-government protests might remain more politically active and civically engaged than nonparticipants. Furthermore, protest participation might influence the career trajectories of individuals. In addition, involvement in civil resistance is likely to enhance an individual's sense of political efficacy and attachment to the political community. Finally, participation in the protest movement might have a pronounced impact on interpersonal relations and trust in compatriots. Data from oral history projects illustrate the transformative impact of participation in the Revolution of Dignity on individuals.

Political Identity

The Revolution of Dignity fostered the development of collective identity in contemporary Ukraine. People from different backgrounds formed a united front against the ruling elite. "We felt that we were a nation," said Ukrainian writer and librarian Olha Strashenko. "People felt that they were making history."[115] This growing sense of political efficacy facilitated fierce resistance to Russia's invasion. "There emerged a brotherhood that is now clearly seen during wartime," pointed out Oksana Belska, a healthcare professional who provided psychological counseling for participants in the Revolution of Dignity and subsequently became a psychologist for the military.[116] Fighting for a common cause strengthened citizens' resolve to build an independent, democratic state.

Ukrainians have finally and definitely formed as a nation that beyond any doubt deserves the right to national sovereignty, the right to be a master in their home, determine their destiny, and bear responsibility for it.[117]

Engagement in Euromaidan made some people realize how much they loved their homeland and how many sacrifices they were willing to make to defend

---

[114] For an overview of the literature, see Florence Passy and Gian-Andrea Monsch. 2019. "Biographical Consequences of Activism." In *The Wiley Blackwell Companion to Social Movements*, eds. David A. Snow, Sarah A. Soule, Hanspeter Kriesi, and Holly J. McCammon. Hoboken: Wiley Blackwell, pp. 499–514; Sara Vestergren, John Drury, and Eva Hammar Chiriac. 2017. "The Biographical Consequences of Protest and Activism: A Systematic Review and a New Typology." *Social Movement Studies* 16 (2): 203–21.
[115] UINP interview with Olha Strashenko, September 18, 2015.
[116] UINP interview with Oksana Belska, December 16, 2014.
[117] UINP interview with Nataliia Sokolenko, January 14, 2015.

Ukraine's independence. Evheniia Yanchenko, for example, noted greater self-awareness of her patriotism.

> I would never have thought that I was such a patriot until I got here. Frankly speaking, I even did not know all the lyrics of the national anthem. And I would never have thought that I would sacrifice everything and I would stand here like many others who are standing here and are not going anywhere.[118]

A shift in the linguistic practices of Russian-language protesters signified the gradual development of national identity. Individuals who grew up speaking Russian began to switch to Ukrainian to reclaim their Ukrainian identity and distance themselves from Russia's aggressive foreign policy in the region. Anastasiia Dmytruk, for example, started speaking and writing in Ukrainian.

> I mainly spoke Russian at the Institute because most of the people around me were Russophones. The [protest] events triggered a reevaluation of my values and made me think about the importance of the language issue in our country. Now I speak Ukrainian and have more poems written in Ukrainian.[119]

Civic Activism

The Revolution of Dignity created a fertile ground for the development of horizontal networks and the growth of civil society. As a result of anti-regime mobilization, Independence Square became a meeting place for civic activists from different communities. The AutoMaidan activist Kateryna Kuvita, for example, emphasized the long-term positive effects of mass mobilization for civil society.

> Since Maidan lasted for a long time, there emerged a coordination of action and the separation of genuine civil society and real activists from "grant-eating" organizations. Many people got acquainted, tested each other's flexibility, honesty, decency, professionalism. Such a number of acquaintances that took place on Maidan would simply be impossible under normal circumstances, without these [protest] events.[120]

Russia's military intervention in February 2014 led to the transformation and growth of preexisting social networks to raise funds for the military and provide assistance for internally displaced persons (IDPs). Following Russia's aggression, Iryna Kyselova, for example, quitted her full-time job and fully focused on her volunteer work.

> Volunteer work required so much time in 2014 that I quitted my job and focused solely on it. It was necessary to buy this, do that ... For half a year I was dependent on my spouse's income. When he was hungry and tired, he occasionally got angry with

---

[118] NaUKMA interview with Evheniia Yanchenko. Qtd. from *Maidan. Svidchennia. Kyiv, 2013–2014 roky*, p. 262.
[119] UINP interview with Anastasiia Dmytruk, April 15, 2016.
[120] UINP interview with Kateryna Kuvita, September 23, 2015.

me because I was never at home, but he stoically endured it. In 2015 I went back to work.[121]

On an individual level, participation in the Revolution of Dignity provided an incentive for the continuation of civic engagement during wartime. Once again, everyone tried to do their bit to advance a common cause. Yuliia Datsenko, for example, observed how all her friends who participated in the revolution helped the war effort as much as they could.

Nowadays everyone reaffirms through their work that we did not stand on Maidan in vain. Someone went to serve the country. Someone is currently on the eastern front. Someone regularly goes there with volunteers. Someone delivers humanitarian aid. Someone makes balaclavas. Someone makes camouflage nets. We went to work in the Ministry of Culture because culture is a weapon.[122]

Fighting on the cultural front, Ukrainian female artists and musicians organized concerts for the Ukrainian troops. Between 2014 and 2018, the art collective *Narodna Filarmoniia* (The Folk Philharmonic), for example, held over 500 charity concerts for Ukrainian soldiers near the battlefront or in training centers and military hospitals.[123] Ruslana Lotsman, a musician and a former Euromaidan participant, was a cofounder of this civic initiative:

We [Narodna Filarmoniia], along with patriots who performed on Maidan's stage, with artists, poets, composers, musicians, and bards, tour to support our warriors, defend our Ukraine, our independence in the same manner as we used to do on Maidan's stage.[124]

Many former Euromaidan participants established civic organizations to raise funds and collect supplies for the armed forces and volunteer battalions. Formed by a group of Euromaidan activists and based on the left bank of Kyiv, the civic initiative the Left Bank (*Livyi bereh*) initially sought to maintain public order and expose illegal casinos in the neighborhood.[125] However, in response to Russia's military intervention, the Left Bank channeled its resources toward the provision of critical resources for their compatriots on the frontlines.[126]

Moreover, some civic organizations established by former Euromaidan participants focused on the provision of legal and mental health services for families of Ukrainian soldiers. Formed by three women, Natalia Didyk, Olha Verzhykivska, and Nelia Vterkovska, the civic organization Women's Power of Ukraine (*Zhinocha syla Ukrainy*) sought to provide legal aid and psychological

---

[121] UINP interview with Iryna Kyselova, March 7, 2017.
[122] UINP interview with Yuliia Datsenko, July 24, 2015.
[123] For an overview of the projects completed by the Folk Philharmonic, visit the webpage www.fph.org.ua/node/84.
[124] UINP interview with Ruslana Lotsman, October 30, 2014.
[125] On the activities of the civic organization, see its Facebook page, www.facebook.com/samooborona.dneprovskogo/about_details.
[126] UINP interview with Anastasiia Maksymchuk, November 12, 2014.

counseling for female relatives of Ukrainian soldiers. Many activists believed that the volunteer movement was "Ukraine's secret weapon" against a more powerful opponent.[127]

Opinion polls indicate that the frequency of volunteering has markedly increased since the onset of the Russia–Ukraine war. Though the same proportion of the adult population reported volunteering in 2012 (10.2 percent) and 2015 (13 percent), there was a considerable increase in the intensity of volunteering: 22.6 percent of volunteers in 2015, compared to only 5.8 percent in 2012, weekly donated several hours for a cause.[128] Two-thirds of donated time and money was channeled toward support for the Armed Forces of Ukraine.

Volunteering on the Battlefront

On the basis of self-defense units that were active during Euromaidan, several volunteer battalions were formed in 2014 to fight against Russia's aggression on the eastern front.[129] Iryna Tsvilla, for example, joined the volunteer battalion *Sich* named after a military structure formed by Zaporozhian Cossacks in the sixteenth century:

> Everything for me, as well as for many others, began with Maidan. When the war started, staying on the sidelines was out of the question. The question was, "How should I get involved in it?" I did not have any military experience, I did not know how to use weapons, and I did not see myself as a high-quality military item ... But I had some experience in civic activism, working with a group of people ... I knew them from Maidan and from pre-Maidan activities – protest rallies and pickets – when we jointly defended our rights. There was a community, and it was not so scary [to join a battalion] because at least I knew who would be next to me.[130]

Many women who provided urgent medical care during the Euromaidan protests volunteered to serve as paramedics on the frontlines. Among them was Yuliia Paievska, later known as Taira. With the fifth *dan* (rank) in the Japanese martial art Aikido, Paievska was initially a member of the protest movement's security team that patrolled the encampment area and prevented provocations by the police. On January 19, 2014, given an escalation in police violence,

---

[127] On this point, see Liubov Eremicheva and Halyna Zhovtko. 2015. "Zhinocha syla Ukrainy: My mozhemo dopomohty zvesty nebo z zemleiu." *Hromadskii Prostir*, March 3. www.prostir.ua/?focus=zhinocha-syla-ukrajiny-my-mozhemo-dopomohty-zvesty-nebo-z-zemleyu.

[128] Democratic Initiatives Foundation. 2017. "Blahodiinist i volonterstvo-2016: rezultaty sotsialnoho doslidzhennia." February 21. https://dif.org.ua/article/blagodiynist-i-volonterstvo-2016-rezultati-sotsiologichnogo-doslidzhennya.

[129] For an overview, see Michael Cohen and Matthew Green. 2016. "Ukraine's Volunteer Battalions." *Infantry Magazine* 6 (1): 1–5.

[130] Evheniia Podobna, ed. 2018. *Divchata zrizauit' kosy: Knyha spohadiv/rosiiska-ukrainska viina*. Kyiv: Liuta sprava and the Ukrainian Institute of National Remembrance, p. 276. https://uinp.gov.ua/elektronni-vydannya/divchata-zrizayut-kosy-knyga-pro-zhinok-na-viyni.

Biographical Consequences of Activism

Paievska joined a medical team and started providing critical care for injured protesters.[131] Following Russia's military aggression in the eastern part of Ukraine, Paievska developed a course on tactical medicine and founded the volunteer paramedics group *Taira's Angels* to provide tactical medicine and evacuate people from the war zone.

For many women, fighting in the Russia–Ukraine war was a logical continuation of their struggle for Ukraine's independence on Maidan. In her *Live Journal* blog, the Ukrainian journalist and blogger Olena Bilozerska provided a daily account of mass mobilization against *khamovlada* (rule of the cad).[132] As she was standing on Maidan, she realized that her friends and she would go to the frontline in case of the war.[133] Bilozerska subsequently joined the Ukrainian Volunteer Corps (*Dobrovolchyi ukrainskii korpus*) and became a sniper.[134] As noted by Yuliia Filipovich, a participant in the Euromaidan movement and later a grenade launcher in a volunteer battalion, "Patriotism does not have a gender. If you love your country, you love it regardless of the fact that you are a man or a woman."[135]

Career Change

Participation in the Revolution of Dignity influenced the career trajectories of some participants, especially young people. Having volunteered for the civic initiative Euromaidan SOS, Mariia Ivanyk decided to make a drastic change in her life. "I completely changed my lifestyle," Ivanyk said. "Until then [2014], human rights work was something that I was interested in and I did it during my leisure time. Now it is my full-time professional activity."[136] Likewise, seventeen-year-old high school student Sophia changed her career plans after volunteering at a medical station during Euromaidan:

> I was planning to apply for a program in philology, but now I want to take a gap year after high school, travel as a volunteer and think about what I would like to do next. There are a lot of qualified, superb doctors [in Ukraine], but they cannot help people. There are no syringes, no masks, there is no financing; instead, there is a great deal of injustice, profiteering, bureaucracy, petty theft, human egoism at all levels, throughout the whole state hierarchy. I would like to somehow fight against it, participate in the

---

[131] Olena Sharhovska. 2020. "Taira – komandyr 'anheliv'. Yuliia Paievska ta ii shliakh iz Maidanu u frontovi paramedyky, a zvidty na Invictus Games." *Novynarnia*, March 4. https://novynarnia.com/2020/03/04/tayra.

[132] Olena Bilozerska. 2013. "EvroMaidan 21.11.2013" [blog entry] *Live Journal*, November 22. https://bilozerska.livejournal.com/2013/11/22.

[133] Ukrainky. n.d. "Ia snaiperka – istoriia Oleny Bilozerskii." https://ukrainky.com.ua/ya-snajperka-istoriya-oleny-bilozerskoyi.

[134] Olena Bilozerska. 2020. *Shchodennyk nelehalnoho soldata* [Diary of an Illegal Solder]. Kyiv: Itek Servis.

[135] Podobna. *Divchata zrizauit' kosy*, p. 108.

[136] UINP interview with Mariia Ivanyk, August 12, 2014.

implementation of reforms. For this purpose, I am trying to choose a niche in which I would be most effective.[137]

Gender Relations

The data from the oral history projects suggest that the Revolution of Dignity not only created an opportunity for women's contestation of dominant gender norms but also triggered men's display of masculinity at a critical juncture in Ukrainian history. Several female participants in the revolution acknowledged that men's behavior inside the encampment made them believe that not every man had turned into a couch potato. As a psychologist, Viktoriia Kochubei interacted with a large number of people, and she was impressed with everyone's commitment to civil resistance.[138] Likewise, Mila Ivantsova observed a high concentration of "real" (*spravzhni*) men inside the encampment.

Until Maidan, I had an impression, maybe a feminist one, that real men had disappeared in Ukraine. There were mama's boys or total losers who gave up on themselves, or some non-traditional men. Maidan impressed upon me the idea that a real Ukrainian man had woken up.[139]

Drawing on data from in-depth interviews with female participants in the revolution, it is safe to conclude that men's heroic resistance to the regime appeared to have improved the image of men in Ukrainian society. Women's positive comments imply that the existing pool of marital partners might have been larger than they initially assumed.

Engagement in civil resistance provided abundant opportunities for the development of romantic relationships among Euromaidan participants. A few women dubbed "Brides of the Revolution" (*narecheni revoluitsii*) or "Brides of Maidan" got married during the Revolution of Dignity, which was widely covered in the mass media.[140] On February 5, 2014, movement participants celebrated the wedding of Yuliia and Bohdan. Volunteering in a field kitchen, Yuliia cut her finger and went to the on-site medical station wherein Bohdan provided first aid for her. It was love at first sight, according to the newlyweds.[141] Originally from Chernivtsi oblast, Halyna Yeremytsia and Oleksandr Chaban also fell in love on Maidan. On February 9, 2014, the date of the tenth people's assembly (*viche*), Oleksandr made a proposal to Halyna

---

[137] Dmytro Desiateryk. 2014. "Druhyi front: Istoriia odnoho z volonteriv Maidanu." *Day*, April 25. https://day.kyiv.ua/uk/article/cuspilstvo/vtoroy-front.
[138] UINP interview with Viktoriia Kochubei, February 16, 2015.
[139] UINP interview with Mila Ivantsova, October 21, 2014.
[140] Olha Robeiko. 2022. "Narecheni revoluitsii: iak siohodni zhyvut pary, iaki odruzhylys na Maidani." *UNIAN*, November 21. www.unian.ua/society/narecheni-revolyuciji-yak-sogodni-zhivut-pari-yaki-odruzhilis-na-maydani-video-novini-kiyeva-12052992.html.
[141] UaModna. 2014. "Pershe vesillia na Maidani – 2014." February 6. https://uamodna.com/articles/pershe-vesillya-na-maydani-2014.

from Maidan's main stage, holding a bouquet of roses and a ring in his hand.[142] The two civil resisters got married on the premises of the encampment on February 14, St. Valentine's Day. Another couple tied the knot on February 15. Khrystyna Kryvdyk and Danylo Klekh have known each other since childhood, and they were planning to get married in the summer of 2014. However, the couple changed their wedding plans to share this special moment in their lives with their newly found friends. "Maidan has become a part of our lives," Khrystyna said. "We met here a lot of people, and we were eager to share with them our happiness."[143] Such weddings were hailed as a symbol of civil resistance to the brutal regime and people's triumph over adversity.

CONCLUSION

Gender outcomes of the Revolution of Dignity and the Russia–Ukraine war are multifaceted. From a political standpoint, women's activism on Maidan provided an impetus for women's pursuit of political ambitions. A sizeable proportion of women competed for seats in the national parliament and lower-level legislative bodies to influence policymaking processes. To some extent, it was a product of learning a lesson from the 2004 Orange Revolution. Participants in the Revolution of Dignity realized they should not withdraw from politics in the postrevolutionary period and should keep up public pressure on the ruling elite to implement structural reforms. Furthermore, many women remained active in civil society and volunteered to support the war effort. In the economic sphere, women pressed for the breakdown of occupational segregation. In particular, women gained access to combat positions in the military and contested dominant gender norms inside the Armed Forces of Ukraine. In line with a hybrid model of women's participation in a revolution, the level of progress in different domains varied in the postrevolutionary period. It might take a few decades to unravel the long-term effects of the Revolution of Dignity and the ensuing war on the status of women in Ukrainian society.

---

[142] Chas. 2014. "Bukovyntsi odruzhatsia na stolycnomu Evromaidani u Den vsikh zakokhanykh." February 14. https://chas.cv.ua/socium/16275-bukovinc-odruzhatsya-na-stolichnomu-yevromaydan-u-den-vsh-zakohanih.html.
[143] Viktoriia Savitska. 2014. "'Pomizh boiamy narodylas nova sim'ia'." *Lvivska Poshta*, February 18. https://lvivpost.net/ukraine/n/24174.

6

Conclusion

Over the past several decades, women played a prominent role in mass mobilization against authoritarianism. From Tunisia (2010) and Turkey (2013) to Sudan (2019) and Belarus (2020), citizens rose against long-serving incumbents to press for political change. Regime opponents employed a wide range of nonviolent tactics to contest dominant power relations. People occupied urban spaces, spray-painted graffiti, formed human chains, and performed protest songs. In most cases, revolutionary movements represented a cross-cutting coalition of social forces, bringing together individuals with diverse backgrounds. Women's participation in the revolutionary struggle was driven by a gamut of motives, took multiple forms, and produced various outcomes.

The book proposes a typology of women's participation in a revolution. In particular, a hybrid model of women's participation in a contemporary revolution assumes a variety of motivations for women's engagement in a revolution, underscores the diversity of women's roles over the course of mass mobilization, and acknowledges various degrees of success in gender equality in different spheres. Using the case of the Revolution of Dignity in Ukraine, the book demonstrates various motivations for women's involvement in a revolution, diverse domains of women's engagement, and multifaceted outcomes of mass mobilization. As shown in the book, Ukrainian women performed a variety of tasks, including the coordination of volunteers, provision of supplies, communication of movement ideas, and organization of street actions. Furthermore, the book examines the impact of women's engagement on gender equality in the aftermath of the incumbent's ouster.

To explore the applicability of the proposed typology to other cases and further illustrate the breadth of women's engagement in a revolution, the concluding chapter briefly discusses the 2013 Gezi Park uprising in Turkey and the 2020 electoral revolution in Belarus. Despite considerable political and cultural differences, the two countries have recently witnessed an escalation in authoritarianism and a resurgence in the incumbent's emphasis on traditional values. In turn, citizens tried to thwart the government's infringement on political rights and civil liberties through nonviolent action. Originally, these two cases were selected to represent different models of women's engagement in a revolution. The government's crackdown on women's rights provided an incentive for many young college-educated women in Turkey to get involved in the 2013 protests, which is in line with an emancipatory model of women's participation. In contrast, Tsikhanouskaya's emphasis on the love of her spouse and her children as a key motive for her presidential run fits in well with a patriarchal model of women's participation. Yet, a closer look at patterns of women's activism in these societies reveals a more complex mosaic of civil resistance. Some female participants in the Gezi movement invoked their maternal identity to protect youthful protesters against police violence, which aligns with a patriarchal model of women's participation. Meanwhile, women's defiance of the tyrant's patriarchal norms and women's leadership role in nonviolent resistance in Belarus can be construed as an example of the emancipatory model of women's participation. What emerges from this additional empirical analysis is that a hybrid model of women's participation in a revolution appears to prevail in many contemporary societies.

IMPLICATIONS

The findings presented in the book have several implications for the study of contentious politics. First, the book enhances our knowledge of different modes of citizens' participation in a revolution. Second, the book speaks to a key debate about the drivers of mass mobilization. Specifically, the book sheds some light on the interplay between state repression and nonviolent resistance. Furthermore, the study deepens our understanding of policy outcomes and the biographical consequences of women's participation in a revolution.

Conceptualization of Participation in a Revolution

The book calls for a broader conceptualization of citizens' participation in a revolution. A conventional gender-based division of labor within the revolutionary movement tends to place men on the barricades and assign women to the performance of the so-called support tasks. The case of the Revolution of Dignity in Ukraine, on the contrary, demonstrates that women can assume a wide range of roles over the course of mass mobilization against the regime. Women sustain the resilience of a movement not only by managing the steady provision of food and medical services but also by conceiving and leading numerous civic initiatives. In acknowledging women's multiple contributions to a revolutionary cause, scholars can provide a more inclusive account of the liberation struggle.

Furthermore, the book tells a cautionary tale against viewing women's physical absence from the encampment as an indicator of women's withdrawal from the revolution. Currently, the ubiquitous use of information and communication technologies blurs the boundaries of participation in a revolution. Data from oral history projects reveal that many women who were physically absent from Independence Square performed such critical tasks as crowdsourcing, legal aid, and public outreach. On-site opinion polls and participant observation might not capture a full spectrum of participants in a revolutionary movement. Instead, in-depth interviews with regime opponents might enable scholars to sketch a more detailed portrait of movement participants based inside and outside the main protest site.

Drivers of Women's Participation in a Revolution

An in-depth analysis of women's participation in the Revolution of Dignity challenges the idea that women are unlikely to get involved in high-risk activism. Since the brutal dispersion of peaceful protests in November 2013, there has been a high probability of recurrent police violence and imprisonment of regime opponents. Nonetheless, thousands of men and women persevered in their struggle against the incumbent government. Notably, college-educated women represented a sizeable share of movement participants.

The book contributes to contentious politics literature by uncovering a wide range of motivations for women's engagement in a revolution. As shown in Chapter 3, dissatisfaction with the quality of governance, outrage over police violence, professional service, civic duty, motherhood, or solidarity with protesters might serve as a catalyst for women's activism under precarious conditions. These findings bring into focus the idea that women should not be seen as a homogeneous group. Rather, women have multiple grievances and social identities, which affects their decision to get involved in a revolution.

A related finding that emerges from oral history projects is that feminism is rarely mentioned as a primary reason for getting involved in the revolution. Apparently, the concept of feminism continues to be riddled with controversy in postcommunist Europe. In turn, some women seem to eschew an overt articulation of feminist ideas to avoid a public backlash. In post-socialist Albania, for example, several women activists prefaced their self-description of activism with the phrase "I am not a feminist but...."[1] A similar pattern was observed over the past centennial in Ukrainian society. In documenting the rise of a modern women's movement in pre-WWII Ukraine, Bohachevsky-Chomiak finds that women engaged in the work of women's organizations "gingerly acknowledged feminism."[2] Likewise, the interviewed Ukrainian activists rarely brought up the concept of feminism in their narratives about Euromaidan. Nonetheless, female participants in the revolution contested patriarchal norms

---

[1] Ermira Danaj. 2018. "'I Am Not a Feminist But...': Women's Activism in Post-1991 Albania." *Gender, Place and Culture* 25 (7): 994–1009.

[2] Martha Bohachevsky-Chomiak. 2021. "*Feminists despite Themselves*: A Look Back." *Kyiv-Mohyla Humanities Journal* 8: 164–67, 166.

and reasserted women's agency. Under such circumstances, women's actions might speak louder than words.

Another contribution of the book lies in identifying various social networks conducive to women's participation in a revolution. As seen in Chapter 3, women were embedded in a wide range of mixed-gender social networks, including professional associations, civic organizations, universities, and religious institutions. Data from oral history projects indicate that Facebook served as an important source of information about protest events in the mid-2010s. Specifically, individuals with weak social ties were more likely to get galvanized into action via social media. For others, friendship ties or professional networks were more influential. An implication of these findings is that offline social networks remain vital for mass mobilization despite the growth of social media use.

The book illuminates the added value of taking a long-term perspective on contentious politics in society by unraveling cross-time patterns of women's activism in the Russian Empire, the Soviet Union, and postcommunist Ukraine. The empirical analysis concentrates on three episodes of contention: the 1917–1921 Ukrainian Revolution, the 1990 Revolution on Granite, and the 2004 Orange Revolution. A recurrent narrative in Ukrainian historiography is that women activists were compelled to subordinate "their feminist agenda to the goals of the national liberation struggle."[3] An examination of women's activism suggests that women tried to advance gender equality despite the primacy of the national drive for independence. The gender-specific networks prevailed at the start of the twentieth century, while many women were involved in educational and cultural initiatives in the Ukrainian National Republic. Over time, however, social networks appear to have become more diverse. Female and male students who took part in the 1990 student hunger strike were mobilized via coed universities and mixed-gender civic organizations. More recently, given women's active participation in the labor market, many Euromaidan participants were galvanized into action through their professional networks. This finding suggests that patterns of women's mobilization are contingent on the dominant gender norms in the country.

State Repression and Nonviolent Resistance

The book speaks to a debate about the effects of repression on the scope and methods of resistance.[4] Repressive measures can crush dissent or fuel mass mobilization. Furthermore, state violence reinvigorates intra-movement

---

[3] For an overview of major trends in Ukrainian women's history, see Oksana Kis. 2012. "Restoring the Broken Continuity: Women's History in Post-Soviet Ukraine." *Aspasia: The International Yearbook of Central, Eastern, and Southeastern European Women's and Gender History* 6: 171–83, 175.

[4] Erica Chenoweth, Evan Perkoski, and Sooyeon Kang. 2017. "State Repression and Nonviolent Resistance." *Journal of Conflict Resolution* 61 (9): 1950–69.

deliberations over the use of nonviolent action. The case of the Revolution of Dignity illuminates conditions under which state repression ignites further collective action. As shown in the previous chapters, police violence against peaceful protesters might cause a backlash and lead to the radicalization of regime opponents.

In addition, the book sheds some light on the relationship between gender and nonviolent action. Consistent with civil resistance literature, the book documents the positive impact of women on the movement's commitment to nonviolence. For weeks, Ukrainian women organized street actions and pleaded with the police against the use of force. However, the findings call into question a widely held assumption that women unconditionally reject the deployment of force against their adversaries. Once regime opponents and the ruling elite arrived at the conclusion that they had reached a point of no return, the likelihood of using radical tactics dramatically increased. In February 2014, women and men joined forces to fight against the regime by building barricades, making Molotov cocktails, and burning tires. It was the protesters' threat of storming the president's palace that reportedly prompted the incumbent's departure from the capital city and ended a cycle of police violence.

Women and Autocratization

The book contributes to comparative politics literature by placing women's role in the struggle against autocratization at the center of empirical analysis. The early 1990s saw a boom in democratization studies. A sizeable literature scrutinized the growth of civil society in Eastern Europe.[5] In particular, scholars analyzed the emergence of women's organizations and the contestation of gender norms during the transition from communism.[6] More recently, numerous studies have investigated how women in the Middle East raised their voices against authoritarianism and patriarchy in the 2010s. Far less attention has focused on women's engagement in contemporary revolutions aimed at

---

[5] Grzegorz Ekiert and Jan Kubik. 2001. *Rebellious Civil Society: Popular Protest and Democratic Consolidation in Poland, 1989–1993*. Ann Arbor: University of Michigan Press; Marc Morjé Howard. 2003. *The Weakness of Civil Society in Post-Communist Europe*. New York: Cambridge University Press; Sarah E. Mendelson and John K. Glenn. 2002. *The Power and Limits of NGOs: A Critical Look at Building Democracy in Eastern Europe and Eurasia*. New York: Columbia University Press; Sabrina P. Ramet. 1995. *Social Currents in Eastern Europe: The Sources and Consequences of the Great Transformation*, 2nd ed. Durham: Duke University Press.

[6] Barbara Einhorn. 1993. *Cinderella Goes to Market: Citizenship, Gender and Women's Movements in East Central Europe*. New York: Verso; Yvonne Galligan, Sara Clavero, and Marina Calloni. 2007. *Gender, Politics and Democracy in Post-Socialist Europe*. Farmington Hills: Barbara Budrich; Jane Jacquette and Sharon Wolchik, eds. 1998. *Women and Democracy: Latin America and Central and Eastern Europe*. Baltimore: John Hopkins University Press; Janet E. Johnson and Jean C. Robinson, eds. 2006. *Living Gender After Communism*. Bloomington: Indiana University Press.

overturning the entrenchment of authoritarianism in the post-Soviet region. The book seeks to address this oversight in the literature.

ADDITIONAL CASES

A concise overview of women's engagement in the 2013 Gezi Park uprising in Turkey and the 2020 electoral revolution in Belarus places an analysis of Ukraine's Euromaidan in a comparative perspective. In each case, mass mobilization unfolded in a repressive political regime, albeit the degree of political openness varied across the countries. Anti-government protests were initially triggered by a very specific issue – the demolition of a park, the EU–Ukraine Association Agreement, or electoral malpractices – but police violence against peaceful protesters caused a backlash and broadened the base of support for political change.[7] Another salient feature of civil resistance in Belarus, Turkey, and Ukraine was that urban areas and in particular main squares in large cities served as a major site for a protracted confrontation between the ruling elite and ordinary citizens. Unlike Ukraine's Revolution of Dignity, civil resistance in Turkey (2013) and Belarus (2020) did not culminate in the removal of the incumbent from power. Still, these uprisings had a profound impact on domestic politics and civil society. In Turkey, for example, the Gezi uprising "transformed the culture of political protests in the country and paved the way for the emergence of affirmative resistance, radical imagination, and a new politics of desire and dignity against authoritarian and neoliberal policies."[8] Overall, the additional cases underscore the idea that there might be multiple forms of women's activism and substantial variation in women's empowerment in different domains.

The 2013 Gezi Park Uprising in Turkey

Like Ukraine, Turkey was designated a "partly free" country in 2013, signifying systematic violations of political rights and civil liberties.[9] As a former mayor of Istanbul, Recep Tayyip Erdogan catapulted himself into national politics with the establishment of the Justice and Development Party (*Adalet ve Kalkınma Partisi*, AK Party) in 2001.[10] Advancing a conservative agenda and propagating "family values," AK Party won a sweeping victory in

---

[7] On this point, see S. Erdem Aytaç, Luis Schiumerini, and Susan Stokes. 2017. "Protests and Repression in New Democracies." *Perspectives on Politics* 15 (1): 62–82.
[8] Zafer Yılmaz. 2018. "Revising the Culture of Political Protest After the Gezi Uprising in Turkey: Radical Imagination, Affirmative Resistance, and the New Politics of Desire and Dignity." *Mediterranean Quarterly* 29 (3): 55–77.
[9] The country scores are retrieved from Freedom House, https://freedomhouse.org/sites/default/files/2023-02/All_data_FIW_2013-2023.xlsx.
[10] Alev Çınar. 2011. "The Justice and Development Party: Turkey's Experience with Islam, Democracy, Liberalism, and Secularism." *International Journal of Middle East Studies* 43 (3): 529–41.

2002 and received the plurality of the vote in the 2007 and 2011 elections to the Grand National Assembly. Between 2004 and 2013, Erdogan served three terms as the prime minister. He subsequently assumed the post of the President of Turkey (2014–present). Over the span of two decades, the strongman moved the country in "a profoundly illiberal, authoritarian direction."[11] In 2013, however, scores of people rose against the entrenchment of authoritarianism in Turkey.[12]

Mass protests were initially triggered by the government's decision to demolish a small park in Taksim Square, a popular meeting point in the European part of Istanbul, and build a shopping mall instead. Gezi Park was one of the few remaining green spaces in the city's center.[13] What further angered many Istanbul residents was that the new shopping mall was designed to emulate the style of *Topçu Kışlası*, Ottoman-era military barracks and headquarters of the 1909 mutiny in favor of the reestablishment of Sharia.[14] Like Independence Square in Kyiv, Taksim Square has been a popular venue for mass gatherings. The square was the site of the May 1st demonstration that ended in the deaths of at least thirty-four people in 1977.[15] Between 1980 and 2009, the government banned the organization of Labor Day demonstrations. The ban was lifted for two years and then reinstated in 2012, which was a source of discontent within the Turkish labor movement. In late May 2013, a few dozen environmental activists gathered in the park to disrupt the construction work. They occupied the public space and pitched tents. On May 31, the police attempted to clear the square by using tear gas against protesters and burning the tents.[16]

---

[11] Halil Karaveli. 2016. "Erdogan's Journey: Conservatism and Authoritarianism in Turkey." *Foreign Affairs* 95 (6): 121–30, 121. See alsoÜmit Akçay. 2021. "Authoritarian Consolidation Dynamics in Turkey." *Contemporary Politics* 27 (1): 79–104; Berk Esen and Sebnem Gumuscu. 2016. "Rising Competitive Authoritarianism in Turkey." *Third World Quarterly* 37 (9): 1581–1606.

[12] This episode of contention is frequently described as an uprising by Turkish scholars. See, for example, Emre Eren Korkmaz. 2013. "The June Uprising in Turkey." *SEER: Journal for Labour and Social Affairs in Eastern Europe* 16 (3): 325–46; Özge Yaka and Serhat Karakayali. 2017. "Four: Emergent Infrastructures: Solidarity, Spontaneity and Encounter at Istanbul's Gezi Park Uprising." In *Protest Camps in International Context: Spaces, Infrastructures and Media of Resistance*, eds. Gavin Brown, Anna Feigenbaum, Fabian Frenzel, and Patrick McCurdy. Bristol, UK: Policy Press, pp. 53–70; Yılmaz. "Revising the Culture of Political Protest After the Gezi Uprising in Turkey"; Erdem Yörük. 2014. "The Long Summer of Turkey: The Gezi Uprising and Its Historical Roots." *South Atlantic Quarterly* 113 (2): 419–26.

[13] BBC. 2013. "Turkey Clashes: Why Are Gezi Park and Taksim Square So Important?" June 7. www.bbc.com/news/world-europe-22753752.

[14] On the 1909 mutiny, see Paul Farkas. 2010. *Palace Revolution and Counterrevolution in Turkey (March–April 1909)*. Piscataway: Gorgias Press.

[15] IPS Communication Foundation. 2021. *1 May '77 The Voices of Those Who Lost Their Loved Ones. 1 May '77 and Impunity*. https://bianet.org/kadin/politics/241954-1-may-1977-e-book-is-online.

[16] Hurriyet: Daily News. 2013. "Raid on 'Occupy Taksim Park' Demonstrators Triggers Outcry." May 31. www.hurriyetdailynews.com/raid-on-occupy-taksim-park-demonstrators-triggers-outcry-47870.

An image of a young woman in the red dress, standing her ground despite being pepper sprayed by a heavily armored police officer, became a symbol of civil resistance to the regime. Being a researcher at Istanbul Technical University, Ceyda Sungur became known as the Woman in Red (*Kirmizili Kadin*). "Every citizen defending their human rights, every worker defending their human rights, and every student defending university rights has witnessed the police violence I experienced," Sungur said.[17] The photo taken by *Reuters* photographer Osman Orsal went viral on social media, and it inspired numerous cartoons and memes. A *Reuters* journalist described the image as a "leitmotif for Istanbul's female protesters."[18] Max Fisher of *The Washington Post* summarized the symbolic meaning of the photo as follows:

The dynamic between the woman in red and the police officer in the photo is fascinating, a microcosm of the relationship between outraged Turks and not just the police but perhaps the Turkish government itself, which they see as increasingly authoritarian. The policeman is hunched over slightly as if braced for combat as he, in almost Orwellian cruelty, sprays a few tablespoons of what appears to be pepper spray directly into the face of a young woman who is clearly a threat to no one. But what's most remarkable is her stance: head slightly bowed but she stands her ground, neither charging the officer nor running away.[19]

Police violence against peaceful protesters backfired.[20] On June 1, tens of thousands of people filled the square. For two weeks, this public space was transformed into a major site of civil resistance.[21] Didem Basir, the twenty-nine-year-old actress, noted in her blog how the government's action against protesters became a turning point for many critics of the incumbent government:

Gezi Park was the sparkle, in June 1, we woke up a new day ... Then a resistance began. A resistance that me, my friends, our parents have never seen before ... A resistance of ordinary people without any leader, a political movement or any political party. And now Gezi Park has become a symbol of our fight against fascism and our demand for democracy.[22]

---

[17] Paul Vale. 2013. "'Woman in Red' Becomes Iconic Image for Turkey Activists." *The Huffington Post*, June 5. www.huffingtonpost.co.uk/2013/06/05/turkey-uprising-ceyda-sungur_n_3388712.html?utm_hp_ref=tw.

[18] Alexandra Hudson. 2013. "Woman in Red Becomes Leitmotif for Istanbul's Female Protesters." *Reuters*, June 3. www.reuters.com/article/us-turkey-protests-women/woman-in-red-becomes-leitmotif-for-istanbuls-female-protesters-idUSBRE95217B20130603.

[19] Max Fisher. 2013. "The Photo That Encapsulates Turkey's Protests and the Severe Police Crackdown." *The Washington Post*, June 3. www.washingtonpost.com/blogs/worldviews/wp/2013/06/03/the-photo-that-encapsulates-turkeys-protests-and-the-severe-police-crackdown.

[20] On the government's crackdown, see Amnesty International. 2013. *Gezi Park Protests: Brutal Denial of the Right to Peaceful Assembly in Turkey*. October 2. www.amnesty.org/en/documents/EUR44/022/2013/en/.

[21] Yaka and Karakayali. "Emergent Infrastructures".

[22] Severin. 2013. "An Insider's View from Turkey: Occupy Taksim." *EyEem*. www.eyeem.com/blog/an-insiders-view-from-turkey-occupy-taksim.

An on-site survey conducted by KONDA Research and Consultancy in Gezi Park on June 6–8, 2013, sketches a portrait of participants in anti-government protests.[23] Women represented 50.8 percent of protesters. The average age of protesters was twenty-eight, which closely corresponded to the average age in Istanbul (30.1) and in Turkey (30.3). However, people with higher education were over-represented in the protest movement. Though only 12.5 percent of Istanbul residents graduated from college, 42.8 percent of protesters received higher education. The survey results also indicate that housewives made up only 2 percent of protesters, compared to 33 percent of Istanbul's population. There is a debate in the literature about the role of different socioeconomic groups in the uprising. In the summer of 2013, the sociologist Cigan Tuğal tentatively defined the Gezi Park movement as "an occasionally multi-class, but predominantly middle-class movement."[24] In contrast, Gürcan and Perher emphasize the participation of "wage-earning classes" in the struggle against "neoliberalism with Islamic characteristics."[25] Nonetheless, the Gezi Park movement brought together a mix of seasoned activists and protest novices, including environmentalists, feminists, socialists, anti-capitalist Muslims, and university students.[26] In addition, the results of the KONDA survey indicate that two-thirds of protesters were not affiliated with any political party or nongovernmental organization. Remarkably, people from diverse backgrounds "found a way to come together and say something."[27]

The on-site survey identifies several main motivations for protest engagement. Police brutality was cited as a catalyst for action by 49.1 percent of the surveyed protesters.[28] Only 19 percent of survey respondents decided to join the protests when a construction company started cutting down trees. An additional 14.2 percent turned out after hearing Erdogan's public statements on the topic. In summarizing the movement's main goal, Taksim Solidarity declared, "Our resistance that began with the intention to stop the slaughter of Gezi Park's trees went beyond the park's borders and joined the anger felt by the people in Istanbul and across Turkey against JDP

[23] A total of 4,411 people were surveyed. For details, see KONDA. 2014. *Gezi Report: Public Perception of the "Gezi Protests." Who Were the People at Gezi Park?* June 5. https://konda.com.tr/report/121/gezi-report?l=en.
[24] Cihan Tuğal. 2013. "'Resistance Everywhere': The Gezi Revolt in Global Perspective." *New Perspectives on Turkey* 49: 157–72, 156.
[25] Efe Can Gürcan and Efe Peker. 2015. "Debunking the Myth of 'Middle Classes': The Class-Structural Background of the GPPs." In *Challenging Neoliberalism at Turkey's Gezi Park: From Private Discontent to Collective Class Action*. New York: Palgrave Macmillan, pp. 33–58.
[26] Anthony Alessandrini, Nazan Üstündag, and Emrah Yildiz, eds. 2013. "Introduction by the Editors: 'Resistance Everywhere': The Gezi Protests and Dissident Visions of Turkey." *JadMag* 1 (4): 4–8; Yörük. "The Long Summer of Turkey."
[27] Sulome Anderson. 2013. "Blood, Tear Gas, and Twitter: On the Front Lines with Turkey's 'Occupy' Kids." *New York Magazine*, June 12. https://nymag.com/intelligencer/2013/06/on-the-front-lines-with-turkeys-occupy-kids.html.
[28] KONDA. *Gezi Report*, p. 20.

Additional Cases

government's eleven-year rule."[29] Similarly, many Ukrainians joined the 2013 anti-government protests in response to police violence against peaceful protesters and the government's disregard of citizens' rights.

Media reports suggest that a sizeable share of young college-educated women protested against Erdogan's conservative agenda, including a call to ban abortions, have at least three children in a household, and enact a more conservative dress code for women.[30] Many young women aspired to have the freedom to pursue different lifestyles in contemporary Turkey. A math student named Esra described her political stance as follows:

I respect women who wear the headscarf, that is their right, but I also want my rights to be protected. I'm not a leftist or an anti-capitalist. I want to be a businesswoman and live in a free Turkey.[31]

For some protesters, the demolition of the park was the last straw that galvanized them into action. A young woman named Meli expressed her pent-up frustration with Erdogan's conservative policies since the start of his tenure as the prime minister.

Day by day, this stuff has been building up, and we just exploded. They are so selfish, and they're harming all the trees and the creatures who live here. They're limiting our freedom. So this park is a symbol of the last ten years we've dealt with.[32]

Taksim Solidarity (*Taksim Dayanismasi*), a coalition of over 100 NGOs, political parties, and labor unions, was formed to coordinate the activities of the protest movement. Representatives of Taksim Solidarity met with the prime minister on June 13, 2013.[33] Among movement leaders (who were later put on trial) were several women.[34] "We started a resistance which was exemplary to the world, which was very peaceful," said Mücella Yapici, head of the Istanbul Chamber of Architects. "But we faced increasing violence each time we took the streets."[35] In addition to Mücella Yapici, the documentary filmmaker Mine

---

[29] Taksim Solidarity. 2013. "Everywhere Taksim, Everywhere Resistance." June 15. www.taksimdayanisma.org/her-yer-taksim-her-yer-direnis?lang=en.

[30] On this point, see Korkmaz. "The June Uprising in Turkey," p. 340.

[31] Hudson. "Woman in Red Becomes Leitmotif for Istanbul's Female Protesters". www.reuters.com/article/us-turkey-protests-women/woman-in-red-becomes-leitmotif-for-istanbuls-female-protesters-idUSBRE95217B20130603.

[32] Anderson. "Blood, Tear Gas, and Twitter". https://nymag.com/intelligencer/2013/06/on-the-front-lines-with-turkeys-occupy-kids.html.

[33] Taksim Solidarity. 2013. "Last Minute: Taksim Solidarity Is Going to PM's Office for a Meeting." June 13. www.taksimdayanisma.org/duyuru-taksim-dayanismasi-gorusme-icin-basbakanliga-dogru-yola-ciktilar?lang=en.

[34] For an overview of the trial, see International Commission of Jurists. 2020. *The Gezi Park Case: A Trial Monitoring Report*. Geneva: ICJ.

[35] Hurriyet: Daily News. 2014. "Turkey Stages 'Show Trial' of Taksim Solidarity Platform Members for 'Organizing' Gezi Protests." June 13. www.hurriyetdailynews.com/turkey-stages-show-trial-of-taksim-solidarity-platform-members-for-organizing-gezi-protests-67678.

Özerden and the film producer Çiğdem Mater, as well as three men, were sentenced to eighteen years in prison for the alleged attempt to overthrow the government.[36]

Over the course of two weeks of lull in June 2013, a carnivalesque atmosphere prevailed inside the encampment.[37] Youthful protesters shouted the slogan "Everywhere is Taksim, Everywhere is resistance." There was a "fairground of thoughts" wherein different organizations presented their ideas to a wide audience.[38] On the one hand, some protesters invoked the image of a headscarf-wearing middle-aged auntie (*teyze*) to provide a humorous description of participants in the uprising.[39] One of the tweets, for example, declared, "Mothers have arrived at the resistance. Tomorrow morning when we get up, we may find AKM's facade to have a motherly touch."[40] On the other hand, feminists organized events and demonstrations to draw public attention to women's rights. "Our specific political contribution was to link the 'public' matters that were politicized during the protests to the less visible 'private' matters, in particular to women's oppression in the familial sphere," said Selin Cagatay, a founding member of the Socialist Feminist Collective (*Sosyalist Feminist Kolektif*).[41]

The situation dramatically changed when the police moved in to dismantle the encampment and tear gas protesters in mid-June. According to the Turkish Medical Association, at least 4,755 people were injured in Istanbul between May 31 and July 10.[42] Many doctors volunteered to provide first aid for the injured. In response, the government passed a law in January 2014, imposing severe penalties for the provision of urgent medical care without state authorization.[43] Moreover, given the mass arrests of participants in the Gezi Park protests, dozens of lawyers provided pro bono legal aid for protesters and were

---

[36] The seventh co-defender, Osman Kavala, was sentenced to life imprisonment without parole. For details, see Amnesty International. 2022. "Türkiye: Free the Gezi 7." June 17. www.amnesty.org/en/latest/campaigns/2022/06/turkiye-free-the-gezi-7/.

[37] Zeynep Baykal and Nezihe Başak Ergin. 2013. "Turkey's Rebellion: Gezi Park, The Art of Resistance." *Global Dialogue* 3 (5): 21–23.

[38] Coskun Tastan. 2013. "The Gezi Park Protests in Turkey: A Qualitative Field Research." *Insight Turkey* 15 (3): 27–38, 32.

[39] Perin Gurel. 2015. "Bilingual Humor, Authentic Aunties, and the Transnational Vernacular at Gezi Park." *Journal of Transnational American Studies* 6 (1): 1–30.

[40] Mahiye Seçil Dağtaş. 2016. "'Down With Some Things!' The Politics of Humour and Humour as Politics in Turkey's Gezi Protests." *Etnofoor* 28 (1): 11–34, 26.

[41] Mattia Gallo. 2015. "Sosyalist Feminist Kolektif: Fighting for Women's Rights in Turkey. An Interview with Selin Cagatay." *LeftEast*, February 18. https://lefteast.org/sosyalist-feminist-kolektif/.

[42] Turkish Medical Association. 2013. "Health Status of Demonstrators: Data Collected from the Chambers of Medicine and Physicians (May 31–July 10)." www.ttb.org.tr/images/stories/file/english.doc.

[43] Ola Claësson. 2014. "Doctors Urged to Condemn Turkey's Emergency Care Law." *The Lancet* 383: 941. https://doi.org/10.1016/S0140-6736(14)60466-9.

themselves harassed by the police. Lawyer Burcu Öztoprak, for example, reported to Amnesty International that the police insulted and assaulted her for representing the interests of a challenger organization.[44] Scores of journalists also supported the movement's cause by providing media coverage of protests despite the threat of dismissal and police harassment.

Following a crackdown on participants in the Gezi Park protests, the incumbent tried to tighten his control over society and bolster his support among conservative voters.[45] With the support of AK Party, the women's organization Women and Democracy Association (*Kadın ve Demokrasi Derneği*, KADEM) was established to mobilize women in support of the party's conservative agenda.[46] The AK Party also tried to create additional obstacles to restrict women's right to abortion, which was legalized in 1983.[47] Amendments to the Law on the Civil Registration Services, allowing muftis – religious civil servants – to perform and register civil marriages, were seen as another assault on secularism and women's rights.[48] Moreover, in March 2021, Erdogan signed a presidential decree, unilaterally declaring Turkey's withdrawal from the Council of Europe Convention on Preventing and Combating Violence against Women and Domestic Violence, known as the Istanbul Convention.[49] To challenge the incumbent's move and raise public awareness of legal norms about the protection of women against different forms of violence, women took to the streets and campaigned via social media.[50] On International Women's

---

[44] Amnesty International. *Gezi Park Protests*, p. 49.
[45] Akçay. "Authoritarian Consolidation Dynamics in Turkey"; Koray Çalışkan. 2018. "Toward a New Political Regime in Turkey: From Competitive toward Full Authoritarianism." *New Perspectives on Turkey* 58: 5–33; Esen and Gumuscu. "Rising Competitive Authoritarianism in Turkey"; Bertil Emrah Oder. 2021. "Turkey's Democratic Erosion: On Backsliding and the Constitution." *Social Research: An International Quarterly* 88 (2): 473–500.
[46] Yeşim Arat. 2022. "Democratic Backsliding and the Instrumentalization of Women's Rights in Turkey." *Politics and Gender* 18 (4): 911–41, 933–34; Çağla Diner. 2018. "Gender Politics and GONGOs in Turkey." *Turkish Policy Quarterly* 16 (4): 101–108.
[47] Sinem Esengen. 2024. "'We Had that Abortion Together': Abortion Networks and Access to Il/legal Abortions in Turkey." *Culture, Health and Sexuality* 26 (9): 1119–1133. https://doi.org/10.1080/13691058.2023.2301410; Hatice Kübra Ercoşkun Şenol and Pelin Ercoşkun. 2023. "The Right to Terminate Pregnancy (Abortion): Reflections from Turkey." *Journal of Law and the Biosciences* 10 (2): lsado23. https://doi.org/10.1093/jlb/lsado23.
[48] Heinrich Böll Stiftung Turkey. 2017. "The Mufti Law." November 8. https://tr.boell.org/en/2017/11/08/mufti-law.
[49] Selver B. Sahin. 2022. "Combatting Violence Against Women in Turkey: Structural Obstacles." *Contemporary Politics* 28 (2): 204–24.
[50] Özlem Altan-Olcay and Bertil Emrah Oder. 2021. "Why Turkey's Withdrawal from the Istanbul Convention Is a Global Problem." *Open Democracy*, June 2. www.opendemocracy.net/en/can-europe-make-it/why-turkeys-withdrawal-from-the-istanbul-convention-is-a-global-problem/; Müge Öztunç. 2023. "Digital Activism in Turkey: Istanbul Convention as a Symbol of Women's Movement." *The Turkish Online Journal of Design, Art and Communication* 13 (2): 407–23; Esra Yalcinalp. 2021. "Turkey Erdogan: Women Rise Up Over Withdrawal from Istanbul Convention." *BBC*, March 25. www.bbc.com/news/world-europe-56516462.

Day, for example, women's rights activists organized protest marches to draw public attention to the high incidence of femicides in Turkish society.[51]

Meanwhile, some civil society organizations sought to counteract democratic backsliding by tackling such issues as urban development and electoral integrity.[52] A salient outcome of the Gezi Park uprising was the emergence of the so-called city defenses, advocating citizens' rights to the city and tackling the issue of urban renewal.[53] Istanbul City Defense, for example, was a large network of activists concerned with urban development in the city. A related civic initiative was the Northern Forests Defense, with a focus on the protection of the environment in the area north of Istanbul. Another cluster of civic initiatives, including the election monitoring organization Vote and Beyond (*Oy ve Ötesi*), focused on the quality of elections.[54] Furthermore, the results of the 2024 municipal elections debunked the myth that Turkish voters would not cast a ballot for a female candidate. According to the Platform for Equality for Women, women were elected as mayors in five of thirty metropolitan municipalities and six provincial municipalities.[55] In particular, electoral victories in "conservative areas" were hailed as a marker of women's success in the electoral arena.[56]

An examination of mass mobilization in Turkey shows that (1) women from different backgrounds joined the Gezi Park movement, (2) women performed a variety of tasks during mass mobilization, and (3) activists achieved different degrees of success in national and local politics. As noted by Cagatay, women with different political leanings joined the protests, including "Kemalists,

---

[51] Hürriyet Daily News. 2022. "Turkish Women Hold Rallies against Male Violence on Women's Day." March 8. www.hurriyetdailynews.com/turkish-women-hold-rallies-against-male-violence-on-womens-day-172030; Elif Shafak. 2015. "After Years of Silence, Turkey's Women Are Going Into Battle Against Oppression." *The Guardian*, February 17. www.theguardian.com/commentisfree/2015/feb/17/turkey-women-battle-oppression-protest.

[52] For an overview, see Özge Zihnioğlu. 2019. "The Legacy of the Gezi Protests in Turkey." In *After Protest: Pathways Beyond Mass Mobilization*, ed. Richard Youngs. Washington, DC: Carnegie Endowment for International Peace, pp. 11–17; Özge Zihnioğlu. 2023. "Strategizing Post-Protest Activism in Abeyance: Retaining Activist Capital Under Political Constraint." *Social Movement Studies* 22 (1): 122–37.

[53] Gözde Pelivan. 2020. "Going Beyond the Divides: Coalition Attempts in the Follow-Up Networks to the Gezi Movement in Istanbul." *Territory, Politics, Governance* 8 (4): 496–514.

[54] Sercan Çelebi. 2015. "Civic Engagement in Turkey's Democracy: The Case of Oy ve Ötesi." *Turkish Policy Quarterly* 13 (24): 71–78; Işıl Zeynep Türkan İpek. 2018. "Electoral Integrity and Election Monitoring in Turkey." *Marmara Üniversitesi Siyasal Bilimler Dergisi* [Marmara University Journal of Political Science] 6: 143–68.

[55] SES Equality, Justice, Women Platform. 2024. "The Platform for Equality for Women: Myth of 'Voters Don't Vote for Women' Debunked." April 5. https://esitlikadaletkadin.org/the-platform-for-equality-for-women-myth-of-voters-dont-vote-for-women-debunked/.

[56] Barçın Yinanç. 2024. "Women Sent a Message of Democratic Resilience in Turkey's Municipal Elections." *Enheduanna* [a blog of the Middle East Women's Initiative, Woodrow Wilson International Center for Scholars], April 17. www.wilsoncenter.org/blog-post/women-sent-message-democratic-resilience-turkeys-municipal-elections.

Kurds, worker's unions, left/socialist organizations, LGBT activists, anti-capitalist Muslims."[57] Given the heterogeneity of the protest movement, women assumed various roles within the movement. Women sustained civil resistance through their volunteer work as doctors, lawyers, and journalists. Furthermore, female activists were represented in the movement's leadership structure. Many college-educated women were vocal in their disapproval of the ruling party's conservative agenda and in particular the government's encroachment on women's rights. Upon the dismantlement of the encampment, there emerged various civic initiatives aimed at addressing such issues as urban development, electoral integrity, and gender inequality. However, the Gezi Party formed in October 2013 failed to overcome institutional barriers to compete in national elections.[58] Overall, these findings reveal diverse forms of women's activism and the complexity of gender politics, signifying a mixed record of feminists' success in different domains.

The 2020 Revolution in Belarus

Belarus under Lukashenka has become known as one of the most repressive political regimes in contemporary Europe.[59] The former Soviet republic experienced a short period of political liberalization and market reforms in the 1990s. However, since the election of Lukashenka as the president in 1994, there has been a rollback of democratic reforms and the entrenchment of authoritarianism. In 1995, the incumbent orchestrated a national referendum that brought back Soviet-style state symbols and elevated the legal status of the Russian language.[60] Another referendum held in 1996 expanded the presidential powers and extended his first presidential term until 2001. The incumbent disbanded the popularly elected parliament and stepped up repression against opposition political parties. Moreover, Lukashenka inhibited the development of independent media, civic organizations, and independent trade unions to crush dissent and consolidate his grip on power.[61] The KGB of Belarus kept its

---

[57] Gallo. "Sosyalist Feminist Kolektif". https://lefteast.org/sosyalist-feminist-kolektif/.
[58] Under electoral rules until 2022, political parties were required to receive at least 10 percent of the vote to enter the national parliament. In 2022, the threshold was lowered from 10 percent to 7 percent. On party politics in the post-2013 period, see, for example, Şebnem Yardımcı-Geyikçi. 2014. "Gezi Park Protests in Turkey: A Party Politics View." *The Political Quarterly* 85 (4): 445–53.
[59] Andrew Wilson. 2011. *Belarus: The Last European Dictatorship*. New Haven: Yale University Press.
[60] According to the 1995 referendum, Russian was granted an equal status to Belarusian. In reality, however, the incumbent government inhibited the use of the Belarusian language in the education sector and the mass media.
[61] David R. Marples. 2009. "Outpost of Tyranny? The Failure of Democratization in Belarus." *Democratization* 16 (4): 756–76; Vitali Silitski. 2005. "Preempting Democracy: The Case of Belarus." *Journal of Democracy* 16 (4): 83–97.

Soviet-era name and deployed an arsenal of repressive measures to create a climate of fear in society.

In addition, the tyrant was notorious for his espousal of patriarchal values. In his public statements, Lukashenka frequently peddled the idea of women's primary responsibility to bear children. In March 2019, for example, the president urged women to increase the country's birth rate. "I wish women had more children: it is a good thing for us, men, and for the country," Lukashenka said.[62] Another recurrent theme in the incumbent's rhetoric was that women were physically unfit to lead the nation. "The president in our country deals with many issues – from security to economy – that a person in a skirt is probably not able to tackle," stated Lukashenka during the 2015 presidential election campaign.[63] The incumbent also claimed that a woman would not be able to shoulder the heavy burden of the presidency because the national constitution was not designed to accommodate the possibility of a female head of the executive branch.[64] "I would never concede the president's office to a representative of the weaker sex," Lukashenka stated in 2018.[65]

Another theme in the official discourse was the idea that women should stay out of contentious politics. Government officials, along with state-controlled media, framed female protesters as women with loose morals. In December 2010, for example, Lidziya Yarmoshina, head of the Central Election Commission of the Republic of Belarus, shamed female participants in postelection protests against gross violations of democratic procedures and admonished them to "stay at home, cook borsch, and not run around the square."[66] The incumbent emphasized the idea that politics is a man's domain.

Against this backdrop, Sviatlana Tsikhanouskaya, thirty-seven-year-old spouse of the jailed blogger and mother of two underage children, declared her run for the presidency in the summer of 2020. By that time, several men with political ambitions, including a well-known banker Viktar Babaryka, a cofounder of the Belarusian Christian Democracy Party Paval Seviarynets, a leader of the Belarusian Social Democratic Party (*Hramada*) Mikalai Statkevich, a blogger Siarhei Tsikhanouski, and a founder of a Minsk-based

[62] Nastasia Zanko. 2019. "Rozhaite pobolshe detei. Nu vam zhe prosto: dvoe detei – eto vashi, a tretii – eto moi." Lukashenko o demografischeskoi situatsii. *Onliner.by*, March 1. https://people.onliner.by/2019/03/01/lukashenko-233.

[63] Radio Svaboda. 2015. "Lukashenka Calls Female Opponent a 'Person in a Skirt'." October 11. www.svaboda.org/a/27300320.html.

[64] Franak Viacorka and Melinda Haring. 2020. "Women Make the Difference in Belarus." *The Washington Post*, August 15. www.washingtonpost.com/opinions/2020/08/15/women-make-difference-belarus/.

[65] Elena Spasiuk. 2018. "'V vas – nasha sila i muzhestvo'. Chto govoril Lukashenko o zhenshchinakh." *Naviny.by*, March 8. https://naviny.online/article/20180308/1520486411-v-vas-nasha-sila-i-muzhestvo-chto-govoril-lukashenko-o-zhenshchinah.

[66] Naviny.by. 2010. "Yermoshina o zhenshchinakh na Ploshchadi: sideli by doma, borsch varili." December 20. https://naviny.online/rubrics/elections/2010/12/20/ic_news_623_357675.

Additional Cases

hi-tech park Valery Tsapkala, had been imprisoned or forced to flee the country out of fear of state reprisal. Tsikhanouskaya teamed up with Veranika Tsapkala, a spouse of a presidential hopeful, and Maryia Kalesnikava, a member of Babaryka's election campaign team, to challenge the incumbent at the polls. "We had to replace our men," Tsikhanouskaya explained. In her election campaign speeches, Tsikhanouskaya pledged to create favorable conditions for the conduct of free and fair elections within the first six months of her presidency and then resign from the post. She conveyed the idea that she entered the presidential race out of love for her spouse and her children:

I am not a politician; my husband Siarhei Tsikhanouski wanted to become the President and now he is in prison ... My husband Siarhei Tsikhanouski is imprisoned because he wanted a better life for the Belarusians; my children keep asking when their dad is coming home; and I want to become the President to restore justice in this country.[67]

To mobilize the electorate against the incumbent, Tsikhanouskaya urged her compatriots to overcome their fear of state reprisal. "I am tired of putting up [with the regime], tired of being silent, tired of being afraid," declared the presidential contender at a campaign rally on July 30.[68] Likewise, Kalesnikava pleaded with citizens to overcome their fear of the coercive apparatus. "Do not fear a physical threat. Do not fear the police. The police are merely people," said Kalesnikava.[69]

Furthermore, Kalesnikava positioned herself as a feminist. Being a flutist, she criticized a glass ceiling in the musical profession. "When we come together to form small or large orchestras, when we set ourselves the tremendously inspiring goal of creating something together, then we will succeed in producing true masterpieces," she said at a musical festival in Minsk in 2017.[70] In a media interview during the 2020 election campaign, Kalesnikava stated, "This is not a struggle for power, this is a struggle for human dignity ... and for love that is stronger than fear."[71]

Numerous media reports and opinion polls indicate that Tsikhanouskaya has garnered considerable electoral support. There was a high turnout at her campaign rallies. On August 1, for example, over 10,000 people attended a

---

[67] Presidential candidate Sviatlana Tsikhanouskaya's speech, July 21, 2020. https://babariko.vision/en/news-en/presidential-candidate-sviatlana-tsikhanouskayas-speech.

[68] Naviny.by. 2020. "Tikhanovskaia – OMONu: Ne idite protiv svoei sovesti, ne idite protiv svoego naroda." July 30. https://naviny.by/new/20200730/1596136075-tihanovskayaomonu-ne-idite-protiv-svoey-sovesti-ne-idite-protiv-svoego.

[69] Tatiana Matveeva. 2020. "V Glubokom miting s Tikhanovskoi sobral okolo tysiachi chelovek, v Novopolotske – okolo trekh tysiach." *Tut.by*, July 30. https://news.tut.by/economics/693684.html.

[70] Qtd. from Olga Shparaga. 2023. "Risking All in the Fight for Democracy." *Eurozine*, January 9. www.eurozine.com/risking-all-in-the-fight-for-democracy/.

[71] Maria Kalesnikova [official X account]. September 20, 2023. https://x.com/by_kalesnikava/status/1704546740811034876.

public rally in Hrodna, the fifth largest city in Belarus, with a population of 355,932 people.[72] Tsikhanouskaya's campaign also drew large crowds in small towns across Belarus. In July 2020, for example, over 1,000 people turned out to meet with the presidential candidate in the town of Glybokae, with a total population of 17,000 people.[73] The results of a parallel vote count organized by the civic initiatives Holos (Voice/Vote), Zubr (Bison), and Sumlennyia liudzi (Honest People) show that Tsikhanouskaya received over 81 percent of the vote at 1,310 of 5,767 polling stations.[74] Public opinion research also suggests that the majority of voters cast their ballot for the incumbent's opponent. According to the results of an online survey conducted by the Berlin-based Centre for East European and International Studies (ZOiS), 52.5 percent of voters in urban areas voted for Tsikhanouskaya, 18.6 percent declined to answer the question, and only 17.6 percent claimed to vote for Lukashenka.[75] Yet, the Central Election Commission declared that the incumbent secured 80.1 percent of the vote, and Tsikhanouskaya reportedly received only 10.1 percent. The magnitude of electoral fraud caused public outrage.

Furthermore, the disproportionate use of violence against participants in peaceful postelection protests and the systematic use of torture in detention centers fueled civil resistance.[76] According to some estimates, over 200,000 people joined Sunday marches of solidarity on August 16, August 23, and August 30. The online publication *Charter 97* reported that as many as half a million people participated in the March for Freedom held in Minsk on August 16.[77] An online survey conducted by the Centre for East European and International Studies (ZOiS) in December 2020 found that 20 percent of survey respondents had experienced police violence or personally had known a

---

[72] Belsat. 2020. "Sviatlana Tsikhanouskaya u Horadni. Videa, fota." August 1. https://belsat.eu/news/svyatlana-tsihanouskaya-syonnya-pravodzits-pikety-na-zahadze-belarusi.

[73] Belsat. 2020. "Na mitynhu Tsikhanouskau u Glybokim bolsh za 1000 chalavek." July 24. https://belsat.eu/news/na-mityngu-tsihanouskaj-u-glybokim-sabralisya-sotni-lyudzej.

[74] Voice of Belarus. 2020. "Golos Platform Presents the Final Report on the Presidential Election." August 20. www.voiceofbelarus.com/golos-final-election-report.

[75] Nadja Douglas, Regina Elsner, Félix Krawatzek, Julia Langbein, and Gwendolyn Sasse. 2021. *Belarus at a Crossroads: Attitudes on Social and Political Change*. ZOiS Report 3. www.zois-berlin.de/fileadmin/media/Dateien/3-Publikationen/ZOiS_Reports/2021/ZOiS_Report_3_2021_01.pdf.

[76] On police violence and torture in detention centers, see Human Rights Watch. 2020. "Belarus: Systematic Beatings, Torture of Protesters." September 15. www.hrw.org/news/2020/09/15/belarus-systematic-beatings-torture-protesters; International Partnership for Human Rights and Truth Hounds. 2020. *Belarus on Hold: Crackdown on Post-Election Protests. Findings of Fact-Finding Mission to Belarus*. www.civicsolidarity.org/sites/default/files/belarus_report_field_mission_protests_final.pdf; World Organization against Torture. 2021. *Corridor of Truncheons. How Popular Demonstrations Are Net with Massive Police Violence and Denial of Justice*. Geneva: OMCT. www.omct.org/site-resources/files/Doklad_en_Web.pdf.

[77] Charter 97. 2020. "Mensk. 16 zhniunia. Historychnyia padzei." August 16. https://charter97.org/be/news/2020/8/16/389811/.

victim of police brutality, and state violence was cited as the main reason for citizens' involvement in anti-government protests.[78]

Sociological research shows that people with diverse backgrounds, including university students, IT specialists, doctors, industrial workers, and pensioners, joined civil resistance.[79] The project Voice of the Street (*Golos ulitsy*) carried out by Aksana Shelest and her colleagues, for example, finds that people of different ages and various occupations attended protest marches in August 2020.[80] Concerns over the future of their children brought many people into the street. "I am 26 years old, and I haven't seen another president," said a young woman, holding a three-year-old daughter in her hands. "I want these little creatures [children] to live in a cool, free Belarus, wherein they would like to raise their children."[81] Professional service was also a motive for women's activism, especially among doctors, journalists, and human rights defenders. "As a medic, I cannot turn a blind eye to the fact that people are beaten and subject to violence," stated a fifty-eight-year-old doctor after her trial.[82]

Women's marches were a hallmark of nonviolent resistance to the regime. On August 12, hundreds of women dressed in white formed human chains near the Minski Kamarouski market and marched along the Independence Avenue to condemn police violence.[83] Approximately 10,000 people participated in a women's march of solidarity held on August 29.[84] Several thousand women took to the streets under the slogan "The Girlfriend for the Girlfriend" on September 12, demanding the release of political prisoners.[85] Given the increasing number of arrests, women's marches were transformed into "walks" in the city. On October 3, for example, women were prompted to participate in a

---

[78] Félix Krawatzek and Gwendolyn Sasse. 2021. "Belarus Protests: Why People Have Been Taking to the Streets – New Data." *The Conversation*, February 4. https://theconversation.com/belarus-protests-why-people-have-been-taking-to-the-streets-new-data-154494.

[79] For an overview, see Aksana Shelest and Andrei Kazakevich. 2021. *Sociology of Protests in Belarus and International Assistance* [Policy Brief]. Berlin: Arbeitskreis Belarus. https://ak-belarus.org/eng.

[80] See, for example, Oksana Shelest. 2020. *Golos ulitsy: opros uchastnikov protestnykh aktsii v Belarusi – 19–22 avgusta*. August 23. Centre for European Transformation.

[81] Aleksandra Boguslavskaia. 2024. "Kak proshla samaia massovaia aktsiia za vsiu istoriiu Belarusi." *Deutsche Welle*, August 24. https://p.dw.com/p/3hNhA.

[82] Radyio Svabodnaia Europa/Radyio Svaboda. 2021. "Halasy Belarusi – 2020." www.svaboda.org/a/31578726.html.

[83] Belsat. 2020. "U belym i z kvetkami. Zhanchyny vykhodziats na pikety, kab vykazatstsa suprats hvaltu na vulitsakh Belarusi." August 12. https://belsat.eu/news/u-belym-i-z-kvetkami-zhan chyny-vyjshli-na-piket-kab-vykazatstsa-suprats-gvaltu-na-vulitsah-belarusi.

[84] Ilia Koval, Anastasiia Arinushkina, and Ekaterina Venkina. 2020. "V Minske proshel zhenskii marsh." *Deutsche Welle*, August 29. https://p.dw.com/p/3hiU5.

[85] Radio Free Europe/Radio Liberty. 2020. "Police Arrest Dozens in Minsk as Women Keep Up Protests against Belarus's Lukashenka." September 12. www.rferl.org/a/police-make-arrests-in-minsk-as-women-keep-up-protests-against-belarus-s-lukashenka/30835111.html.

"flower démarche" and stroll downtown in small groups, mingling with pedestrians.[86]

In response, the police stepped up repression against regime opponents and imprisoned thousands of activists to strangulate the protest movement. The Belarusian human rights center Viasna estimated that over 30,000 people were detained for protest participation by November 2020.[87] As a leader of civil resistance, Kalesnikava was arrested and sentenced to eleven years in prison for the alleged conspiracy to seize power, the creation of an extremist group, and actions aimed at threatening national security.[88]

Following an escalation in state repression, thousands of Belarusians fled the country. The number of citizens of Belarus living in Lithuania doubled from 23,440 people in 2020 to 48,800 people in 2022.[89] In addition, the Polish authorities issued 46,000 humanitarian visas and business visas to citizens of Belarus between August 2020 and December 2022.[90] Moreover, at least 207 people were arrested at the border when they were returning to Belarus in 2023, and this policy continued the following year.[91]

Belarusian women in exile assumed a prominent role in sustaining civil resistance to the regime. Upon her forced departure from Belarus on August 11, 2020, Tsikhanouskaya declared that she was willing to step into the role of a "national leader" so that pro-democracy forces could free all the political prisoners and lay the legal groundwork for the conduct of free and fair elections in Belarus.[92] With the support of the Lithuanian government, Tsikhanouskaya set up an office in Vilnius and unveiled the launch of various initiatives aimed at supporting Belarusians abroad and advancing political change in the country.[93] In Latvia, Tsapkala established the Belarus Women's Foundation to combat state repression against women and support women activists. The project

---

[86] Charter 97. 2020. "'Basta!': Plan deistvii na 3 oktiabria." October 3. https://charter97.org/ru/news/2020/10/3/395515.

[87] Viasna. 2020. *Human Rights Situation in Belarus: November 2020.* http://spring96.org/en/news/100777.

[88] Amnesty International. 2021. "Belarus: Maryia Kalesnikava and Maksim Znak Sentenced to Jail over Historic Protests." September 6. www.amnesty.org/en/latest/news/2021/09/belarusian-opposition-leaders-maryia-kalesnikava-and-maksim-znak-sentenced-to-10-and-11-years-respectively/.

[89] Andrei Kazakevich. 2023. *Migration from Belarus to Estonia, Germany, Latvia, Lithuania, Poland: Before and after 2020.* [Policy Brief] Berlin: Arbeitskreis Belarus. https://ak-belarus.org/eng.

[90] Ibid.

[91] Viasna. 2024. "At Least 207 Detained upon Return to Belarus: Current Statistics from Viasna for 2023." January 11. https://spring96.org/en/news/113911.

[92] Sergei Romashenko. 2020. "Tikhanovskaia obiavila o gotovnosti stat natsionalnym liderom." *Deutshe Welle*, August 17. https://p.dw.com/p/3h3lJ.

[93] For a detailed description of the mission of the Office of Sviatlana Tsikhanouskaya, visit the webpage https://tsikhanouskaya.org/be/ofis/nasha-misiya.html.

Unbreakable, for example, sought to raise international awareness of female political prisoners in the country.[94] A host of meetings with world leaders and public events were organized to campaign for democratic change in Belarus.

The 2020 electoral revolution in Belarus was dubbed a "revolution with a female face" due to women's leadership roles during the presidential election campaign and postelection protests.[95] Contrary to the incumbent's patriarchal views, Tsikhanouskaya garnered considerable popular support in Belarusian society. Moreover, women played a prominent role in mass mobilization against the regime in the aftermath of the fraudulent election and police brutality against peaceful protesters. Nonetheless, the protest movement encompassed women with different conceptions of feminism.[96] Hence, a hybrid model of women's participation in a revolution seems to capture best the diversity of the protest movement in Belarus. Further cross-national research is necessary to determine whether the hybrid model applies across a wide range of cases.

WOMEN AND THE RUSSIA–UKRAINE WAR

Russia's military aggression against Ukraine has taken a heavy toll on Ukrainian society. The United Nations Human Rights Monitoring Mission in Ukraine (HRMMU) reported that more than 10,000 civilians, including 587 children, were killed during the first two years since the onset of Russia's invasion of Ukraine in February 2022.[97] Furthermore, UNICEF estimated that "the verified number of children killed in attacks across Ukraine has increased by nearly 40 percent" in 2024, compared to the previous year.[98] The actual number of civilian casualties is considerably higher. The Human Rights Watch, for example, estimated at least 8,034 excess deaths during the first year of full-scale invasion in the port city of Mariupol.[99] Another gruesome outcome of Russia's aggression was the forcible deportation of Ukrainian children to Russia. According to the Children of War platform established by the

---

[94] For a project description, visit the webpage https://belaruswomen.org/en/projects/unbreakable-pages.

[95] Alesia Rudnik. 2023. "The Female Face of Belarusian Resistance." *International Politics and Society*, March 6. www.ips-journal.eu/topics/democracy-and-society/the-female-face-of-belarusian-resistance-6554/.

[96] On this point, see Olga Dryndova. 2021. "Revolution in Belarus: Surprisingly Female?" *Green European Journal*, January 4. www.greeneuropeanjournal.eu/revolution-in-belarus.

[97] The Office of the United Nations High Commissioner for Human Rights. 2024. *Protection of Civilians: Impact of Hostilities on Civilians. Two-Year Update Since 24 February 2022*. February 22. www.ohchr.org/en/documents/country-reports/two-year-update-protection-civilians-impact-hostilities-civilians-24.

[98] UNICEF. 2024. "Significant Increase in Number of Children Killed Across Ukraine This Year, as Deadly Attacks Continue." April 26. www.unicef.org/press-releases/significant-increase-number-children-killed-across-ukraine-year-deadly-attacks.

[99] Human Rights Watch. 2024. *"Our City Was Gone": Russia's Devastation of Mariupol, Ukraine*, p. 147. www.hrw.org/feature/russia-ukraine-war-mariupol/report.

Ministry of Reintegration of the Temporarily Occupied Territories of Ukraine and the National Information Bureau, more than 19,500 children have been deported or forcibly displaced by the Russian authorities.[100] In addition, HRMMU documented over 100 enforced disappearances in Crimea under Russia's occupation since 2014.[101]

Women were particularly vulnerable to conflict-related sexual violence.[102] The Independent International Commission of Inquiry on Ukraine established by the Human Rights Council documented numerous cases of sexual and gender-based violence committed by Russian soldiers in Ukrainian localities under Russia's occupation. Victims of rape were reportedly aged between 15 and 83.[103] Based on more than 100 testimonies, Pramila Patten, Special Representative of the UN Secretary-General on Sexual Violence in Conflict, concluded that the Russian military systematically and deliberately used rape as a weapon of war.[104] Being viewed as guardians of national identity, women were targets of the aggressor state to destroy Ukrainian culture and annihilate the Ukrainian nation.[105] Nonetheless, women should not be seen only as victims of the brutal war.

Ukrainian women played an active role on the battlefront, on the home front, and abroad to reaffirm their agency and repel Russia's invasion of the country.[106] Many participants in Euromaidan went to the frontlines to defend

---

[100] For details, visit the online portal at https://childrenofwar.gov.ua/en.

[101] The Office of the United Nations High Commissioner for Human Rights. 2024. *Ten Years of Occupation by the Russian Federation: Human Rights in the Autonomous Republic of Crimea and the City of Sevastopol, Ukraine*. February 28. www.ohchr.org/en/documents/country-reports/ten-years-occupation-russian-federation-human-rights-autonomous-republic.

[102] For an overview, see OSCE Parliamentary Assembly. 2023. *2023 Gender Report: Understanding and Addressing the Gendered Consequences of the War in Ukraine*. Copenhagen, Denmark: OSCE Parliamentary Assembly. Presented by the Honourable Hedy Fry, OSCE PA Special Representative on Gender Issues. www.oscepa.org/en/documents/special-representatives/gender-issues/report-17/4717-pdf-2023-gender-report-understanding-and-addressing-the-gendered-consequences-of-the-war-in-ukraine-eng/file

[103] *Report of the Independent International Commission of Inquiry on Ukraine to the Human Rights Council*. Prepared for the fifty-fifth session February 26–April 5, 2024. www.ohchr.org/sites/default/files/documents/hrbodies/hrcouncil/coiukraine/a-hrc-55-66-aev.pdf.

[104] Agence France Presse. 2022. "Rape Used in Ukraine as a Russian 'Military Strategy': UN." October 14. www.france24.com/en/live-news/20221014-rape-used-in-ukraine-as-a-russian-military-strategy-un.

[105] On this point, see Mia M. Bloom. 2022. "Rape by Russian Soldiers in Ukraine is the Latest Example of a Despicable Wartime Crime That Spans the Globe." *The Conversation*, April 7. https://theconversation.com/rape-by-russian-soldiers-in-ukraine-is-the-latest-example-of-a-despicable-wartime-crime-that-spans-the-globe-180656.

[106] For an overview of women's resistance, see Iryna Drobovych. 2022. "Liderstvo ukrainskykh zhinok: na viini ta pislia peremohy Ukrainy." *Ukrainska Pravda*, April 21. https://life.pravda.com.ua/columns/2022/04/21/248335/; Olena Nikolayenko. 2024. "Contesting the Gender Binary in Wartime: Ukrainian Women's Resistance to Russia's Aggression." In *Handbook on Gender and Activism*, eds. Jo Reger, Rachel Einwohner, and Kelsy Kretschmer. Northampton: Edward Elgar Publishing; Sarah D. Phillips and Tamara Martsenyuk. 2023. "Women's Agency and Resistance in Russia's War on Ukraine: From Victim of the War to Prominent

the country's territorial integrity and democratic development. Thousands of women joined volunteer battalions and the Armed Forces of Ukraine.[107] In January 2024, 45,587 servicewomen served in the Armed Forces of Ukraine.[108] Furthermore, the women's veteran movement assumed a leadership role in advocating for gender equality in the military.[109] Women activists succeeded in bringing about legal changes and securing women's access to many combat positions. Meanwhile, female artists fought on the cultural front to raise international awareness of Ukrainian culture and history.[110] Likewise, Ukrainian scholars challenged the persistence of Russian narratives in academia and called for decolonization in East European Studies.[111] To address existing inequities in knowledge production, Ukrainian researchers urged the academic community in the West to reimagine "the centres of knowledge production beyond the centre."[112]

A wide array of transnational networks formed during the Revolution of Dignity have been reactivated to deliver humanitarian aid to the IDPs, provide

---

Force." *Women's Studies International Forum* 98: 102731. https://doi.org/10.1016/j.wsif.2023.102731.

[107] Olesya Khromeychuk. 2018. "Experiences of Women at War: Servicewomen During WWII and in the Ukrainian Armed Forces in the Conflict in Donbas." *Baltic Worlds* 4: 58–70; Tamara Martsenyuk, ed. 2016. *Invisible Battalion: Women's Participation in ATO Military Operations (Sociological Research)*. Kyiv: UN Women; Evheniia Podobna, ed. 2020. *Girls Cutting Their Locks: A Book of Memories, the Russo-Ukrainian War*, trans. Mariia Kovalenko. Kyiv: Ukrainian Institute of National Remembrance and Liuta Sprava.

[108] Lesia Leshchenko. 2024. "Stalo vidomo, skilky zhinok sluzhat u ZSU stanom na 2024 rik." *UNIAN*, March 8. www.unian.ua/society/stalo-vidomo-skilki-zhinok-sluzhat-u-zsu-stanom-na-2024-rik-12567048.html.

[109] Jonathan Röders. 2023. "Veteranka: Supporting Ukraine's Female Defenders." November 3. London: Royal United Services Institute. www.rusi.org/explore-our-research/publications/commentary/veteranka-supporting-ukraines-female-defenders.

[110] Svitlana Biedarieva and Hanna Deikun, eds. 2020. *At the Front Line: Ukrainian Art, 2013–2019. La línea del frente. El arte ucraniano 2013–2019*. Mexico City: Editorial Diecisiete; Kateryna Iakovlenko. 2022. "Eyewitness the Russian War in Ukraine: The Matter of Loss and Arts." *Sociologica* 16 (2): 227–38; Yuliya Ilchuk. 2017. "Hearing the Voice of Donbas: Art and Literature as Forms of Cultural Protest During War." *Nationalities Papers* 45 (2): 256–73; Iuliia Lashchuk. 2018. "Displaced Art and the Reconstruction of Memory: Ukrainian Artists from Crimea and Donbas." *Open Cultural Studies* 2: 700–709; Maryna Shevtsova, ed. 2024. *Feminist Perspectives of Russia's War in Ukraine: Hear Our Voices*. Lanham: Lexington Books.

[111] Yuriy Gorodnichenko, Ilona Sologoub, and Tatyana Deryugina. 2023. "Why Russian Studies in the West Failed to Provide a Clue about Russia and Ukraine." *Vox Ukraine*, June 21. https://voxukraine.org/en/why-russian-studies-in-the-west-failed-to-provide-a-clue-about-russia-and-ukraine; Tereza Hendl, Olga Burlyuk, Mila O'Sullivan, and Aizada Arystanbek. 2024. "(En)Countering Epistemic Imperialism: A Critique of 'Westsplaining' and Coloniality in Dominant Debates on Russia's Invasion of Ukraine." *Contemporary Security Policy* 45 (2): 171–209; Maria Sonevytsky. 2022. "What Is Ukraine? Notes on Epistemic Imperialism." *Topos* 2: 21–30, https://doi.org/10.24412/1815-0047-2022-2-21-30.

[112] Oksana Dudko. 2023. "Gate-Crashing 'European' and 'Slavic' Area Studies: Can Ukrainian Studies Transform the Fields?" *Canadian Slavonic Papers* 65 (2): 174–89, 183.

rehabilitation services for the injured, and supply equipment for the military.[113] Founded by the Euromaidan participant and war veteran Mariia Berlinska, the Victory Drones project offered innovative training on the use of modern technologies in warfare.[114] In addition, the massive migration of Ukrainians from the conflict zone to the EU has given rise to the development of new transnational networks in support of the war effort.[115] Appealing to the international community, Ukrainian feminists issued a manifesto, titled *The Right to Resist*.[116] "If Ukrainian society lays down its arms, there will be no Ukrainian society. If Russia lays down its arms, the war will end," the Feminist Initiative Group stated, calling for the supply of weapons to the Ukrainian military.

Furthermore, female journalists, human rights defenders, and lawyers collaborated to document war crimes committed by Russian soldiers on the territory of Ukraine.[117] Founded by the Center for Civil Liberties, the Kharkiv Human Rights Protection Group, and the Ukrainian Helsinki Human Rights Union, the global initiative "Tribunal for Putin" documented 54,000 war crimes during the first eighteen months of Russia's full-scale invasion.[118] The Reckoning Project is another international initiative cofounded by the American journalist Janine di Giovanni, the British journalist Peter Pomerantsev, and the Ukrainian journalist Nataliya Gumenyuk to collect fact-based, legally admissible testimonies from witnesses and victims of war crimes in Ukraine.[119]

Taken as a whole, an analysis of women's participation in the Revolution of Dignity sheds some light on sources of fierce resistance to Russian imperialism. Contrary to the Kremlin's propaganda machine, the citizens of Ukraine

---

[113] Serhiy Kovalchuk and Alla Korzh. 2020. "The Transnational Activism of Young Ukrainian Immigrants." In *Democracy, Diaspora, Territory: Europe and Cross-Border Politics*, eds. Olga Oleinikova and Jumana Bayeh. London: Routledge, pp. 127–44.

[114] For a description of the project, see https://en.victory-drones.com.

[115] According to the most recent data released by the Office of the United Nations High Commissioner for Refugees in May 2024, there were 5.9 million refugees from Ukraine in Europe. More than two-thirds of refugees were female. For details, visit the Operational Data Portal, https://data.unhcr.org/en/country/ukr.

[116] Feminist Initiative Group. 2022. "The Right to Resist: A Feminist Manifesto." *Spilne*, July 7. https://commons.com.ua/en/right-resist-feminist-manifesto.

[117] Cynthia M. Horne. 2023. "Accountability for Atrocity Crimes in Ukraine: Gendering Transitional Justice." *Women's Studies International Forum* 96: 102666, https://doi.org/10.1016/j.wsif.2022.102666; Anna Romandash. 2023. *Women of Ukraine: Reportages from the War and Beyond*. Stuttgart: Ibidem Press; Jessica Zychowicz. 2023. "Women's Activism in Ukraine: Anti-discrimination, Anti-disinformation, and Human Rights in Early Civic Documentations of the Ukraine-Russia War." In *Post-Soviet Women: New Challenges and Ways to Empowerment*, eds. Ann-Mari Sätre, Yulia Gradskova, and Vladislava Vladimirova. Switzerland: Palgrave Macmillan.

[118] Council on Foreign Relations. 2024. "Ukraine Update: Pursuing Justice in Wartime with Nobel Peace Prize Recipient Oleksandra Matviichuk." October 24. www.cfr.org/event/ukraine-update-pursuing-justice-wartime-nobel-peace-prize-recipient-oleksandra-matviichuk.

[119] For details, visit the website of the Reckoning Project at www.thereckoningproject.com.

displayed the capacity for self-organization and the resolve to defend their home country against foreign aggression. At the time of this writing (June 2024), the war continues to rage in the country. Ukrainian women exhibited a great deal of resilience, resourcefulness, and valiance in their struggle for national independence, democracy, and cultural heritage. Future research should explore the long-term effects of women's activism on gender equality in the postwar period.

Appendix 1.

List of Interviewees: The Project "Maidan: Oral History" by the Ukrainian Institute of National Remembrance

Interviewee name	Place of birth (oblast)	Age (2014)	Date of interview
Bohdana Babych	Zhytomyr	36	December 9, 2014
Iryna Bekeshkina	Sverdlovsk (Russia)	62	March 3, 2014
Oksana Belska	Volyn	46	December 16, 2014
Mariia Berlinska	Khmelnytskyi	26	July 20, 2015
Evheniia Bilchenko	Kyiv city	34	September 23, 2014
Olha Bohachevska	Volyn	25	July 22, 2015
Odarka Bordun	Lviv	32	December 22, 2015
Sofiia Borysko	Lviv	21	August 19, 2014
Mariia Burdun	Kyiv city	30	September 16, 2014
Kateryna Butko	Kyiv city	26	October 3, 2014
Svitlana Chaplinska	Khmelnytskyi	42	November 30, 2014
Kateryna Chepura	Kyiv city	28	June 12, 2014
Yaryna Chornohuz	Kyiv city	19	August 10, 2014
Yuliia Datsenko	Kyiv city	30	July 24, 2015
Valentyna Davydenko	Cherkasy	59	December 1, 2014
Anastasiia Dmytruk	Chernihiv	23	April 15, 2016
Oleksandra Dubicheva	Dnipropetrovsk	29	September 4, 2014
Olensandra Dvoretska	Crimea AR	24	April 5, 2016
Solomiia Farion	Lviv	25	May 12, 2015
Liubov Halan	Lviv	18	December 17, 2014
Olena Hantsiak-Kaskiv	Kyiv	40	December 25, 2014
Olha Hodovanets	Kyiv city	37	August 27, 2015
Maryna Hohulia	Kyiv	28	August 9, 2014
Olena Hrechaniuk	Kyiv city	22	November 10, 2014
Yelyzaveta Hrynenko	Vinnytsia	23	March 5, 2014
Anhelina Husar	Kyiv city	22	October 15, 2014
Olena Ivanova	Kyiv city	44	August 6, 2014
Mila Ivantsova	Kyiv city	54	October 21, 2014
Mariia Ivanyk	Ivano-Frankivsk	21	August 12, 2014
Nataliia Kadyn-Feseniuk	Kyiv city	35	June 27, 2014
Yuliia Kapshuchenko	Kyiv city	25	2014

(continued)

(continued)

Interviewee name	Place of birth (oblast)	Age (2014)	Date of interview
Rada Kishka	Sumy	23	2014
Liudmyla Knoblokh	Kyiv city	61	March 12, 2014
Viktoriia Kochubei	Kyiv city	45	February 16, 2015
Nataliia Koltsova	Kyiv city	55	August 11, 2015
Kateryna Korniiko	Kyiv	38	September 24, 2015
Nina Krasnova	Donetsk		September 3, 2015
Tetiana Kucher	Dnipropetrovsk	22	July 22, 2016
Kateryna Kuvita	Kyiv city	29	September 23, 2015
Yaryna Kvitka	Lviv	29	2014
Iryna Kyselova	Kyiv	33	March 7, 2017
Olha Lishchynska	Volyn	52	November 11, 2016
Ruslana Lotsman	Cherkasy	26	October 30, 2014
Iryna Lukicheva	Vologda (Russia)	45	July 23, 2015
Nina Makarchuk	Kyiv	59	September 8, 2014
Anastasiia Makarenko	Chernihiv	23	June 10, 2014
Mariia Makhnovets (Volynska)	Volyn	64	July 14, 2014
Anastasiia Maksymchuk	Chernivtsi	27	November 12, 2014
Olesia Mamchych	Kyiv city	33	June 17, 2014
Tamara Martsenyuk	Volyn	33	November 11, 2014
Oleksandra Matviichuk	Kyiv	31	July 5, 2014
Taisiia Melnyk	Dnipropetrovsk	29	April 23, 2015
Maryna Mirzaeva	Kyiv	18	June 23, 2015
Maiia Moskvych	Volyn	25	February 23, 2015
Tetiana Motsak	Kyiv	23	March 24, 2015
Tetiana Movchan	Ternopil	39	August 20, 2014
Iryna Mukhina	Zakarpattia	26	August 27, 2014
Yanina Muliavska	Kyiv city	32	December 16, 2014
Oleksandra Navrotska		28	April 15, 2016
Inna Nerodyk	Volyn	26	November 6, 2014
Maryna Nikolaichuk	Kyiv	37	June 13, 2014
Olena Nozhovnik	Kyiv city	34	September 22, 2015
Iryna Panchenko	Kyiv city	40	September 15, 2015
Yuliia Pishta	Kherson	31	September 18, 2015
Olena Podobed-Frankivska	Ternopil	30	August 21, 2014
Anna Prokhorova	Kyiv city	27	July 14, 2016
Olesia Roi	Odesa	34	15 March
Oksana Romaniuk		35	June 11, 2015
Olha Salo	Lviv	32	January 30, 2015
Nataliia Sholoiko	Chernihiv	52	December 4, 2014
Liudmyla Sivtseva-Klymuk	Volyn	30	February 29, 2016
Maryna Sochenko	Kyiv city	51	October 3, 2014
Nataliia Sokolenko	Kyiv	39	January 14, 2015

Appendices

Interviewee name	Place of birth (oblast)	Age (2014)	Date of interview
Olha Strashenko	Kyiv city	64	September 18, 2015
Olena Sychenko	Rivno	23	August 13, 2015
Kateryna Tkachenko	Kharkiv	34	September 22, 2014
Halyna Tsyhanenko	Cherkasy	43	October 30, 2015
Yuliia Tychkivska	Lviv	25	April 28, 2015
Natalia Vorozhbyt	Kyiv city	39	April 9, 2016
Yuliia Votcher	Vinnytsia	63	December 10, 2014
Nelia Vterkovska	Ivano Frankivsk	30	September 21, 2015
Larysa Yushkevych	Odesa	34	October 28, 2014
Oksana Zabuzhko	Volyn	54	November 4, 2015
Iryna Zemliana	Poltava	27	February 12, 2015
Kateryna Zhytska	Cherkasy	26	October 12, 2014

Note: The list of interviewees is based on data compiled by the Ukrainian Institute of National Remembrance.

Appendix 2.

List of Interviewees: The Project "Maidan. Testimonies" by the National University of Kyiv-Mohyla Academy

Interviewee name	Place of birth	Age (2014)
Svitlana Abaeva	Khmelnytskyi	
Olena Chornousova		60
Natalia Chubata	Ivano-Frankivsk	23
Nataliia Defterenko	Kyiv city	38
Oleksandra Didyk	Ivano-Frankivsk	
Dariia Diehuts	Kyiv city	27
Oleksandra Dubicheva	Dnipropetrovsk	29
Olena Finberg	Kyiv city	61
Maryna Frolova	St. Petersburg (Russia)	31
Olena Herasymiuk	Kyiv city	33
Inna Hryshchenko	Zhytomyr	24
Olena Ivanova	Kyiv city	44
Nina Khodorivska		24
Ivanna Kobeleva	Kyiv city	25
Zoia Konusova	Kyiv city	21
Bohdana Kostiuk	Kyiv city	50
Adelaida Kovalska	Kyiv city	27
Olena Kozachenko	Kyiv city	24
Yaryna Kvitka	Lviv	29
Natalia Leliukh	Chernihiv	40
Olena Litvishko	Poltava	33
Maryna Lysak	Kyiv city	35
Lesia Lytvynova	Kyiv city	38
Olena Maksymenko	Kyiv city	29
Tetiana Mazur	Lviv	32
Tetiana Mohylina	Kyiv city	41
Masha Nazarova	Kyiv city	17
Oleksandra Nazarova	Russia	27
Uliana Onyshchuk	Lviv	
Kateryna Overchenko	Kyiv city	25
Yana Paladieva	Kyiv city	16
Vira Pavliuk	Chernivtsi	56
Anna Poliak	Kharkiv	
Nina Potarska	Kyiv city	30
Maryna Pylypenko	Kyiv city	39

Interviewee name	Place of birth	Age (2014)
Olha Salo	Lviv	32
Natalka Serdiuk	Zaporizhzhia	
Lesia Shevchuk	Kyiv city	33
Zoriana Sokhatska	Ivano-Frankivsk	60
Iryna Soloshenko	Kyiv city	44
Olha Streltsova	Kyiv city	42
Oksana Syvak		40
Halyna Tanai	Dnipropetrovsk	23
Svitlana Tarancnko	Odesa	43
Tetiana Udovytska	Kyiv city	45
Svitlana Umeliukh	Kyiv city	47
Oleksandra Ustynova	Vinnytsia	28
Katrusia Vitvytska		
Anna Volokhova	Kyiv city	
Evheniia Yanchenko	Kyiv city	29
Olesia Zhukovska	Ternopil	21
Olha Zhyzhko	Kyiv city	
Aliona Zinchenko	Donetsk	34
Anzhelika Zozulia	Zakarpattia	20
Halia	Kyiv city	30
Hanna		30
Iryna Petrivna	Kyiv city	70
Kseniia	Kyiv city	
Natalka		
Vasylisa	Kyiv	33

Note: The list of interviewees is compiled based on data reported in *Maidan. Svidchennia. Kyiv, 2013–2014 roky*, eds. Leonid Finberg and Uliana Holovach. Kyiv: Dukh i Litera, 2016.

Index

Art Squad (*Mystetska sotnia*), 113
AutoMaidan, 84, 89, 100, 112, 118–19

Berlinska, Mariia, 87, 188
Bilozerska, Olena, 163
biographical availability, 10–11, 98–100
Bohomolets, Olha, 106, 145, 147
Burmaka, Mariia, 58, 68, 71

Civic Sector of Euromaidan, 106, 111, 114–16, 120–21
corruption, 6, 40, 82–83, 143–44, 150–51
crowdsourcing, 108–10, 161

Euromaidan, 4, *See* Revolution of Dignity
Euromaidan SOS, 102, 112–13, 163
European integration, 20–21, 78–80, 83, 87, 93

FEMEN, 33
feminism, 5, 49, 57, 62, 67, 72, 78, 86–87, 101, 124, 157, 168–69, 176, 181, 185, 188
Feminist Offensive (*Feministychna Ofenzyva*), 33

gender equality, 6, 30–34, 49–52, 60, 70, *See* Feminism
gender quotas, 134–36
gender wage gap, 31, 152–53
Gezi Park Uprising, 171–79

Heavenly Hundred (*Nebesna Sotnia*), 23, 95
Herashchenko, Iryna, 136, 138
Hospital Guard (*Varta v likarni*), 88, 118
human dignity, 19–21, 66, 79–81, 95, 181

Independence Square (*Maidan Nezalezhnosti*), 18–19, 21, 58, 67, 114, 172
International Women's Day, 33, 42, 178

Jaresko, Natalie, 139, 142

Matviichuk, Oleksandra, 102, 112
Mirna, Zinaida, 50, 52
Moloda Prosvita, 66–67
motherhood, 5, 10, 64, 72, 78, 84–85, 117, 176, 181, *See* Biographical availability

National University of Kyiv-Mohyla Academy (NaUKMA), 35, 91–92, 121, 123
nonviolent resistance, 12–13, 115–22, 169–70

occupational segregation, 31, 126, 153
Open University of Maidan, 114–15
Orange Revolution, 62–70

Paievska, Yuliia, 162
Parfan, Nadia, 86, 126
People's Hospital (*Narodnyi hospital*), 110
Pora (youth movement), 66, 83, 92
Prosvita, 46–48, 50, 62

revolution
    case selection, 18–20, 39–41, 166–67, 171
    definition, 17–18
    domains of women's activism, 103
    typology of women's participation, 5–6
Revolution in Belarus, 2000, 179–85

197

Revolution of Dignity
  chronology of events, 21–23
  gender norms, 124–27
  motivations for protesting, 73–77
  outcomes, 129–30
  participants, 23–30
Revolution on Granite, 53–62
Rudnytska, Anzhelika, 59–60
Rukh (Popular Movement of Ukraine for Perestroika), 54–57
Ruslana (Lyzhychko), 68, 118, 120
Rusova, Sofiia, 48–50
Russia-Ukraine War, 17, 132–34, 154–55, 160–63, 185–88

Salo, Olha, 66, 116
Self-Defense of Maidan (*Samooborona Maidanu*), 23, 90, 93, 97–98, 122–24, 126, 162
social media, 18, 21, 73, 86, 88–90, 100, 102, 169
social networks, 11, 16, 26–27, 101, 160, 169
  civic organizations, 93–94
  family and friendship networks, 89–91
  political parties, 97–98
  region of residence, 97, 105
  religious institutions, 94–97, 107–8
  universities, 57–58, 91–93
student hunger strike, 1990, 57–58, *See* Revolution on Granite

Suprun, Ulana, 132, 142
Surovtsova, Nadiia, 48–50

Tymoshenko, Yuliia, 67, 70, 138, 145, 148–49

Ukrainian Central Rada, 46–49
Ukrainian Greek Catholic Church, 22, 95
Ukrainian Helsinki Group, 53–54, 96
Ukrainian Institute of National Remembrance, 34–35, 41
Ukrainian National Republic, 41, *See* Ukrainian Central Rada
Ukrainian Revolution, 1917-1921, 41–53
United Nations Security Council's Resolution 1325, 132

Vidsich (social movement), 92–94

women in government
  Cabinet of Ministers, 138–44
  female presidential candidates, 144–49
  women in legislature, 32–33, 134–37
women's squad (*sotnia*), 16, 123–24, 126

Yasynevych, Yaryna, 66

Zabuzhko, Oksana, 114
Zaporozhian Sich, 105, 111, 122, 162
Zinkevych, Yana, 129

For EU product safety concerns, contact us at Calle de José Abascal, 56–1°, 28003 Madrid, Spain or eugpsr@cambridge.org.